FIRST IMPRESSIONS

first impressions

PERKS, QUIRKS AND JERKS

DENTAL LIFE BEHIND THE MASK

JOY MOORE

First paperback edition Sept 2023

ISBN 979-8-9884852-0-9 (paperback)
ISBN 979-8-9884852-1-6 (ebook)

www.firstimpressionsbook.com

This book is dedicated to one of my favorite people, who continues to provide unwavering support for whatever I cook up.

Thank you, Chuck, for always believing in me.

TABLE OF CONTENTS

quirk (noun)

1. an abrupt twist or curve
2. a unique or peculiar trait: IDIOSYNCRASY
3. an odd or unusual characteristic

A memorable thing about a person's personality that makes them different, weird, or unique. An unusual habit.

Introduction

This is a story about a girl from the great Lone Star state of Texas, more specifically West Texas, who fell into a life in the dental world. Sounds super exciting right? Well, wait until you hear about some of the wacky offices I have worked in. Fortunately for me, there were some amazing ones as well. And if you don't count the time I froze when my Dr. caught his scrub pants on fire, I was an excellent assistant.

Back when I made my way out of Texas and into the big wide world, I made a few self-discoveries that served to shape the way I carved out my place in this universe:

1. I'm a people person. I love meeting new people, but don't expect me to remember your name after two minutes! It's not you, it's my brain. It's more like a sieve than a storage unit.
2. If my life had a bumper sticker, it would say: Don't pee on me and tell me it's raining. So, my BS detector is always on full alert!
3. I thrive when surrounded by supportive, kind caring souls. At the end of the day I just want to be surrounded by people who make me feel happy and appreciated.

I have always been passionate about helping others, so when my path in life led me into the dental field, I was able to use my skills not only to assist dentists, but to do much more than that. I was a chairside therapist, a comedian, a cheerleader, and a ninja all rolled into one. That's me, my name is Joy! I am the one who takes care of you while you were "in the chair." I have seen it all, from the most terrified patients to those I could almost call family. From my position perched high up in my assistant's chair, seated head-to-head with the dentist as we bump knees behind you and silently fight to get the perfect angle to see into your tiny . . . little . . . mouth, I have observed plenty.

Through my work in dentistry, I have had the amazing opportunity to connect with and learn from people of all walks of life. My goal was always to provide quality care with a smile. Usually that smile had red lipstick on it and was hidden behind a mask, but you could always see the sparkle and smile in my blue eyes!

Along the way I started jotting down little stories here and there—things that happened in the office, stories my patients shared with me—and before I knew it, I had this book. This is a collection of stories, experiences, and reflections from a lifetime of days spent in the dental office, (actually, many dental offices). I have tales of working in offices that were not, let's just say, "ideal," and others that were life-changing, amazing office environments. Not to mention the interview process that goes along with landing a job in my field—those stories are an adventure of their own! As I take you through the ups and downs of my roller-coaster life in dentistry, I'll share some pretty wild accounts of things that happened (some of which I still shake my head at in disbelief) as well as introduce you to a little something I call "the Rule of Five."

I sincerely hope that this book will provide you with a good laugh and perhaps a bit of encouragement.

So, climb into "the chair" and allow me to fasten this paper bib around your neck. The dentist will be with you in a moment!

Joy

CHAPTER 1

No, Not Julie – J-O-Y

I'm typically not the first to arrive at my dental office in the morning. My boss, Dr. Huntington, gets in much earlier than me. When I walk in, you can bet he is already seated in the front operatory, doing lab work at his dental bench, which is a huge metal desk with a bright overhead light, an air apparatus that puffs out air, and everything he needs to perform any possible dental lab work. His days are filled with a considerable amount of lab work, along with patient care. The back ledge of his lab bench is lined with random jars and coffee mugs that have funny sayings that hold the well-worn lab tools from his college days. These he uses in his specialty area of dentistry, which is prosthodontics.

Dental prosthodontics is a big name for "complex dentistry." If you've heard of implants, fixed dentures, over partials, implant supported bridges, veneers, or the like, you are on the right track. Prosthodontists do the difficult reconstructions that most general dentists aren't willing to do because of the intricacies involved. It's the last train out of town. If a prosthodontist can't help you, you really are in a pickle. My boss, Dr. Huntington, is a seasoned prosthodontist—a dental specialist who went through two years of pre-dental school, then four more years of dental schooling before....drum roll please, completing the two years in his specialty area of prosthodontics. He spent twenty-six years in the Navy before he retired as a Commander and opened his private practice. So, he's been around the block. As with all dentists he continues to take classes to keep up to date on new information, dental products and techniques in this field. Prosthodontists take on the most complex cases and the most challenging issues being faced by their patients.

As Dr. Huntington's lead dental assistant, I do quite a bit of lab work as well. Lots and lots of lab work! In fact, often I am behind the scenes in my own little room in the back of the dental office doing said lab work. If you come down the hall to my little cave, *please* announce yourself because I startle easily and have been known to scream. Most always, I scream. My brother, thinking it was funny, spent the better part of our childhood dreaming up new ways to scare me. He and I played many epic sibling pranks on each other when we were young. He sure did come up with crazy ways to startle me, just to hear me scream. From hiding plastic bugs in my bedroom, to waiting behind shower curtains in the dark bathroom, to opening doors abruptly when I least expected it! It kept me alert. I would scream loudly as he walked away, laughing. At the dental office, I always tell Dr. Huntington I am going to put a bell around his neck, so I can hear him coming, so I won't scream and scare the patients.

Just so you know, I don't keep my favorite lab tools on Dr. Huntington's lab bench. I keep my own favorite lab instruments hidden in a drawer, because my dear boss tends to misplace things. I like knowing where my stuff is, so when I reach for "said stuff" it is right where I last put it. Also, he is a pen thief. We do a pocket check at the end of every day. My pens have bright instrument-coding tape wrapped around them so I can lay claim to them when he empties his pockets.

I, like most dental professionals, have a very Type A personality!

Are you competitive? Work obsessed?
Do you operate at an urgent pace? Have
you been accused of having a "higher
level" of impatience? Do you multitask?
And are you VERY organized? Then
you, my friend, may be Type A!

Lab work involves a lot of math, skill, artistic ability, and talent. It requires the use of instruments with a fine point, a flame, and scientific understanding of design and fabrication of dental prothesis (try saying that three times fast). I absolutely love it. So does my boss. To me, the methodical rhythm of performing lab tasks is hypnotic. A myriad of repetitious skills come into play when performing a dental wax up, for example. Heating the scooped wax spatula over a Bunsen flame, pressing the hot instrument down into a block of wax that begins to melt around it, then scooping up the pool of newly melted liquid at just the right time and placing it on your study model, all the while ensuring that the mocked-up plastic teeth on your model stay in place—this is my world and I love it. *Doctor* (as we call Dr. Huntington around the office), has perfected the waxing art. It takes a certain finesse to make the final result of a waxed-up model look like a smooth masterpiece, a replica of a patient's mouth and how they will look when treatment is done. It took me a long while to learn the same techniques. Early on, my wax ups looked like lumpy mashed potatoes. Doctor and I each have our favorite waxing instruments and they are worn with years of use. Mine have become so much a part of me over the years that I jokingly suggest my waxing spatula should accompany me in death—fittingly placed in my left hand with homage paid to being a southpaw!

After I unlock the door and enter through the waiting room, I walk down the hall, passing the first operatory, where Doctor is seated.

"Good morning, Doctor!" I say cheerfully, as I pass by his room.

"Good morning, Joy!" he replies.

I can hear the smile in his voice. You know, come to think of it, I can't remember there ever being a day he was in a grumpy mood in the morning.

This little morning ritual is important to me because I have worked in many offices where my "Good Morning" did not get an answer back. No acknowledgment. None. A nod of the head or a quick, meaningless "Mornin'" is all I'm after, but for some people that is just too much to ask. So, I appreciate Doctor's friendly manner. Unfortunately, not everyone in this small office is as cordial. The person who cleans teeth won't acknowledge my existence and can be downright peculiar sometimes. Now, she is a ray of sunshine around the patients—they all think she is wonderful. But no matter how friendly and helpful I have been to her through the years, she's still like an iceberg when it comes to me. Some people just can't be thawed and choose to live in their own little melodrama. Don't even get me started on that time she tailed me after work! Honestly, I still shake my head about that!

———————

After greeting Doctor, I make my way down the short hallway to the bathroom where I change from my street clothes into scrubs. Because there are so many ooglie mooglies bouncing around during patient care, we keep our scrubs at the office where, mostly, I wash them. After changing and hanging up my street clothes, I put detergent in the washer to start a load of the staff's scrubs and lab jackets from the day before. OSHA (the Occupational Safety and Health Administration) governs healthcare facilities and says it's ideal to keep your dental germs at the office, so the scrubs we wear during our workday are laundered here and never leave. Between the office laundry and my laundry at home, it seems I am always doing laundry. It is an uneasy feeling for me to not have a load going somewhere. In the back of my mind, I think I am always tabulating what's in the washer and what's in the dryer. And in case you are wondering, the hygienist doesn't often help me with the laundry, even though her scrubs are getting washed every day as well. Occasionally she'll get them from the dryer and hang them up. When she does, she makes sure to tell me that when I hang them, it's in the wrong direction. I like buttons facing to the right, but she feels the universe and everything in it will only continue to function if they are facing to the left. I've even caught her reversing the ones I've hung up out of the dryer. *Girl, if you have time to do that, you have time to be the one to take them out of the dryer!* But I try not to let it get to me. I'm lying, it gets to me. You know, everyone has quirks. Whether you can tolerate them is the question. And this is one that gets me.

When I first started out in this industry, scrubs were not the norm for dental assistants and hygienists. In those days, the dentists (usually male) wanted their staff (almost exclusively female) to wear long skirts, pantyhose, and nice blouses. I remember the JCPenney store having so many racks of panty hose—from the cheapies to the pricey ones with reinforced toes, girdle panels, thigh squeezers, and gut suckers—you name it, they had it. But sitting in the assistant chair in a skirt was about as practical as riding a horse in a dress:

awkward, constraining, and uncomfortable. Wearing what felt like a corset and trying to be ladylike while assisting the dentist and leaning over patients all day was a struggle. Not only was it difficult to keep a dressy outfit clean, but preventing my hose from getting a run was often a losing battle. Working in a dental environment creates many opportunities to snag or tear delicate nylon stockings and once started, a run would spend the day working its way up the length of your leg. Unless you carried a bottle of clear nail polish (note: after it dries, putting a dab on the fibers could stop a run in its tracks before it grew), you would be treated all day to the sensation of that nylon fabric slowly splitting open. I had to have an entire work wardrobe that was separate from my regular clothes; and I had to launder off every bit of grossness that landed on my outfits in my home machines. So, suffice it to say, I am very grateful that we now work in scrubs!

Once I'm in the office there is a morning routine—tasks to get the day started—that I run through without thinking. Sometimes I feel like a pilot getting my plane ready for takeoff.

- ✓ Start a load of scrubs in the washer.
- ✓ Fill the ultrasonic, which I call the "shaker," with water and cleaning agent. (This is a machine that uses ultrasound to agitate and remove debris from dental instruments, kind of like a dishwasher.)
- ✓ Empty the reservoir in the autoclave, or the "cooker," as I fondly say; top it off with distilled water; and start a load of bagged instruments from the day before. (A dental autoclave uses extreme heat and steam in a pressurized environment to sterilize instruments.)
- ✓ Wipe down the sink and set out clean towels that the day's soiled instruments will be place on as they accumulate. More laundry for me to do!

- ✓ Changed into scrubs and my lab jacket, both of which will be splattered with dental stone powder and no telling what else over the course of the day.
- ✓ Put away sterilized instruments from the day prior and restock rooms.

Next, I head up front to the reception area to grab a copy of the day's schedule—complete with patient names and the treatments they will have—which was printed out by the receptionist before she left for home the previous day. The dental program we use puts this information into time blocks to show how long each appointment will typically last. Before the receptionist arrives, I check the office voice mail for any emergency situations or cancellations.

I use the printed schedule to make notes about each patient's appointment, check for any lab cases that need to be delivered and add personal notes. After the messages are checked I head to the front dental operatory, where Doctor and I mainly work. I like to preset treatment trays for the day, confirm I have all needed instruments, and chat with Dr. Huntington. We talk about football, but I don't follow sports, so these conversations are mostly Doctor raving or light-heartedly grousing about the latest games and me doing my best to keep up. He gets pretty excited about two teams he roots for but doesn't sulk, thankfully, when things don't go their way. He also likes to hunt and watch DVDs of hunting. He plays these on a little TV/DVD combo that he keeps by his lab bench in the front operatory. That unit must be over twenty-five years old, but somehow it still works. I am sure he'll use it for as long as it keeps playing his hunting DVDs. I've peeked over his shoulder at them a few times: grown men dressed as trees with animal urine dabbed behind their ears and rifles thrown over their shoulders as they tromp through the woods. This is what Doctor likes to glance at and listen to while he sets teeth in wax to make a denture set up and does his other lab work.

"You want me to tell you how this one ends?" I would joke.

"Ha-ha," he says, "I know, I know, something dies."

I remind him he has five minutes before our morning huddle. In Dr. Huntington time, that's ten or fifteen minutes. After a few years of working with him, I've learned that you must secretly add an extra cushion to his time if you want him to be somewhere. His inner conductor moves at its own pace. He's as quick as a train rolling through town, as they say. (In case you aren't familiar, trains typically go through towns . . . very . . . slow . . . and . . . steady.) Well, slow and steady does win the race!

At our morning team meeting, we discuss each patient and the progress on the lab cases. Dr. Huntington and I have a short-hand dental language that we use to discuss our plan for the day. While we may set out to have a case follow a certain path, that often doesn't happen, so we try to prepare for obstacles and (should we hit one) have a plan for other directions we can take. Over my many years working with Doctor, one thing that I have come to admire about him is that he has always been open to my suggestions. There are times when he has made me feel like a genius for my ideas! If I propose something that's too far out there, he'll explain why it wouldn't be a possibility, yet never discount my input. Many times he's encouraged me to try what I think might be a good way to do a dental task, just to see if it will work. I can't tell you how many times an idea has failed, and I have felt discouraged, like I wasted my time. But through that trial and error I have learned why certain things won't work and moved on. In my head, I know Dr. Huntington has tried most techniques over the years and knows how to produce the most ideal outcome. I appreciate that he has given me the chance to learn on my own, as this has made me a better assistant.

*A good teacher allows the student
to make mistakes and use them
as an opportunity to learn.*

The receptionist arrives just as we are about to start our morning meeting. Doris has a long drive to the office every day. She is an older woman with gray hair, chickens in her backyard, and a love for Jesus. I like picking on her in a loving way. She's easily rattled and over the years I have tried to shield her from situations that might shake her up, such as disgruntled patients, pushy salesmen, or computer issues. Doris is more honest and innocent than anyone I know. We make a great team, especially when an older patient wants to tell me their medical life story. I typically need to get my next patient and don't have time for the whole story, but I don't want to be rude. Instead, I just park them in front of Doris, and they can compare medical surgeries till the cows come home. When you sit with Doris, she gives you her full attention and listens to every word you say—and without a doubt, I'm sure she'll include anything you tell her in her daily prayers.

Next, in walks the hygienist. She arrives as I'm setting up my room. My "Good Morning!" greetings usually annoy her, so when I'm feeling ornery, I make sure to direct one LOUD and CLEAR in her direction. Most days, I leave her be.

After a few minutes our meeting is called to order. Doris pulls up a chair, Dr. Huntington takes his seat, the hygienist wanders up from her room (playing on her phone), and I seat myself at a desk in front of a computer. We start to discuss the patients scheduled for the day, reading through the block of appointments. I like to look at the schedule on the computer during our discussion and add additional notes.

"Joy, make sure to have the Zimmer implant kit ready for the patient after lunch. He has a loose implant crown," Dr. Huntington starts out. "This was an implant placed ten years ago and I'm hoping once I access the retaining screw, through the occlusal surface of the crown, I will just have to tighten the screw and place a resin filling in the access opening."

(Translation: he needs the little screwdriver from a certain dental company and a spare sterilized screw. He will use a high-speed handpiece with a little bur to cut through the top of the crown until he removes the old filling, which will expose the top of the screw that holds the implant crown in. He will see if it just needs tightening or needs a new screw and then replace the white filling thus sealing the occlusal surface. Then he will check the bite and adjust as needed and ta da, mission completed!) Typically he can perform this task without compromising the existing crown.

"Would you also like a periapical X-ray taken prior?" I ask. This means a single radiograph, or X-ray, of a tooth.

"Yes, please."

"So, worst case scenario would be what?"

"Well, the implant in the bone could be failing, causing mobility. But I really believe the screw has just loosened over the years. If I can't torque it to 15 Newton-Centimeters, then I will replace the screw with a new one."[1]

"Gotcha," I say, knowing I will need to have the sterile replacement screw ready for the procedure.

---

1 A Newton-Centimeter (Ncm) is the desired insertion torque for a dental implant.

Everything looks like it will unfold nicely for the other patients, and we are ready to start our day. The hygienist continues to play on her phone while I leave to transfer the laundry to the dryer, flip the suction compressor on, wash my hands thoroughly, and then head to the front office to seat my first patient about five minutes ahead of schedule.

"Mrs. Livingston? Hi! My name is Joy," I say, as I enter the waiting room. I am ready to escort this new patient back to the dental operatory. She has been filling out paperwork to inform us of her medical and dental past. For many, this takes quite a chunk of time. Doris will go over the paperwork to make sure everything is signed properly, and all medications are listed.

"I am Dr. Huntington's assistant," I say. "Welcome to our prosthodontic practice." I try to speak loudly, enunciating my name, for our patients who are older and may be a little hard of hearing.

"Julie?" she says back, breathlessly getting up from the waiting room chair.

"No, not Julie. J-O-Y. Joy," I say, spelling it out and using my left hand to underline my name tag, "Vanna White style."

My trusty name tag has had the same placement for twenty-nine years. Every workday I dutifully pin it onto the upper corner of my lab jacket, above the left pocket where it's proudly displayed until the workday is over and it is released from duty. How much easier would it make life if we all just wore nametags wherever we went? No more awkwardness at parties or crowded events because you can't remember that one person's name . . . and then like me, having to invent nicknames so they stay in your memory. Funny ones, which always stay safely tucked away inside my head.

They say you're supposed to look someone in the eye when you meet them and say their name three times, and if that isn't enough, use a rhyme to make their name stick in your mind. So, that's what I do. I most often try to remember people's names by something unusual I can associate with them. Mrs. Abbey, who babbles and talks nonstop, becomes "Mrs. Gabby Abbey." Rufus is a doofus (he lost his denture). Ms. Holmes' upper denture has lipstick to spare—hence why she'll forever be known through my stare, as "Ms. Lipstick"! Jack and Joan Filpot, a married pair, bring humor to the office when they come for dental care. See what I did there?

There are many times when Doctor and I play "Name That Patient." We can remember facts about teeth, procedures we've done, a patient's grandkids, and other tidbits, but not your name. Doris can tell you a patient's name based on a surgery they've once told her about, and I'm not kidding!

"Julie?" the new patient says again.

"No ma'am, J-O-Y, like my name tag says," and I once again sweep my finger across my name tag.

I have tried to break myself of pointing to my name tag "Vanna White style" because of a particular incident. My husband and I were at our church, both dressed in our Sunday best; he was standing proudly by my side. At the point in the service where we were told to greet those around us, I turned to a couple beside me who we did not know (they were new to the church) ready to make an introduction.

With a friendly smile I said, "My name is Joy," while using my left hand in my typical "Vanna White style," as if I was wearing my name tag!

The woman looked very confused by my invitation for her to look at my chest, and just said, "Excuse me?"

I repeated, "My name is Joy," as I again ran my hand across the top of my left breast, from right to left, pointing out my nonexistent name tag to this poor couple.

They both smiled, did the polite head nod, and quickly turned to greet someone in the opposite direction.

My husband quietly whispered in my ear, while trying not to bust out laughing, "You aren't wearing your name tag and have just pointed out your left breast to that new couple."

"Oh no!" I whispered back, in complete shock, quickly realizing it was time for me to take some well-deserved R&R from the dental office.

Handing Mrs. Livingston's paperwork to Doris, minus her health history (which Dr. Huntington will go over), I usher my new patient through the waiting room doorway and down the hall to the operatory room.

"Let's have a seat in here, and Doctor will be in to meet you and go over your health history," I say.

But this would be too easy, you don't just bring a patient from the waiting room to the operatory without them needing a detour. I understand this and it doesn't even phase me when she asks for the restroom.

Mrs. Livingston: "I need to use the restroom first, is that all right?"

"Oh, yes, of course you may use the restroom first," I say. Never mind that Mrs. Livingston was thirty minutes early to fill out paperwork, which she completed in twenty minutes, then sat in the waiting room for another ten minutes until she was called back.

"I'll show you where it is, all the way back up front in the waiting room," I say. And in my head I think, *Where you were seated for the past thirty minutes. . . .*

Even if Doris has asked you to please visit the restroom prior to being brought back for your appointment, most everyone asks to use it the minute I come up to the waiting area to get them.

Always.

Five minutes go by. . . .

I am waiting to escort my new patient back to the dental chair. Time is ticking away for this appointment that was scheduled for an hour slot. I know five minutes isn't a lot, but if every patient puts me five or ten minutes behind, before long I'm thirty minutes behind and patients in the waiting room are getting cranky.

At the ten-minute mark, we are headed back to the dental operatory. It's always our plan to stay on schedule, and mentally I am calculating where I will make lost time up throughout my day.

"What brings you in today?" I ask, as she sets her belongings on the counter and takes a seat.

Mrs. Livingston: "First, may I have a cup of water; my mouth is dry from all of my medications."

"Yes, I will gladly get you a cup of water from the water cooler." I then walk back up front to the waiting room—you know, where she was originally seated with time to get a drink and use the restroom—to get her a cup of water from the water cooler.

A moment later, I present her with the requested cup of water, "Here's your water, Mrs. Livingston." *Of course, with the medication she is on, most likely drinking this cup of water will make her need to use the restroom again in a few minutes. But that's all right . . .*

Mrs. Livingston: "I need a tissue please, my eyes constantly water and I always have to have one handy."

A tissue? That you could have grabbed out of the box that sits on the counter . . . right next to where you set your purse before you sat down? Let me come from all the way on the other side of the chair and grab you a tissue.

"Yes, of course, you may have several," I say. "Are you having any discomfort with any of your teeth? Are there any dental concerns for you today?" I start making notes in her file on the computer.

Note: NP (New Patient) 81 yr. old female

Mrs. Livingston: "I hate for you to see my teeth; they are in bad shape, and I forgot to brush. Do you have any mouthwash? May I rinse first?"

"Yes, we do have mouthwash, of course. You can rinse before the dentist does your exam."

I move again to the other side of the chair to get a bit of mouthwash in a plastic cup. I hand her two cups, one with the mouthwash and another to spit in, so she doesn't have to get up and use the sink. This actually grosses me out. I can handle blood and everything else that goes along with being a dental assistant, but foamy spit still gets me.

Resuming my position by the computer, I begin again to ask the questions that the dentist needs to know before he enters the operatory—and now it's twenty minutes into the appointment that was scheduled for an hour. I know Dr. Huntington wants to be thorough with his exam and will take at least forty-five minutes. Once again I'm calculating how we will get our day back on track.

"Do you have any teeth that are causing you concern? Any dental complaints?"

Mrs. Livingston: "No, nothing is bothering me," she says. "I just want a pretty smile. When I was young and married, I put my family first, and now I want to do something for myself. I had three children, and their needs came before mine. I've lost so many teeth and I'm embarrassed to smile, so I don't."

Suddenly I feel for her. None of her little requests and delays matter anymore. I'm used to those, anyway. I'm glad to know her concerns and to work in a profession that can help her. I sit down next to her in my assistant's chair for a moment, and say, "You know, that's more common than you think. Back in the day it was of the mindset to pull teeth if they were bothering you, but that's changed. You've come to the right place! Dr. Huntington will be doing an exam today and discussing with you how we can get you the smile you've always wanted."

Note: NP 81 yr. old female, no dental complaints.
Wants to improve her smile.

Reading through her medical history to confirm all needed information is filled out for the doctor, I see a medical surgery was checked.

"I see you had a surgery on your knee. What year? And I see you are on several medications. Do you have a dry mouth? Also, when was your last cleaning?"

Note: Left knee replacement 2012, NKA (No known
allergies), HH (health history) reviewed, patient states
dry mouth due to meds. Last prophy (cleaning) 2016.

After what probably seems like a million questions, I say, "Let me go get Dr. Huntington and he and I will be with you shortly."

Dr. Huntington and I have a routine when it comes to new patients. I take the patient's full dental history, note their dental concerns, and listen to their stories—then I brief him on the little tidbits before he sees the patient. This allows him to walk into the operatory with his opening line ready and establish a good rapport with someone. For example, Doctor might say to a new patient: "Joy tells me you have three children, and you are originally from here. That's unusual for a Navy town . . ."

And they are off . . .

The new patient exam takes about an hour. In Dr. Huntington time that's about an hour plus ten or fifteen minutes. He likes to get to know his patients, listen to what they have to say about their dental needs, and explain how we can help them achieve the best outcome. While Doctor describes what he can offer a patient, in my mind I play a game of "dental chess." *If we make this move and do this procedure, then we will have to make another move and do this other procedure.* I can see the pieces moving on the gameboard, just as I can see Mrs. Livingston's mouth start to change into the beautiful smile she is dreaming of. I absolutely love this part of being a prosthodontic dental assistant. I can envision many complex procedures and how they will progress over multiple appointments for a patient. Years of working alongside Dr. Huntington, being his copilot, and observing his techniques and expertise have brought me to this level of understanding. I have seen him work miracles for many patients.

Dr. Huntington quickly explains the process of taking the digital X-rays and the needed preliminary upper and lower impressions before leaving us alone in the room.

As soon as he leaves, Mrs. Livingston turns to me with an anxious look and says, "So, how do we start? What should I expect when you take those upper and lower impressions?

I pat her hand reassuringly and begin to explain that although the process may be a little uncomfortable, the impressions will capture every detail of her mouth, so we can create an accurate model of her teeth as they are now. Then, Dr. Huntington will lay out the treatment we will follow to make that beautiful new smile she desires so much!

I see a glimmer of hope twinkling in her eyes and my heart warms at the thought that we are about to make this long-awaited dream a reality. Helping people have confident smiles is definitely one of the perks of being a dental professional.

"Mrs. Livingston, we're going to help you get that new, beautiful smile you want. I'll be with you every step of the way. Now, let's take those first impressions!"

PART I

The Beginning Years

CHAPTER 2

The Game of Life

I grew up in Odessa, Texas, an oil field town that went bust in the early 80s. If you passed through during that time (and for many years) you would see blocks of abandoned stores, closed oil field operations, and rundown homes. On your way out of town nothing but empty fields would sprawl for as far as your eye could see. There's a joke in West Texas about the land being so flat and void of trees that you can watch your dog run away for three days. The landscape is dry and punctuated with mesquite bushes, cacti, and pump jacks. In wintertime, to add flair to our front porches, we built snowmen out of tumbleweeds that the winds often lined up against fences. For a teenager in Odessa in the later part of that disparaging decade, there was absolutely nothing to do except waste gas cruising "the drag." The drag was a three-mile stretch of highway that ran through the center of town. We would drive back and forth, over and over, turning around in parking lots that sat at each end. The hope was to see someone you knew (or wanted to get to know) from one of the two high schools. We would drive and drive, loop after loop, chasing dreams, love, and adventure . . . trying to create our own excitement. Once, I exchanged snow cones with a stranger in the next car while my friend drove—our two cars way too close as we traveled down the road, side by side—cute boys in that car, being daring and making the most of a moment in time.

My parents (my mom and my stepdad) were both in law enforcement so I grew up spending a lot of time at the sheriff's department. I knew most of the officers and staff, which meant that everywhere I went I would make eye contact with an officer who would most likely report my whereabouts to my parents.

My brother, Brian, was one year, one month, and six days older than me and in every way my exact opposite. I was involved in all the classes, clubs, and events, whereas he stayed in his room or out in his wood-working shop building something by himself. In our younger years when we would spend holidays and summers at my grandparents' home in San Angelo, Texas, my brother was forced to interact more with me. They had almost two acres of land with a large garden. There was always something to be picked, snapped, shelled, canned, shucked, or watered. After harvesting produce, and we would all sit on the back porch and chat while our hands busily prepared ripened produce for cooking or canning.

If it was not too hot my brother and I would pull out the Jarts and start a game. Jarts were lawn darts that were more like long, weighted daggers you would hurl at targets placed on the lawn. Their sharp, pointy tips would pierce the ground so the oversized dart would stick where it landed. It was the kind of activity that was all the rage until people and pets started getting injured and killed from being hit with a stray Jart. This led to the game being banned in 1988. For years before the ban, they couldn't be sold in toy stores or without an explicit warning label—and here we were, two young kids throwing them every which way.

We did not watch television unless Grandma and Grandpa turned on the news or *Wheel of Fortune*, so Brian and I had to find other ways each day to entertain ourselves. Grandpa had a wooden can crusher, built with his own hands, that we used to crush aluminum coke or beer cans. (In the south, everything soda-wise is called a "coke.") The crushed cans would then be sold for cash at a scrap-metal place. My brother and I would walk the neighborhood looking for cans, or my grandpa would gather empty cans from our relatives' households. Brian didn't care so much about the crushing, but I would smash can after can, pulling the wooden lever to bring a block of wood down on the pliable aluminum until it was just a little disk. We also played dominos when the heat of the day was too much and kept us inside, which was often the case by midmorning during a sweltering West Texas summer. My brother would join us for a few rounds, then lose interest because my grandpa was a math genius (even though he only had a third-grade education) and would win almost every game. Looking back, I thought I had beaten him every so often; but in reality, Grandpa sometimes let me win so I would keep playing.

In 1989, at barely eighteen years old, I married my high school sweetheart. I was a senior with a few weeks still to go before graduation; but my soon-to-be husband had finished high school early and enlisted in the Navy. We were married as soon as he finished boot camp and was able to come back home for a week. Within days he left for Connecticut to attend his first Navy training, called "A" School. We were so in love and felt we could conquer the world and anything else that was put in front of us. After I graduated, my parents drove me and my meager belongings up to the Northeast so I could join my new husband. Despite being really excited for my new married life, saying goodbye to my mom was difficult, and I found myself in tears every other day. It helped to have a new part of the country to explore, though. Everything was so different from Texas. Though we were as poor as a church mice, even with me working at a child development center, we found ways to discover what the area offered.

Six months later, my husband had finished his schooling and the Navy informed us that he would be stationed at Naval Submarine Base Bangor (now Bangor Trident Base), in Washington State. We moved over Christmas time with our cash savings in a little cedar box, and quickly discovered that the Pacific Northwest was breathtakingly beautiful. Night and day from West Texas and the tumbleweeds.

Our lives now became a seemingly endless cycle of my husband's deployments—out to sea on a submarine for three months, then back home for three months, only to go back out again. It was difficult for me to adjust to the changes that came with this lifestyle, even though I thought of myself as independent and capable. I tried to make friends with the other military wives, but they were mostly older and had kids, so we just didn't click. They would often meet up at the local bars, but I was only eighteen, so this left me out. Fortunately, I met Laura, a Navy wife from Montana who was my age. She was warm and kindhearted with a flair for fashion that made her stand out. As new wives who were also new to the military lifestyle, on top of still being teenagers and living far from home, we hit it off immediately. Neither of us had children yet, so we set out to have fun on those long weekends while our spouses were away. We enjoyed going shopping, exploring the Seattle area, and sharing stories of what life was like back home. She introduced this West Texas girl to gyros from a food truck, scones fresh from the bakery, clam chowder, and a world of other foods that were not typical in my upbringing.

By chance, I also had the opportunity to meet and develop a lifelong friendship with my upstairs apartment neighbor, Lynn. She was tremendously pregnant at the time and struggling to cope with the oppressive heat of the summer season. Our apartment building did not have air conditioning, which was not unusual for that part of the country because it was only hot for a few weeks in the summer. One evening I had my large bedroom window open in an attempt to cool the place off a bit. Lynn's bedroom was directly above mine and apparently her window was open as well.

"Hellloooo . . ." I heard, coming from somewhere, as I put laundry away in the bedroom dresser.

"Um . . . hello??" I replied to no one.

"Were you good today?" the voice asked.

"I um, well, I did have a piece of cake, but otherwise, I would say, YES."

I heard loud laughter and then footsteps moving through the apartment above me. A few moments later there was a knock on my apartment door. When I opened it, my very pregnant neighbor was standing in front of me, smiling.

"Hey! I live above you and was just talking to my cat; I think you might have thought I was a crazy lady shouting out a screened window."

"Well, not so crazy that I did not answer you!"

We both laughed and introduced ourselves, and in that moment became instant friends. She was a military brat who had grown up with a father in the Navy, which gave her an understanding of the struggles I was facing. We continued building our friendship as the days went by. Before long, she welcomed a precious little boy into the world. Our bond continued to grow over time and years, and we could always stand by each other through thick and thin. Lynn showed me the value of true friendship.

Another chance encounter that changed my life forever was meeting Liz in the apartment laundry room. As we sorted through our respective piles of laundry, we noticed the same insignia on some of our T-shirts—a design that only those who served on a particular submarine would have. This realization opened a conversation between us and soon enough, we were sharing stories.

Liz was from Florida, and it turned out that our husbands were on the same submarine. That chance meeting led to us being best friends for life. When our husbands were in from sea, we didn't see much of each other; but as soon as they shipped out again, we would pick up right where we left off—traveling to tulip festivals, pizza nights, craft shows, driving up mountains to take in the beautiful views, or whatever amazing adventures we could discover.

Friends come and go like the waves of the ocean . . . but true ones stick, like an octopus on your face. — Unknown

---

I quickly found out you can't live off love and an E-2 income, so I looked for a job that I would genuinely enjoy and found one as a nanny for three little kids in Poulsbo, which was a twenty-minute drive from our apartment. I'd done plenty of babysitting in Texas, starting at age twelve with the children of my parents' co-workers at the sheriff's department, so taking care of little ones seemed like a natural way for me to supplement our income. For this position, I would be responsible for a newborn boy, a three-year-old girl, and a four-year-old boy. The parents were very strict about their children not watching watch TV, so they did not even have one in the house. Unusual in today's world where technology reigns supreme. We did lots of fun crafts such as paper chains, coloring, and making paper airplanes to throw around the backyard. We played games like tag and hide-and-seek; we also got creative by putting together obstacle courses made out of pillows and cushions. For the most part, not a bad job for a teenager—which I still was—even though the newborn was using *cloth diapers*. Seriously, google cloth diapers and feel sorry for young me.

The days went along fairly smoothly, or at least as smooth as juggling three kids can be, until . . . "THE DAY" came along that would remain forever etched in my memory. The day that changed my mind about being a nanny. . . .

The mom was still breast feeding the newborn, so she would come home to nurse him as often as her job allowed. On this particular day she pulled me aside to fill me in on a little tidbit: The baby was having difficulty pooping. I was completely taken aback, this wasn't exactly a topic I had discussed with anyone before, but here she was giving me the entire lowdown on her baby's bowel movements like it was no big deal. My initial thought was: *Ewww, gross! How do I handle this?* I wanted to appear confident and professional. I was a nanny, right? This was all part of my job description. But it wasn't sitting well with me. As she explained in vivid detail about her infant's condition and that I would need to apply an ointment to his butthole as well as stimulate his anus to help with his bowel movements, my stomach literally turned. At that point, I think my very soul fainted inside me at the thought of having to perform such an intimate task for a child who wasn't even mine. Keep in mind, she was on child THREE. She was in "just-do-what's-necessary" mode, while I was in "Oh heavens do what?!??"- She went on and on about his severe diaper rash and how he was starting to associate pooping with pain, so he was holding back on his bowel movements. . . . I felt the blood drain from my face. Shouldn't this mom have noticed that for me the room was spinning, and I could no longer follow exactly what she was saying? But she continued on with her instructions, giving me every detail, step by step, telling me how and where to apply the *ointment* and to stimulate his *anus*. With. My. Fingers. My mind began spinning out of control and I could no longer make sense of what she was saying. Words swirled together into a jumbled mess as they reverberated through my head: "stimulate," "poop," "anus," "fingers." I think I mentally checked out when the word "poop" was first mentioned.

Now let's be clear, I was just eighteen years old. I was not ready to stimulate another human's anus!

That same day, the three-year-old had a snotty nose that she would wipe on her dress or blow snot bubbles if I was not quick enough with a tissue. Coughing, nose running down her face, she constantly followed me asking for another snack, which was okay because it kept her within reach so I could wipe her nose. To add to the list, she was on medication which I had to stay on top of throughout the day and get her to take. The four-year-old, not to be outdone, had just thrown up for the second time (after the mom went back to work). This meant that my day consisted of wiping noses, cleaning up vomit, bathing children and trying everything in my power to help a baby go poop (which at this point felt like an insurmountable challenge)!

When the time came, I dutifully took the baby to the changing table to do the deed as per the mom's instructions. By now I was covered in every type of fluid that could come out of a human, what's one more? I did my best to follow the mom's steps, trying not to gag as I applied the ointment to his cherry red bottom. Placing the cloth diaper on him followed by a pair of rubber pants, I picked him up and seconds later IT happened. An explosive release of what can only be described as putrid breast-fed-baby poo erupted from his bottom! His cloth diaper was no match for the sheer volume of liquid that came flying out like water from a firehose. In an instant, mustard yellow liquid oozed and spurted in all directions—covering not only the little guy in smelly, runny baby poo, but me, too!

This, my friends, was the last straw. Right then and there I decided that nannying multiple young children was not my calling. I tended to every need of each child until their parents came home, and with much regret I dropped the axe (with a little notice so they could find a replacement nanny). As my days in that home dwindled down, I looked forward to hanging up my proverbial nanny hat. I would no longer be wiping someone else's child's snotty nose, erupting vomit, or chapped butt.

I. Was. Done.

CHAPTER 3

Finding the Next Step

Now a retired nanny, it was time to find another way to supplement our income. In high school I had always been passionate about theater arts and might have even pursued a degree in this field if I hadn't gotten married and moved away. Now that I was living almost 2,000 miles from home and needing an income, going for a four-year degree didn't seem feasible. I set my sites on finding something that would be a good career and have me working before too long. To make an informed decision, I decided to visit a local technical college and meet with an advisor to find out about the programs they offered and what the cost commitments would entail. I've often wondered if this advisor was short on student enrollment for dental assistants because without hesitation she pushed me toward dentistry. Although the thought was intriguing, I wasn't sure it was the perfect fit for me. The dentist was not my favorite place to be. When I was three, my mom and grandma had taken me to a dentist who, to my young eyes, looked like a big, scary giant. In fact, I got so scared that I urinated in the dental chair. The office had a foul smell that I could still recall, and I was sure I had heard kids screaming and crying in the other exam rooms.

In high school I had taken a career placement test, as was common at that time. I had always pegged myself for something worldly sounding: paranormal investigator, smokejumper, spy, or actress. Imagine my surprise when my placement test results indicated I would make an excellent plumber!

The advisor at this technical school said I had only two choices: dental assisting or medical assisting. Had I taken typing in high school, she said, I could have studied to be a receptionist. With only two options put before me, I had to decide which end I wanted to work on, the mouth end or the hind end. I really didn't know if medical assisting would involve the hind end, but visions of bed pans started dancing through my head. I took that as a sign. I'd already had six years of wiping hind ends at this point, so I chose dental assisting to try the mouth end.

I started the program, but after only a few weeks I didn't feel any more confident in my choice. I mean, who enjoys sucking spit out of another person's mouth or seeing them spit into the cuspidor (a chairside dental spit bowl that was still common in those days)? I was the one who hadn't wanted to stimulate an anus and now here I was at the other end watching people spit, drool, and gag?!? I started looking for a way out, another option. I was certain I was not on the path the Lord had meant for my life to take. *Were paranormal investigators subjected to such gross atrocities?* I wondered.

In this school, the dress code consisted of white pants and a coordinating top. In the 1990 world of wearing very bright, vivid, neon colors, I didn't own any muted tops, much less with white in them. I prayed out loud, *Lord, we don't have the money for new clothes. If it's meant for me to be a dental assistant, place in front of*

me a way to get the clothes I need to continue with this career path.
On the way home from class the next day I stopped at a yard sale.
In a pile of clothes, I found almost new, white scrub pants in my
size and several coordinating tops—all for a song and a dance.
Finding these clothes on that day, literally, was the reason I stayed
in dental assisting school.

I excelled at learning the book portion of dentistry. Using
my husband's mouth to count teeth and study the shape of each
tooth, I was able to visually see much of what was described and
illustrated in the book. I memorized the components for the X-ray
machine, the names for instruments, and the types of dental materials. In class we practiced on each other, taking impressions and
hard dental X-rays, looking in the little dental mirror, loading the
dental syringe for the dentist to give an injection, and counting
teeth while using your finger to fulcrum (using a finger as a support from which to pivot). We took dental-alginate impressions
until we were able to get all the landmarks. Over and over. My
gag reflex is super sensitive, so I had a very hard time when my
classmates took dental impressions or X-rays in my mouth, but
thankfully they didn't ask me to be their "patient" very often. My
sensitivities, however, made me hyper aware of the difficulties and
sensitivities any patient might have, and I have worked hard to keep
impressions from being traumatizing for my patients throughout
my career. For a final test grade, I convinced a friend to let me take
a full series of sixteen hard X-rays on her. It took over three hours
to take the images, develop and mount them, then get graded, but
it turned out well. God bless her!

I was hired by a general dentist for the six-week-externship
portion of my dental assisting program. It was typical for this on-
the-job training to be unpaid. As luck would have it, however,
this dentist was not only willing to train me with pay, but he also

offered me a dental assistant position after my externship. My new boss was quiet and wore all white from head to toe, because of his Mormon religion. He apparently hired me for my book smarts, because I had no experience being in a patient's mouth. It takes years of practice to develop a gentle manner, to learn how not to jab the patient with a sharp instrument or your fingernails, and to master keeping the dentist's working field clean and visible while staying out of their way with the suction.

My first week I would have many meltdowns. I felt overwhelmed and inexperienced. But the seasoned hygienist kindly whispered in my ear, "Fake it till you make it. It will come to you in time."

I have heard her whispered words every time I have started a new endeavor.

This dentist wanted his assistants to wear the usual white pants with a coordinating shirt. As I've mentioned, he wore white as well, so in my head I nicknamed him "Dr. Whitepants." He told me that in his religion this was a sign of purity. I'm not the tidiest person and dentistry can be a messy profession, so I did my best to keep my whites clean.

A few weeks into working at this practice, I was assisting Dr. Whitepants in an extraction procedure. Just when he thought the tooth was coming out nicely, the crown, or the top part, of the tooth snapped off (as can happen) and he was left to get the root tip out of the bone. Think of getting a tiny splinter out of your finger. This can be difficult—sometimes very difficult. The goal when removing a tooth is always to preserve bone, but the entire root tip must come out. At times the dentist will use a high-speed handpiece with a surgical bur to remove a small amount of bone to get enough leverage to pop the root tip out. In moments like these it's very important for the assistant to suction the seepage from the extraction site while keeping the suction tip out of the way, to ensure the dentist has a clear view of what they are doing.

"Suction," Doctor said, as he grabbed his large, metal extraction forceps from a tray.

I placed the tip of the plastic surgical suction near the site where he was working.

"Suction," he said more sternly.

He repeated his requests for suction, and each time I gently placed the surgical suction into the site. Surgical suction tips have a tiny little opening so you can get them right into the tooth socket. I kept suctioning the area but, of course, seconds later the socket fill up again with blood, blocking Doctor's view of the root tip.

"Suction, suction . . ." Whitepants growled over and over, *"Suction! Suction!! SUCTION!!!"*

As the tone of his demands escalated so did my stress! I was still honing my skills but trying to be an efficient assistant for both Doctor and patient.

I see the next part in slow motion. Dissatisfied with my suctioning skills, Dr. Whitepants grabbed the suction from me in frustration, only to find that the suction tip wasn't securely in place. The surgical suction tip popped out of the high-volume evacuation hose, splattering blood all over his white clothes. I froze. *What just happened?!?* I grabbed the hose portion from

Doctor as the suction hissed loudly without the buffer of the tip. Doctor now stood there in his now blood-stained clothes, looking like a murder victim, as the slightly dripping, bloody suction tip dangled from his fingers. Tears started to well up in my eyes and the moment forever etched itself into my brain. *What have I done?* My bloodied boss just glared at me, but before my emotional response could fully brew, he snapped his fingers, pointed toward the patient (who had somehow been spared from the mess) and mouthed, "No! Not now!" Apparently, I was to have my little break down later because we needed to get that root tip out. From there, we managed to complete the procedure without further incident, despite the tense and strained atmosphere.

Some talk about "baptism by fire," but I think mine was a baptism by blood!

Can I say it one more time? And can I get an *Amen?!?* Thank the heavens above that we now wear scrubs and protective jackets that stay at the office to be laundered, with extra sets available in case the day comes when there is a situation, and we need to change! And, as God as my witness, I have checked to make sure the high-volume suction tip is securely in place before every procedure since that day!

———————

I think it's fair to say that this wasn't going to be my forever office. In a way, it was helpful to learn early on that there would be "good" offices and "bad" ones, that things might not always click, and that the dentist or the staff might not all become my closest friends. But it was a very tough lesson to learn during my first time out in the field, and I went through a lot of professional growing pains because of it.

My First Dental Assistant Job – Lessons Learned

✓ How to deal with in-office and in-the-moment tensions.

✓ How to keep my cool when Doctor is losing his.

✓ How to keep moving through a procedure, no matter what.

✓ Always put the patient first, even if tensions are rising.

———

Another piece of the puzzle I learned about quickly in my first dental job—and one that I had absolutely no prior experience with—had to do with office culture. The social game.

A dental office is a very small world and ecosystem unto itself. Like a band with each musician playing an instrument in rhythm with the group, the song will either come out magically and effortlessly, or an off note will float through and mess everything up. Each player must learn their part and know how to best contribute to the whole. But I was just learning all of this. I knew I wanted to function within a friendly, respectful workplace (Don't we all?) but I would have a few more barefoot jaunts across hot coals before I would know how to navigate the layered dynamics of a dental office.

I carried on, trying to march to the beat, seeking to find the rhythm. I quickly learned that not everyone in an office wants to find that rhythm. Some people just won't play with the band no matter what. Some will constantly go against the grain. You know how there's always that one person at every job? You know the one . . . with the little remarks and the less than helpful attitude. Mona was that person in this office. She was a seasoned assistant who had been working in the profession for years. I had hoped to get into an office with an experienced assistant who might help me learn the ropes, but she wasn't too keen on helping me learn anything. She did her job and tolerated me, and that's where it ended. No tips or suggestions would be offered from the all-wise, all-knowing assistant. Now, it wasn't all bad. We had some good moments thanks to the patients' fascination with us. Mona was from New Orleans and had an accent that contrasted mine. Between my West Texas cadence and her New Orleans drawl, we kept the patients in stitches and well entertained. Her tales of Mardi Gras were particularly captivating: she described the floats as being elaborately decorated, with beads, moon pies, and other trinkets being thrown from them into the crowds that lined the streets. I couldn't even begin to imagine that kind of party atmosphere. She was married and wanted to have a baby and shared this often when we chatted. Despite her disinterest in helping me professionally, at least we did talk. The receptionist was another matter entirely—she blatantly ignored me because I had taken the job that her friend had previously held before leaving for hygiene school. Learning the basics of dental assisting was easy, but I was not prepared for the politics and personalities among the staff. Everyone seemed to have their own quirks and it took time to become accustomed to them.

I kept my head down and stayed focused on my work, trying to build the practical experience I so desperately needed. Becoming familiar with the dental techniques came easily to me; but the hardest part of my new career was learning *how* to work in people's mouths. Being gentle yet confident in what I was doing was my biggest hurdle. One day, I was assisting on a bridge procedure with Dr. Whitepants. I guess the appointment ran long, because suddenly the entire staff was ready to go to lunch and waiting on him to join them. He had prepped the patient's teeth (meaning he reduced each tooth by a millimeter all around, so the lab could make a bridge that would fit over them) and then we took a final impression. This involved sliding a quadrant tray lined with foul-tasting puddy—with a thin layer of another type of impression material drizzled on top—into the patient's mouth for him to bite down on, and there it would stay for ten minutes. Well, Dr. Whitepants and staff skipped off to lunch as soon as he inspected the impression we had taken. This left me behind with this nice gentleman patient. I set about making a temporary acrylic resin bridge by hand, for him to use while the lab made his permanent bridge. I had only made one or two temporary bridges or temporary crowns at this point, so I wasn't very familiar with the smelly material I was working with in his mouth. It starts off as a runny liquid, but within a few minutes it begins to harden and slightly heat up. At the heat stage it should be ready to come out of the mouth to be contoured. If you have any undercuts, or the preps aren't one hundred percent parallel, the acrylic can lock into place. It's all about the timing when using this material: remove it too soon and it will still be runny and make a mess, remove it too late and guess what . . .

It will have no give and you'll find it has locked onto the teeth . . .

It won't come out . . .

By this point in my life, I carried with me a few golden nuggets that I learned from my stepdad. First, if you drive in snow and spin out, turn the wheel in the direction of the skid. He always said it was an easy way to regain control of your car. Second, keep your hands at ten and two on the steering wheel. *My stepdad was in law enforcement, so he was all about keeping control of your vehicle—best to avoid the kinds of accident scenes he came upon in his line of work.* Third, and this is probably the single most important piece of advice he ever gave me: If you ever get lost, stay put! Statically speaking, someone is more likely to find you if you aren't moving around. This also serves as a great reminder for when mistakes are made—just STOP! Your issue is more likely not to need as much correction if you stop early and make a plan.

So, there I was with this nice patient, trying to make a temporary bridge. I was using an acrylic material, kinda like fake fingernails are made from, with an acute smell that would get in your nose and mouth. It hit the heat stage and I tried to remove it from the patient's mouth, but it was locked onto his teeth. Not a little bit locked on, but FULL ON not coming off. I couldn't budge it! *Oh crap,* I thought, *Doctor and the rest of the staff are out to lunch!* I could not believe my luck and here was this poor man in the chair expecting me to be all done with his temporary in a few minutes. I was really up a creek without a paddle, so I did the only thing I could do: STOP and make a plan. I leveled with the guy. I told him, "I got your temporary locked on and you won't be able to fully bite down. The dentist will have to use a handpiece with a dental bur to cut it off, but he's not here at the moment. He'll be back soon, but until then we're just going to have to chat for the next forty-five minutes or so." I felt awful that this had happened at all, let alone so early in the lunch hour. Never mind that no one had considered when or if I would have lunch that day. Despite all this, the patient was very understanding of the situation, and I learned a lot about him while we waited for the dentist to come back. Mind you, these were the days before cell phones, so I had no way of tracking the staff down and filling them in on what was happening in the office. When Dr. Whitepants and staff returned, he was not thrilled (OK, he was mad), but he quickly burred off the stuck material and we made a new temporary and sent the patient on his way. I would later see that patient around town, and we would have a chuckle every time about me getting this tempo-rary bridge locked in his mouth, and who the heck leaves a new assistant alone with a patient to make a temporary?!? But what else could I have done? *If you ever get lost . . . stay put, someone will eventually find you. If you mess something up, STOP, and get help—unless the help is at lunch, in which case wait for help to finish his leisurely lunch and come back.*

I can't remember how long I worked in that office. It felt like years, but it was only about six months. My personality was much too bubbly for such a serious place. The life lessons I learned while there were invaluable though, and I found a way to take lemons and make lemonade. If I had been old enough I would have swapped the lemons for limes, added tequila, and made a margarita. I was the lowest on the totem pole but instead of simply wallowing in my low-level position, I decided to embrace it and do my absolute best. It's not uncommon for the bottom of the food chain to be tasked with some of the least desirable duties. In a dental office this includes emptying the main suction trap. What's that, you say? Well, it's about the worst sludge task a human can do, and yes, it's as gross as it sounds. If I never, ever have to do that again, I'm good. Remember the suction I use to keep the dentist's working field clear? Well, you know what it's sucking up, right? Blood, sa-liva, amalgam, and ooky stuff. Well, where did you think that was all going? You probably imagined that it was being flushed away, like when you flush a toilet, and that everything you never wanted to see again was simply being whisked underground by a magical piping system that takes it out of sight and out of mind, right? WRONG (and I wish)! I'm sorry to report that all that yuck is collected in a trap that must be periodically emptied. That's right, my friends, emptied. Manually. And modern advances have un-fortunately not replaced the need for this to be done by a human who gets an up close and personal view of the dark depths of its contents. Me. In this office there was a ginormous, main trap as well as the little chairside traps.

To add to my daily challenges, Dr. Whitepants didn't always have the patience of a saint, especially when it came to the art of taking dental X-rays. Ideally, you get the tooth and the root (apex) in the center of the film. With a hard X-ray, you wouldn't know if you got the image you needed until the film developed completely, which could take seven minutes or more! If I messed up a hard X-ray, (cone cutting, contacts weren't open, blurry image, cut off apex) I had to quickly retake it and try to buy another few minutes of time before the dentist figured out that I had just wasted over fifteen minutes trying to complete one single X-ray. Chair time is valuable in dental offices, so those minutes lost were not taken lightly. Doctor had a low tolerance level for missed X-ray angles.

About four months after I started with this office, my husband and I had the exciting news that we were expecting a baby. He was still in the U.S. Navy and was out to sea for three months, then back on shore for three months, year-round. The dental office was not super excited about my news because I was a new hire. The other assistant, Mona, was even less excited because she wanted a baby so badly but so far hadn't gotten pregnant. She would always come up to me and rub my tummy with a smile, hoping for good luck. Unfortunately, my happiness at becoming a mother did not last long. Nine weeks into the pregnancy, I had a miscarriage. This came as a complete shock to both me and my husband who had already bought some baby clothes and furniture in preparation for welcoming our little one into the world. To make matters worse, he had to leave just days later for sea duty, which meant I was left alone to deal with our sudden loss.

I only took one day off to gather myself, which wasn't nearly enough and left me feeling like an emotional wreck. Upon my return Mona wouldn't use the restroom after me, saying she was afraid my bad luck would rub off on her. Ouch! How could she think such a thing? Why would she say it out loud? I worked through my devastation in that office, surrounded by an unsupportive and unsympathetic staff—something I wouldn't wish on anyone.

Only a few weeks later I was let go. The assistant I replaced couldn't get into hygiene school and came back, so that was that. All in all, it was for the best because I didn't fit in there.

Determined to find a better match, I started looking for another dental office, but this time with more caution than enthusiasm. The whole experience kicked off my habit of keeping a little pros and cons list for each office I worked in (or interviewed to work in). I noted information about how each workplace operated, its staff interactions, as well as how they treated me. Over time this became something of a ritual before stepping into any new environment. Arming myself with knowledge beforehand allowed me to feel more secure. There would be plenty of varied work experiences and environments waiting for me in the years to come. As I floated from little world to little world, and office to office, and ecosystem to ecosystem—sometimes just filling in temporarily, sometimes interviewing for a permanent position, and sometimes following-up an interview with an often unpaid "trial" day of work to show my knowledge and skills—I started to notice certain patterns in how each office was run, how the staff interacted, and how I might be treated. I took mental notes throughout the day and kept a running tally of things that went well and (most importantly) things that were red flags and had the potential to be trouble in the future. I called the red flags "quirks" and devised a system for spotting them and analyzing how serious they might potentially be. Needless to say, Dr. Whitepants easily had five quirks that I would not miss:

Quirks (Dr. Whitepants)
1. All white uniforms, difficult to keep clean (mine and Doctor's).
2. No patience with staff.
3. Staff must be silent while Doctor reads the paper.
4. Introvert.
5. Doesn't get my humor.

CHAPTER 4

The Quirk List

Around the time that I left Dr. Whitepants' office and started looking for my "forever" job, I decided my quest in life was also to find joy; after all, Joy *is* my name. To help manifest this, I came up with the Rule of Five.

Under the Rule of Five, for everyone you meet, there are usually five things that you like. As well, there are usually five things that annoy you—I call these "quirks." There are also—if you pay attention—five things that you will realize you have in common with most other people. If you are hired by, dating, or friends with another person, you must decide if you can live with their five quirks. ("Quirks" being defined as things that are unique to that person, and perhaps a little odd to you.) For me, a "quirk" might be, for instance, snapping gum constantly or chewing gum like a cow chewing its cud, nervous pen clicking or -gasp! -sniffing their nose constantly. *Do you need a tissue? No? Then stop it!* Now, one person's quirk might be another person's "just fine." Everyone is different, and each of us may tune into or get turned off by different quirks.

Ah, quirks. We all have them. Is the person next to you chewing their food more loudly than necessary and then trying to chat with you, turns to talk to you with their mouth full? Is that person really texting during the movie in the dark movie theater? Do your coworkers not replace the empty toilet paper roll? Does your boss leave cabinet doors open ? (Dr. Huntington I see you!) Is your OCD friend obsessed with keeping the hand towels arranged just so in her bathroom? Does she overreact if you don't replace them in just the right way? Is the dentist you are working for a screamer? A grumbler? An old schooler? An instrument thrower? And most importantly, important to me, does anyone returned your morning greeting at the office?

---

*A difference of opinion is what makes
a good horse race. — Will Rogers*

There are five things that every person you meet wants you to remember, to know, and to always be aware of—no matter what. Five "love 'em or leave 'em" things. And these five expectations are different for every boss you work for, every person you date, and every friend you make. Can you live with the five things that are important to your boss, partner, or friend? These five things may annoy *you,* but you must tolerate them because they are super important to the other person, and you are in each other's lives.

Why not look inwards and ask ourselves: What are my five things? What five demanding things do I need from people I let get close to me? Once we understand our own "five" we can appreciate other people's five items too!

Okay, I'll go first.

1. Don't be late. I'm always fifteen minutes early and it super annoys me if you are late.
2. Be open and honest. But not brutally honest, or you will hurt my feelings. I'm a delicate flower.
3. Understand my independence.
4. Be able to carry a conversation/hear what I'm saying.
5. Be adventurous.

It took many years for me to find someone who makes my five needs a priority. Early in the relationship with my now husband, he learned that arriving early helps me feel in control. I suffer from panic attacks, especially in crowds, and scoping out a scene before any event or appointment helps keep the elephant off my chest. And my husband's five? Number one is loyalty. Two, a sense of humor. He hit the lottery on that one, because I am hilarious! Three, affection. Number four, give and take. Five, be adventurous.

So, the secret to a happy marriage is to find a mate whose five annoying things you can tolerate. Want a harmonious workplace? Find a boss with five things you can handle to make their life happy. Want to experience rich, wonderful friendships? Find friends with whom you can give each other's five annoying things safe harbor. These things may frustrate you, but it's about finding people with *tolerable* quirks: annoying but *tolerable* habits that you cringe at (but put up with) or abide by so that everyone can live in peace. I developed this philosophy during my quest to find another job after my stint with Dr. Whitepants. So, while I was frustrated with Dr. Whitepants' five annoy habits, he had staff that overlooked them. During my hunt for a full-time dental assistant position, I spent my time filling in at various dental offices. This gave me plenty of opportunity to identify and think about the "five things" As I encountered a wide variety of dentists and staff.

Filling in at a dental office is much like dating. You go in hopeful, but then you start to see those quirks—the five things—and listen, if it gets over five, you know you've got a problem.

———

Around this time, I was asked to fill in at a holistic dental office for a few weeks, out in this fancy town. I wasn't at all familiar with this type of dentistry and no one in the office took the time to explain how they did things or what to expect. The dentist (let's call him "Dr. Earthy") and his wife were Asian. I never spoke with the wife because she did not speak any English. She oversaw setting up trays and sterilization. Okay, that works for me because every dentist wants different instruments and dental materials ready for the procedures. Sterilization is nothing exciting, anyway. She went around wrapping anything and everything we had touched during a procedure in gauze that had been soaked in something smelly and placing timers nearby to remind her to unwrap them a few minutes later. Timers were always going off throughout the office. I'm not sure what the heck she was using as a disinfectant, but it smelled awful.

Every new patient exam took over two hours and involved a lot of things I had not seen in a dental practice before or since. With the patient standing up, Dr. Earthy would have me place a neutral object (unknown to me) in one of the patient's hands and then place different metals or other objects, one at a time, in their other hand. The patient would then hold their arms straight out on each side, at shoulder level. If the side with the metal or other testing object caused the arm to dip, that meant their body reacted to the item and they had an allergy or sensitivity. We documented many different metals and sensitivities using this technique. Needless to say, it was a very slow and time-consuming process.

The quirks were adding up quickly:
1. Wrapping anything that was touched in gauze that smelled like formaldehyde.
2. Timers going off everywhere.
3. Spending hours testing for allergies via items placed in the patient's hands.

When I assisted Doctor Earthy with the removal of a silver filling (amalgam), he insisted that we first put on hazmat suits. These big bulky suits would protect us from any airborne mercury. To me it felt like I was preparing to go on a space mission in one of those bulky, astronaut-like outfits! As if we were on the moon, Dr. Earthy would get into his suit and then announce to the office that we were working in a hazard zone and to keep their distance. In contrast to our elaborate protective attire, the patient wasn't given any extra protection, only the small bib draped from their neck as a splatter guard—just like any other dental office. The removal process itself was a strange sight, with both Doctor Earthy and I looking quite cosmically comical in our respective hazmat suits as we drilled out the filling and suctioned up any debris. Once done with this task, we would shed the cumbersome costumes and return to the patient and fill the tooth with a white composite material.

One more for the quirk list:
4. Changing in and out of hazmat suits throughout the day. (And were they laundered?!?)

My first time assisting while Doctor administered anesthetic with a dental syringe, to numb a patient's tooth and surrounding gums, also felt like I had somehow found my way into a dental office on another planet. I had just brought the patient back to the dental chair, put the bib around his neck, and laid him back.

"Joy, center the patient," Dr. Earthy requested matter-of-factly.

Okay . . . I thought. I guessed that Doctor must have felt that the patient's head was not laying correctly in the chair, so I moved his head a little bit to make sure it was centered on the headrest.

"No, Joy. Center the patient," Doctor stated again, this time more sternly.

Well, okay, I must still be missing something . . . move patient's head a tad more to the left???

"No, Joy!" he snapped, "You must rub the patient's temples and hum *'OHMMMMMMM'* to help him center while I give the injections."

Now, I don't particularly like touching patients in a nonmedical way, so this request did not come easily to me. Very awkwardly, I did my best to rub the patient's temples and chant while Doctor gave the shots, feeling uncomfortable the entire time. (I guess this was somewhat better than the dentist who made me jiggle the patient's ear lobes while he gave a shot, but not by much . . . and that's a different story!)

Bingo. We hit number five:

5. Expected to rub a patient's temples and meditate over them while Doctor gives injections.

It's funny about paths in life. I always think of that board game, "The Game of Life." You can take this path or that path. You see the board in front of you and know that if you move your little car this way, this is the possible outcome. If you move your little car that way, there is another possible outcome. It would be nice if, in real life, you could see what's in front of you when you step out on a new path. Life can be an adventure; we just have to choose which paths we want to explore first. In this case, however, if I had seen a hazmat suit and chanting up ahead, I might have taken a detour.

CHAPTER 5

Swimming Upstream

I have never felt like I quite fit in—I mean who does, really? We all have moments, days, or even longer stretches of time when we feel like we don't understand the world and our place in it. I know I spent most of my formative years trying to be like my peers, doing what they did and wearing what they wore and generally trying to fit in. A feeling of being different, of being separate from everyone else, started to grow in me when I was young. It's hard to say when exactly this feeling began, but by the time elementary school rolled around it had sprouted into something more substantial than just a passing thought. Its seeds had taken root over time, growing and climbing like vines up a trellis, until the feeling of being an outsider consumed my every waking moment.

When I was in fourth grade, my single mom moved my brother and I from the very small town of Kermit, Texas, to the bigger small town of Odessa, about an hour away. When school started, I naively hoped that my big brother would protect me as we navigated being the new kids who had not yet made friends. I was terrified by all the unfamiliar faces—everyone seemed so different from us. I had a pretty bad bowl haircut, and I was teased that first week at our new school. Bullies trapped me in a corner against the school's cement stairs as we lined up to go to our classroom, chanting, "Joy, boy, the big fat cowboy..." My brother, one grade ahead of me, saw what was happening but just walked on past, not wanting to make himself a target by stepping in. I felt abandoned, like nothing that happened to me could possibly matter to him. During those first years in a town that felt new, strange, and scary, I ate my unhappiness, which made the bullying worse. At one point I was the largest girl at the school. Walking up the stairs one day I was followed by a bully who pointed out that my thighs were rubbing together in my corduroy pants, and he was afraid they would catch on fire.

We had not taken a bus to school back in Kermit, but in Odessa my brother and I rode a big yellow bus. The smell of diesel and the bumpy rides morning and afternoon were nothing to look forward to as a timid fourth grader. To make it worse, no one wanted to sit next to me. The school seemed enormous with hallways that sprawled on forever, and on my first day I wasn't even sure where my classroom was located, though I was shown the day I enrolled. I spotted two redheaded girls on my bus, and I was pretty sure one was in my class. I secretly followed her to a classroom, only to find out I didn't belong there. I had followed the wrong one. The teacher in the wrong classroom got me turned around and heading to the right classroom, where I nervously had to make a second "first entrance," my stomach filled with butterflies. All eyes were on me as I made my way to the desk that had been assigned to me. I could feel my face turning bright red from embarrassment and the anxiety of being late. I barely heard a word when the teacher introduced me to the class, all I could focus on was how out of place I felt in this strange new school. For weeks it felt like I was the only one in the room no one wanted to talk to or be friends with. Even my new teacher, Mr. D., didn't seem to show much interest in me. He let all the other little girls have a turn sitting on his lap before the morning bell, but not me. I now see that his behavior was a bit questionable, but at the time it made me feel left out.

I wanted so badly to giggle with others about the things girls that age giggle about, but my classmates seemed to already have all the friends they needed. My loneliness led me to come up with a plan. We were all preparing for the school spelling bee, so I decided if no one would talk to me, then I would spend my time studying to be the fourth-grade spelling bee champion. I stuck my nose in my spelling book and practiced every word over and over. On the bus I went over the words and quizzed myself to make sure I was learning them. The day of the spelling bee came . . . and I won! I have never spelled big words correctly since then (thank goodness for spell-check nowadays), but on that day I couldn't be stopped. Opponent after opponent was eliminated, yet I remained—spelling word after complex word, to the amazement of everyone. Thanks to winning that spelling bee, I was at least seen as the "smart girl," and before long some of the girls in my class started talking to me.

I began making friends and I was finally asked to join in on the fun at recess, playing jacks and tether ball. I was pretty darn good at jacks because my hand-eye coordination was spot on, so I was the girl to beat. To play jacks you start by scattering the little metal pieces called "jacks" across the concrete. The first player bounces a ball and while it's in the air they pick up one metal jack with the same hand and then catch the ball before it bounces again. The game becomes increasingly difficult as it goes on, because you have to pick up more and more jacks each time before catching the ball.

You keep going and picking up more jacks until you "foul" (drop a jack or fail to catch the ball), making it the next player's turn. Back in my elementary school days, the winner of each game would be rewarded with a marble from their opponent's collection. It made me feel like I was on top of the world every time I won! I still have the leather pouch that housed my prized marbles.

As the school year progressed, I made more friends, lost some weight, and even caught the attention of a boy. In those days, a sign of true love was to steal a girl's comb out of her back pants pocket. This boy would snap up my comb and then run, and we would spend the entire recess chasing each other and playing keep away. I would play the part of the girl who was upset that a boy took her comb, but the truth is I was happy to have a boy looking my way. I put his name in big letters on my closet door at home and pined away for us to be married. I confessed all this to him at our twentieth high school reunion. We laughed and laughed, remembering those innocent times.

Things went well for a while; I made some new friends and was really starting to enjoy my new school and the town I lived in. But then one day those vines of self-doubt started to grow again, silently wrapping themselves around me and pulling me back down. You know those monkey bar climbing domes that sit in most school playgrounds—the kind you climb all over and hang from as soon as you are tall enough and strong enough, but by the time you are a girl in fourth grade it's more fun to just park yourself at the very top with one or two friends and talk? So there I was, perched atop this dome at recess with a girlfriend when out of the blue another girl (someone I thought was my friend) walked by, stopped in her tracks, and pointed straight up at me. She proceeded to announce in the loudest voice possible that all the kids playing nearby should come look at my left ear, shouting that it was flat. My hair was pulled back into a ponytail, which did show my ears. My left ear indeed doesn't have the curve at the top like my right ear. My grandma had the same flat ear. Several kids gathered around the climbing dome, laughed and pointed making up silly rhymes about my ear. It was awful and went on until the end of recess. Bullies had me cornered again. It was one of those moments that becomes indelible in your mind and in your heart. After that day, I stopped wearing my hair up and once again felt alienated from my peers. There is nothing worse than being eleven years old and not looking like everyone else. I carried those feelings with me for a very long time.

Soon enough the days of middle school hit (in Texas, we call it junior high). When the dreaded physical education classes came around, I immediately knew what to expect: no one would ever pick me to be on their team. I am the least athletic person I know, then and now. One day the gym teacher took us outside to play football, a game I have no interest in even though I'm from a town and state that lives and breathes football. I was so proud when I finally caught the ball. A moment of triumph! As I took off running I could hear my teammates shouting, so I ran faster and faster toward the goal line. I thought I heard an encouraging, "Go! Go! GO!" but in reality, they were shouting, "No! No! NO!" It turned out I was running in the wrong direction and scored for the other team! Talk about not fitting in!

To get out of taking P.E., I joined band and tried to blend in while holding a large shiny brass baritone. My family was on a tight budget, so we couldn't afford to buy an expensive band instrument. I had to rely on the school-provided baritone chosen for me by the band teacher (if only I'd had enough rhythm for drums). I had hoped to play the saxophone so I could sit with the girls who played woodwind instruments and try to befriend them, but a sax would have cost too much. Instead, I was the only girl in the brass section sitting next to all male tuba players. I was encouraged to bring that baritone home every day, so I could practice. It was huge, and the ginormous black case was clunky and nothing but trouble as I lugged it on and off the bus. This provided yet another excuse for kids to tease and pick on me. Needless to say, being in band did not help my social life or feelings of not fitting in one bit!

Sometime in seventh grade, however, I fell in with a group of girls who were all in band. We ate lunch together and shared stories that we all giggled over. These girls were obsessed with the British new wave band Duran Duran. I had to love the group as well to fit in with them, which seemed like a fair trade for their friendship. I was assigned one of the band members to be my everything, the only one not taken by the other girls. I had a gray hat with the group name on it and a little pin with my guy's face on it that I fixed to the hat. We would go over to each other's houses and watch MTV and wait for a Duran Duran video to come on so we could each swoon over our guy. It was good to feel accepted, even if I wasn't quite as gaga over Duran Duran as they thought.

By the end of junior high, I had the best friend I had always wanted! She quickly became my soul sister—my confidant. We were an unstoppable force: through our teenage years we created this amazing world for ourselves where we both fit in and felt understood. She and I were inseparable as we navigated our high school years together. Those days spent together laughing, dreaming the dreams only teens can dream . . . are some of my most beloved, happiest memories! She accepted me for who I was, at least until much later in life when she had "the talk" with me at a nice restaurant. She mentioned feeling like our friendship had evolved to the point where she no longer felt a connection with me, and

I didn't fit in to her life. She needed space. My heart plummeted; the world around me seemed to stand still as her words sunk in. I never again returned to that restaurant. To this day, there is an empty space in my heart left by her absence.

And now here I was, let go from my very first dental assistant job. I felt a whirlwind of emotions, from sadness to relief. Even though I hadn't been happy there, losing it was tough. After all, I had gone into that dental office expecting to gain experience and grow professionally, only to find myself in an environment that simply didn't work for me. I had tried my best to adapt to the dynamics of the office, but I lacked the necessary training experience and (I'll admit it) maturity. Nevertheless, I decided to look positively on the six months I spent with Dr. Whitepants, and to appreciate the insights I gained. That experience taught me valuable lessons. It also gave me a better understanding of how different personalities can interact within small teams and how important it is to be aware of these dynamics. Now I knew what I wanted out of my career path moving forward! The fear of moving on to another job was slowly being replaced with excitement. This was an opportunity to find something that fit better with who I was and where I wanted to go in life. With newfound confidence in my abilities, I vowed to face each challenge head-on and with wit and resilience—a skill set which has served me well ever since!

CHAPTER 6

Dr. Albright (My Happy Place)

You know what they say, "When one door closes another one opens." It wasn't long before I was hired at the office that would make me truly fall in love with dentistry. My new boss, Dr. Albright, was an old school, older dentist who attended to his patients with more love and care than I had ever seen before. He believed his patients expected to be seen by him when they came in, and so he was the one they would see—even for cleanings. He had truly mastered the art of dentistry, for instance, he made his own gold crowns (a complicated process of casting and polishing). He scaled, polished, and flossed his patients' teeth, rather than having a hygienist perform these duties. He filed teeth by hand when they needed root canals instead of using a root canal handpiece designed to make the job quicker. He also showed me the art of placing gold foil on the buccal surface of a molar—a long and laborious process which requires the utmost skill and craftsmanship. He taught me to order the dental supplies, a task he had never entrusted to anyone else. He got my humor and welcomed me into not only his office, but into his family. I also loved the receptionist, Rosemary, and grew close with her over the years. I fit in. I loved waking up and going to work. Doctor enjoyed my stories and encouraged me to go on adventures and make new memories in my life. Both he and Rosemary would listen attentively to tales of my beloved Texas and how life was so different there. I still can hear the little silver bell that Rosemary would "Ding!" throughout the day, each time a patient arrived.

There were a few quirks, as will always be the case in any type of job. But remember, I described finding a working situation with *tolerable* quirks you can live with. I was happy to tolerate Dr. Albright's quirks because they were far outweighed by working in such a loving, respectful environment. I had finally found my happy place!

Dr. Albright's Easy-to-Live-With Quirks
1. Hand developing hard dental X-rays and maintaining a water tank temperature.
2. Limited assisting duties. (Doctor does it all.)
3. Prefers the office scrubs to be ironed (but will allow me to do this at the office during his two-hour lunch break, during which he went home and took a nap).
4. Committed to old school dental procedures and materials (won't try newer, easier ones).
5. Patients spit in a cuspidor (and I have to watch).

Five Things to Love About Working in Dr. Albright's Office
1. Doctor is upbeat, always smiling, and makes a mean salmon dip.
2. Rosemary was quickly becoming my favorite person (hated her bell, though).
3. The patients felt very cared for and were so friendly.
4. Doctor took the time to teach me the *whys* of dentistry.

5. Within walking distance of three coffee huts and wild blackberry bushes. (I often went berry picking at lunch.)

Working with Dr. Albright was an unforgettable experience that taught me so much about the craft of dentistry, as well as the importance of providing ethical and moral patient care. His receptionist, Rosemary, was a delight—her easy-going personality was so welcoming, and she always greeted you with a warm and genuine smile. I loved that she laughed with her whole heart, her face lighting up as she took in a funny comment or story. She was guarded, yet insightful, and so caring. She sometimes got frustrated because the front desk was run in an old-school style (Dr. Albright style!)—with paper and pencil to make appointments, which she then typed up on a typewriter to create our daily schedule, no computer! But she kept on top of everything. From day one we connected. I still think of her often and reach out every now and then just to make her smile, mailing a short note or a watercolor card I've painted. Dr. Albright's patients also appreciated Rosemary's compassion and positive attitude through the many years she spent behind the front desk. It's just another reminder of how vital it is for offices to find individuals who can make an impact beyond their job description.

Most ways of doing dentistry in this office came from the tried-and-true methods Doctor learned in dental school. He went by the book, the one he had been taught from decades earlier when he was a dental student. So . . . X-rays at the office were still taken with the little hard-edged dental films everyone hates. Patients would awkwardly bite down on the bulky intraoral tabs, and then we would follow the monotonous steps required to develop them. Doctor never fussed if I missed an angle. He would just kindly ask me to retake the X-ray, which I would, repeating the slow process until a better image was developed. By this time, the industry transition to digital X-rays that yielded images instantly on a computer screen was well underway, but this technology was expensive. Plus, such advances had not yet reached Dr. Albright's office. Instead, we hand dipped those hard films to develop every single tooth image. While this was the most economical way to process an X-ray image, and the resolution was excellent, each film would take seven to ten minutes to develop. As well, the X-ray tank water had to be kept at a certain temperature for the solutions to process correctly. In Washington state it's typically chilly, so keeping an eye on the water temperature was required throughout the day.

Every day at lunch time Dr. Albright would take a two-hour break and go home for a meal and a nap. During this time, I would spend about thirty minutes ironing our scrubs because back then the material they were made of came out of the dryer very wrinkled. If blackberries were in season, I would go down the hill for a little berry-picking adventure near our office where they grew wild. On days when I needed an extra boost of energy, I would walk to one of the coffee huts nearby and get a cup of espresso. The perks were numerous at this office!

There was something special about our little office family. I felt very accepted and to top things off, Dr. Albright got my humor! Rosemary handled patient scheduling and check-in/out procedures with ease and efficiency, always announcing patients' arrivals with her trademark silver bell dinging loudly throughout the hallway. This was annoying to take day in and day out, but it had been her signal to Dr. Albright since long before I arrived. How else would Doctor and I know a patient was in the waiting room? That bell was one of the quirks I chose to tolerate, but it was years before I could go to Waffle House and not jump when they hit their bell to alert the server that an order was up.

"Hi! Welcome to our practice, my name is Joy," I would say as I swung open the wooden waiting-room door to call a patient back for their appointment.

"Before I seat you in a room, Doctor has requested an X-ray called a panoramic."

I would walk the patient to an area where the big panoramic X-ray machine was housed. Back then, this was a machine you sat down in, and the X-ray head would rotate around you. It would stop at the midline of your face, then your seat would shift, and the X-ray head would continue its rotation until it had taken a complete panoramic of your head. The machine was old and slow, taking nearly ten minutes to finish imaging a patient. Also, because it stopped and repositioned itself on the midline of your face (down the center) it would not take images of your front teeth. Those had to be taken with manually with hard X-rays.

"If you follow me to the exam room, I will seat you and then I'll go and develop your X-ray and be right back," I would say, as I removed the weighted lead apron from the patient and walked them down the hall.

Dr. Albright was a perfectionist when it came to dentistry, taking his craft very seriously. Prior to me, he had an assistant he trained "apprentice style." (Meaning she hadn't gone through an assisting program, as is allowed in Washington State.) Breaking in a new assistant can be difficult for any dentist, but I was eager to learn. We quickly fell into our respective roles and worked together smoothly. As Doctor scaled the patient's teeth to remove the hard plaque that builds up between cleanings, I would hold out a little 2"x2" square of gauze for him to wipe the scaler with as he went. Rinse and repeat. Then he would get ready to use the prophy cup on the slow-speed handpiece to polish the patient's teeth. In my right hand, I would hold a little dappen dish that I had filled with prophy paste. In my left hand

I would hold the high-volume suction that had a swivel end and keep the saliva at bay. Dr. Albright liked to save money by having me use a very large tub of this prophy paste—scooping it out with a little mixing spatula and placing some in the small reservoir of a dappen dish. I would then seal the dish up with foil saved from the X-ray film. This was part of my morning prep for any cleaning patients scheduled for the day. Prophy paste comes in little disposable dappen dishes just like this now. These days, a hygienist will drop one into a holder worn on a finger like a ring, making it easy to swirl the prophy onto their polishing tool as they go. When the patient had been flossed, he had them rinse with cinnamon flavored mouthwash and spit in the cuspidor.

Dentistry is an art form like no other that requires skill and finesse. Dr. Alright was an expert at carving amalgam or silver fillings to create a tooth surface that was similar to the patient's original tooth (before the cavity.) He could seamlessly place a "white" or resin filling on a front tooth. But perhaps his most impressive technique was his ability to create and cast his own gold crowns, rather than having them made in a dental laboratory. This requires an immense amount of skill, and I had the pleasure of observing him as he crafted many crowns with tremendous attention to detail and pride in his work. Gold crowns are the friendliest restoration you can have in your mouth and last for many years. I'm a huge fan of them! I have one on a molar to this day that I received when I was in my twenties. I also feel so fortunate to have assisted in the placement of that one gold foil filling—such a beautiful form of long-term restoration that is no longer taught in dental schools. It takes hours and hours to complete. Imagine a cavity the size of the head of a pin. After the decay is removed, these teeny tiny, little bitty pieces of gold foil are laid over the prepped site and then gently pounded into place with the lightest malleating. This process essentially adheres the gold foil to the tooth, filling the prepped area in a form of cold welding. Tiny tools are used to manipulate layer upon layer of the gold dental foil. The procedure is very methodical and the outcome of this type of restoration is pure beauty, not to mention long lasting.

Doctor and I worked nose to nose for over eight hours a day. After a while he began to understand (and even seemed to appreciate) my "unique" personality. He would even ask me questions about my beloved Texas and the foods that were common to my upbringing. In turn, he taught me the history of the Northwest and brought in smoked salmon dip and kimchi for me to try. He said he had buried the kimchi in his backyard. It smelled like it!

In Dr. Albright's office, we used a type of dental-impression material called polysulfide (more commonly known as rubber base) that, early on in dentistry, was used for everything. It has a very unique, distinctive smell and could be a challenge to remove from a patient's skin if a little got onto their lips or cheek. Trying to get it out of clothes was an even bigger ordeal! To activate the material, I would mix two pastes together on a big mixing pad using a large spatula, summoning all my strength in my left hand to get it incorporated evenly. After placing the gooey mess in a dental tray, I would hand it off to doctor and he would place it in the patient's mouth. The set time on this material was crazy long, between seven and ten minutes. To pass the time, I would hold up the mixing pad with the leftover material for Doctor to look at and we would do the ink blot test. I might see a goat flying a kite. He might see a hamburger with extra pickles. This became our game every time there was an impression taken. I am glad he joined in and played along with me (for years!), as this is now one of my fondest memories of working with him.

That job provided me with a comfort zone. Every Monday through Thursday I eagerly anticipated spending time with Dr.

Albright, Rosemary, and the patients—it was like my own little sanctuary! I fit in. We laughed as we swapped stories about our lives and worked well as a team, even after he added an additional assistant.

Rosemary became like a mother figure to me. I would ask her for advice and listen to the things she said I needed to do to become a successful adult: have a mortgage, don't buy an expensive house that you can't afford easily, understand the repairs that come with owning a home, make an extra house payment every year to drop your principle (money owed). I followed her sage advice to the letter when I bought my last house, because even thirty years later Rosemary had given me rock-solid guidance.

Dr. Albright also warmed up to me and constantly gave me fatherly advice.

He stressed for me to start a retirement fund and never, ever, touch it—even if things got bad. He said he would start my first retirement fund if I made this promise. I have never touched that money, and things did get really bad at one time for me. . . .

You know what they say, never
squat with your spurs on.

The office loved my Texas sayings. I never knew my sayings were unusual until I would say something, and Doctor or Rosemary would laugh and ask what in the world it meant.

That patient made me
madder than a wet hen!

While I was waiting for a patient to get numb, I once told Dr. Albright I would "just go on about my rat killing." That got his attention!

It's all fun and games
until it gores your ox.

And an office favorite:

He's all hat and no cattle.

I even convinced Doctor to have a cowboy boot day. We all donned boots and denim jeans. I still have the picture with our smiles from ear to ear: Rosemary with the biggest grin, standing in the office hallway all decked out in her cowboy boots and jeans, and Doctor Albright laughing behind her.

If a big holiday fell when my husband was out to sea, I was welcomed into Dr. Albright's home for his family gathering. I would bring southern dishes for everyone to try. For Thanksgiving it was a pecan pie, which oddly they'd never had; and I was introduced to oyster dressing.

The staff also assembled at Doctor's house for our yearly CPR and First Aid refresher courses, along with some interesting creature company. The first time I attended, it was intriguing to see a family of alien-like bald cats running around. Apparently they were hairless cats, which his wife bred because they were in demand and worth quite a bit. My goodness, I wondered, maybe they were in need of little kitty coats to keep them warm. And then there was Earl T., an African Grey parrot who was quite a lively character.

As the instructor started our training, I heard the microwave beep. A few minutes later I heard the same noise again: the microwave beeping. This went on and on, and I couldn't imagine who was using the microwave for that length of time. After a while a voice from the kitchen started saying "Here Pecos, here Pecos . . ." over and over. The culprit turned out to be Earl T. Gray, Dr. Albright's African Gray parrot! Earl T. had been impersonating the microwave and calling to Pecos, one of Mrs. Albright's cats. Doctor finally excused himself to go tell Earl T. to knock it off!

"Can I ask you a question?" said Rosemary one day, while I was standing at the front desk waiting for a patient who was running behind.

"Sure," I said, but with a look of puzzlement. When someone leads with that, they are usually not asking what you brought for lunch.

"Do you have any regrets in life—things you would change?"

I was all of twenty.

"I have zero regrets," I said. "I am where I need to be in life. I have a happy marriage, a cute house that we just bought, great friends, and an amazing job. I can't ask for anything else."

I have thought back to that conversation many times throughout the years. I'm not sure where things got derailed. When my marriage started spiraling it devastated me—this was a person I had married the minute I turned eighteen. I was filled with hope and optimism. I had believed in us. Our marriage, which once seemed unshakeable, was falling apart. When it started to go wrong, it quickly snowballed into something that was too big to fix.

Faults are thick where love is thin. — Danish proverb

The months after we decided to separate, and he moved out, were the most emotionally difficult time of my life. It hurt to breathe. It hurt to be awake. It hurt to be alone, but it was torturous to be around people. I didn't know if I could make it through the pain. It felt like a part of my body was missing. Thankfully, I had my close friend, Lynn (my former upstairs neighbor), who came to my rescue when I needed it the most. You wouldn't put us together as friends. We didn't have much in common at first, but we have the same sense of humor. Let it be noted, she also has excellent penmanship. We clicked and have been friends ever since that night we inadvertently called to each other through our open windows. I would absolutely, if asked, walk over molten lava for her to this day. My marriage was crumbling, and I felt utterly alone. That's when Lynn became my saving grace—her voice the beacon of hope in a dark time. No matter what the hour, she would be there to talk me out of my despair; telling me her most mundane everyday news, funny stories about her boys, what she was cooking for dinner, or the latest thing her beloved dog had done. She may not realize it, but without question she saved my life back then.

Marrying someone in the military is like entering a mysterious and captivating world—it's thrilling, but it can all be turned upside down at any moment. Your life is dictated by what the military says you should do or the place you are told to live. When you are on a submarine, or a surface ship, or deployed to a foreign country, your home life is placed on pause. You focus on the task at hand, defending your country. This role changes and matures you but blurs your connection to your family. You cannot just pick up where you left off months prior, because life happens while you are away. The dog's water bowl has been relocated because it was constantly being stumbled over. You find you must jiggle the handle on the toilet to make it not stick. Your spouse's new school schedule means they have hours of homework. The routines you left three months ago have been replaced with new routines.

The life events that you and your partner tackle together are the moments that shape you into more mature individuals. Day-to-day experiences provide opportunities to grow as a couple. You play the "what's for dinner game" on a daily basis. You learn what to do when the dishwasher floods your apartment (call the manager and soak up the water). The car needs an oil change, so you take it to the oil-changing place, where they forget to put the oil cap back on and oil is blown all over the engine. Car repairs, emergency vet visits, and every other type of life event happens, and you put your heads together and deal with them. But if one of you is serving in the Navy and out to sea for extended periods, it can be especially challenging. The lack of communication, physical connection, and day-to-day contact can put a strain on the relationship that takes dedication and hard work to overcome.

The rigors of life in the Navy are not something I take lightly. I was fortunate enough to go on a family "cruise" on the submarine he was attached to, and I have so much respect for those sailors and the small spaces they live and work in for months at a time. The feeling of being confined made me very apprehensive, and it was only for one day.

After many years of being regularly separated for extended periods of time, coupled with not being able to fully reconnect when we were together, our relationship began to break down. When he was home, he simply wanted to stay in the comfort of his own familiar surroundings. But I wanted to get out together and do things, wanting to escape from the prison-like feeling of the house while he was gone. Those special *"Remember the time when we . . ."* moments that you can both laugh at, became fewer and farther between:

> *Remember the time we took the ferry to Seattle, and I wore high heels, not knowing it was uphill both ways? I did not want us to pay for a taxi, so I walked barefoot to the restaurant that was thirty minutes away. You laughed as we held hands, me pointing out every sharp rock I stepped on. We enjoyed our meal by candlelight that night. You convinced me to get a taxi on the way back because my feet were so sore, and you rubbed them while we sat on the ferry watching the Seattle skyline drift away . . .*

> *Remember the whitewater rafting trip that threw me over the side in rough rapids? I was trapped under the raft for a few seconds. You were as shaken up as me.*

> *Remember when I wanted a dog because I was so lonely without you? We found a dachshund puppy for sale up in the mountains. Remember we drove for hours to get her and when we arrived, the breeders were truly mountain people living off the grid,*

*with no running water or teeth? I loved that dog
for sixteen years and felt so blessed to be her mom.*

For every good *"Remember when . . ."* story, we started having
more and more stories that were not so good:

*Remember when I was twenty-one and needed to
have my tonsils out because I was sick all the time?
Oh, that's right, you were out to sea. I had to fly my
mom in from Texas to care for me.*

*Remember the time I missed you so much and
could not imagine how I could survive the hurt of
you being away for three months, and I was living
for a maildrop that was finally scheduled a month
after you left? (A maildrop was our only communication with our loved ones at sea, but the wives
never knew when we could send an envelope, so I
always had something ready to go.) I wrote you
every day so you would know what was going on
at home, but I didn't get a letter from you. And
on the second maildrop I still did not get a letter.
Cruise after cruise you would come up with excuses
as to why you could not find a minute to write me a
letter, not even one sentence, to help me get through
the pain of missing you. Not even when I packed
addressed envelopes and paper in your bag.*

*Remember when I would get the call that your sub-
marine would finally be pulling in (we were not
told when to expect the sailors home until shortly*

before their arrival), so I would excitedly take the day off from work? I would get dressed up and join the other wives on the bus that would take us down to the lower base to welcome our sailors back after three months without them. One by one, each wife would be reunited with her husband. The joy and excitement surrounding each reunion was electric. I would wait and wait, and you would be one of the last off the ship, and then I would only see you for a few minutes because you had volunteered for first duty back and wouldn't really be coming home for many more days. You didn't seem to want to spend time with me.

Remember when I was stuck at home for three months while you were out to sea, and I was looking forward to the things we would do on your return, only when you came back you just wanted to stay home and play video games?

Remember the Christmas you told me we could not fly home to Texas and see my family, so I sat crying on the floor and you kicked me and told me to get over it?

Remember when we started growing apart?

Remember when we decided on a phone call, when you were in port, drunk, in San Diego, that we would get a divorce?

Remember how you did not even fight to keep me in your life, and when you returned from that submarine cruise you quickly moved in with some single guys? And remember how you immediately started sleeping with every girl you could ... taking polaroid pictures of their (usually) bra-clad breasts as proof of your conquests and leaving them for me to find?

Remember that you were the person with whom I shared all my greatest love, pain, joy, grief, and trust—and my most heartfelt intimate moments?

———

During this period when my marriage was ending, I felt an immense amount of emotional turbulence. Thankfully, with Lynn by my side, I found a new group of friends and we ended up getting involved in country dancing. We spent the weekends line dancing and two-stepping; this was not something I had done before, and it kept my otherwise preoccupied mind occupied. I realized that socializing with new people would help me cope as I adjusted to being single. The friendships that formed from these nights out became incredibly important to me over time; they provided much needed emotional support during a very tumultuous period in my life. But ... I missed Texas.

When the divorce was final, I decided I needed to go back to my people, to my support system. I have Texas blood and I missed my true home. One weekend I went over to Dr. Albright's house. He was refurbishing an Airstream travel trailer. I joined him in the trailer and told him I had to leave and go back to Texas. He smiled and said he knew this day had been coming and wished me well. It broke my heart to leave that office, but I needed a way to find myself again, and to find out who I could be.

Life Lesson: This was just a chapter, not the whole story.

PART II

NEW DIRECTION

CHAPTER 7

Homeward Bound

I set a moving date and started planning for my mom to arrive days before, to help me drive back to Texas. We packed a U-Haul van with all my cherished belongings and towed my car behind it on an open trailer. From house plants to household goods to my male and female dachshunds, everything was ready to go. My female had a litter of puppies just two weeks before I was to leave, so my mom and I placed an open cardboard box between our bucket seats in the front cab and nestled her and the little ones down into it, with the proud daddy sitting alongside. Minutes before we drove away, my ex-husband arrived from out of nowhere and begged me to give us one more chance. His presence brought back a flood of emotions. Nostalgia for the good times we had shared together, sorrow over our eventual separation, sadness for our divorce. In my heart I knew if I gave in to his plea, it would only be delaying the inevitable.

*People tell you who they are, but
often we ignore them—sometimes
for years—because we want them
to be who we want them to be.*

Mom and I drove away, leaving him standing by the curb. I just had to go, to drive away from that life and toward something else, anything else.

We drove long days, stopping only for dog potty breaks or food, and at times to open the back doors of the moving van and give my house plants some air and light. At one point in the steep Colorado mountains, the van got vapor locked causing us to sit on the side of a busy interstate for hours. Good times. We sought out camping cabins when we stopped for the night because they were cheap and back then you couldn't have pets in hotel rooms. It was a long trip. I was hurting from my failed marriage, leaving a town I liked, friends I adored, and a job I loved. I wasn't sure this was the path I was meant to take and found myself doubting my every step and decision. Moving back to my parent's house was not an ideal solution—I was an adult, after all—but it was my next step.

In a small New Mexico desert town, just before the Texas border, my mom and I made a pit stop at a hamburger place to grab a bite and let the dogs walk around. As was my routine by this time, I opened the back of the moving van to tend to my beloved plants. They were all lined up just inside the big back doors, from the floor of the van to the roof, looking like a wild green jungle.

Relieved to know that we were nearing the end of our trip, I took a turn at the wheel as we left New Mexico behind us. The van had a limiter that prevented the vehicle from going faster than fifty-five miles per hour, so I was driving along in the right-hand slow lane when I noticed a law enforcement vehicle to my left. At first, I wasn't too concerned, as I was well within the speed limit. But he pulled in front of me and slowed down, and then two more patrol cars came up: one flanking me on my left side and the other hovering just behind me. No lights or sirens, but this continued for miles with the vehicles keeping speed with me and staying glued to my left, front, and tail. My mom thought I must be speeding and told me to slow down. Annoyed and feeling my tensions rise, I barked back that I was definitely below the speed limit. We crossed over into another county and, quick as a whip, all three law enforcement vehicles pulled back; but just as soon as they left, another three official vehicles from the county we were now in replaced them. The new vehicles immediately took over the positions of the previous cars. We were becoming rattled to say the least. I tried to keep my cool and just drive along uneventfully, but my fear was escalating. My mom worked at the sheriff department in my hometown, so I quizzed her repeatedly, asking why on earth so many law enforcement vehicles would be following me. Suddenly, all three cars turned on their lights and signaled for me to pull over. The one behind me fell back to allow me to merge onto the shoulder and stop. Dry, desolate Texas plains sprawled out for miles as a backdrop to this bizarre scene as our little van coasted and then parked, the three squad cars doing the same. Clouds of dust and gravel stirred up by our tires hung in the air before settling back to the ground. I was completely baffled by what was happening. Rolling down the window, I continued to argue with my mom over how I could be pulled over for doing nothing wrong. We were exhausted from days of travel and this unexpected scene had me feeling more than unhinged. I caught a glimpse of an approaching officer in the long driver's side mirror. His back pressed against my vehicle; he was slowly sliding down the side of the van toward my driver's door with his weapon pulled. Fear swept through me from head to toe.

"Mom, he's got his weapon drawn!"

"JOY," my mom ordered, "JUST SIT STILL!"

I held my breath and braced for whatever might happen next, knowing that this officer would not approach with his gun pulled unless he had reason to believe he might have to use deadly force. Once more before he reached my door I blurted out,

"Mom! I don't understand what's happening!"

"I'm just as confused as you, Joy," was my mother's measured reply, her voice tense. "I have no idea what this is about, but we will find out soon enough."

The officer moved a few inches closer to my open driver's window, but then seemed to freeze, as if something had caught his attention. In an instant he lowered his weapon, relaxed his stance, and poked his head into my open driver's side window.

He took a good look at both of us, and then to my mom he said, "Susan! Is that you?!?"

I glanced at my mother in utter confusion. "Mom! Do you know him?!?" I asked.

My heart was pounding in my throat as I turned my head in slow motion back to the face of the police officer who was peering into our moving van. Just a second before, this officer's weapon had been out and ready for use. Panic and adrenalin surged through me, as I saw the now friendly face peering in at us. Trying to catch my breath and process the change in atmosphere, I slowly wrapped my head around the fact that instead of something terrible and tragic happening, this officer was now greeting my mother like an old friend! As he and my mom chatted, he commented on my dachshunds who were barking up a storm, trying to protect us from this "stranger." Then, he casually asked us to step out of the van and open the back, while the rest of the officers got out of their cars and peered in. To our surprise, upon seeing my jungle of houseplants, the officers roared with laughter and began to explain the whole incident to us. Apparently, an APB (All Points Bulletin) had been sent out on my moving van, stating that I was transporting marijuana plants in the back and had viscous attack dogs in the front. Now, I'm not saying my wiener dogs wouldn't bite your ankles, but that's about as far as their viscousness might go. When my mom returned to work the next day, she read the entire APB report. Apparently, a vehicle with the same make and model of my car, which we had towed on an open trailer behind the van, had been stolen. When we stopped for a bite in that town in New Mexico, just before crossing into Texas, someone thought they were spotting that stolen vehicle and called us in. They must have added "illegal plants and attack dogs" to the story as they observed me caring for my houseplants and walking my dachshunds.

Welcome back to Texas, Joy! We've missed you!!

Right or wrong, when you start over, you have to take a step in a direction. Any direction. I've always hated making big life decisions, and at that fragile time I lacked the confidence in myself to make a choice. Until then I had always viewed life as black or white, and when I made up my mind, I went all in. But after my divorce, I couldn't decide on an entirely new path, so I took what I felt was the easy way out by going back home. At least it was a start, one step.

My dogs and I settled in with my parents. It took me awhile to get used to being back in my childhood bedroom and living in the town where I grew up—the same town where my ex-husband

and I had fallen in love and gotten married. After a few weeks, I decided that I needed a diversion, so I decided to contact a guy I had briefly dated before leaving Washington state. He had separated from the military and moved home to Oklahoma. He invited me to come visit him (a seven-hour drive for me). I took him up on his offer, left my dogs and the puppies with my parents, and off I drove.

———————

I was still licking my wounds from my recent divorce and this little town in Oklahoma seemed like the perfect place to hide. I didn't exactly move in with the guy, who lived with his parents, but I was not in any rush to leave. Unfortunately, he wasn't ready to have a girl around all the time, so he began getting up and out of the house very early in the morning. This meant that I was alone all day in his parents' house in this little town. His mom and dad would leave for work each morning, and my guy friend would go to a ranch nearby, to ride horses and learn the skill of breaking them. The days started to get long and tedious, so I decided to look for a dental assisting job. Unfortunately, this small town only had one dentist who was not hiring. Which meant that I had to travel an hour away to find any opportunities. I thought if I could get into a routine, I would start to feel better and rebuild my life, but even after finding a job I was miserable. The dentist was nice, and I enjoyed the office, but something felt *off*. I just couldn't bring myself to totally settle in. The best way to describe it is that, at least for me, putting a Texan into an office with all Oklahomans was like putting a drop of oil into a bowl of water. That little drop of oil would just float or bounce around and around, but it wouldn't mix. I felt I just couldn't relate to the office staff or allow myself to feel at home.

Working for this dentist also had a different type of a learning curve, because he was missing most of his pointer and middle fingers on his right hand, which I discovered the first time I handed him an instrument. I was accustomed to extending an instrument to a dentist at the same distance every time, but when I did so for this dentist, he couldn't reach it. When I looked down, I suddenly realized why! He was very matter of fact as he explained what had happened to his fingers. Apparently, he'd had an accident while he was still in dental school. He was doing some woodworking and wearing latex gloves to protect his hands when the blade caught his right glove and cut off his two fingers. But despite this impairment, he worked with such precise control and skill. It was amazing to see how he had overcome what could have been a career-stopping injury. The dentist was gentle, kind, and caring, and he was hopeful that I would move to the town where the office was located and stay on with his practice, but I was hesitant. Oklahoma did not feel like Texas, and I did not feel like I fit in.

Then one day, about three months after I first arrived, the guy I was dating took me out to a nearby lake to have a talk. He told me in all honesty that he would never be in love with me, and nothing I could do would change his mind.

Challenge accepted, I thought. *I can make you love me.*

Why on earth would I not take his words to heart, I still wonder. Well, I tried to be more of what I thought he wanted, but cupids bow didn't strike him causing him to fall madly in love with me. I came to this realization a few weeks after our talk by that lake. I knew it was my time to leave and gave notice to the dental office where I had been working. While my guy friend was out late one night with his buddies, I packed my little car, planning to leave at daybreak. I bid him a farewell as the sun rose the next morning, and wouldn't you know it, he begged me to stay.

Why now? I wondered. *Why do you want me now that I'm leaving?*

I climbed into my car and off I went with my paper map in hand, headed to new adventures in the great state of . . . Colorado! I had been there for a band competition once in high school and it was a pretty state, so I thought, *Why not?* But following my nose and my paper map proved to be more difficult than I imagined. I got lost and finally had to admit that I was nowhere near the state I was aiming for. Remembering my stepdad's sage advice *If you get lost . . .* I stopped at a payphone and called him collect. Being the wise man that he is, he told me to *"get your ass home"* and gave me directions on how to get back to Texas.

So, there I was, back in my parents' house. I still couldn't decide on a new direction for my life. My parents and brother were no help. By this time my brother had a wife and a child. He was busy building custom cabinets and trying to dodge his own marital issues.

---

*If you knew you wouldn't fail
and could go anywhere or be
anything, what would you do?*

I thought about working on a cruise ship, but I get motion sick easily, so that was a no. Go back to school? Still no. I enjoyed the diversity of dental assisting and didn't want to change careers.

Faced with my typical indecisiveness, I decided to go to the sheriff department, where my mom still worked, to ask for some direction from a man named Roy. My mom had worked with Roy for years, and as a teenager I had always enjoyed chatting with him when I stopped in to see my mom. Roy worked the child-abuse cases and was known for making level-headed decisions. I took my little female longhaired dachshund, Rusty, along for the ride. While I was saying hello to my mom's coworkers, many of whom had known me since I was a child, Rusty somehow managed to get off her leash and ran right up to the Sheriff and bit him! This was out of character for her. With many apologies, I scooped her up and went in search of Roy, a wise man who didn't know it yet, but he was about to change my life.

I plopped down in a chair in Roy's office. He looked up from a file he was reading and focused his eyes on me.

"Hi, Roy," I said. "Can I talk to you for a minute? I need help with what direction to take in my new life."

"And you came to see me?!?" he chuckled. "I'm flattered."

"I need to figure out where to go to start my life over."

"Well," said Roy, his face pensive as he adjusted himself in his seat and put his hands behind his head, "let's start by narrowing down where you might want to live. I understand you tried finding Colorado and got lost before you could get out of Oklahoma."

Geez, word travels fast, I thought. That mix up was going to follow me for the rest of my life! In my defense, this was way before the era of cell phones with GPS, and a kind lady who talks to you from your dashboard and keeps you on the right road!

"Yep. I think I had better stay in Texas."

He reached into his desk drawer and pulled out three darts. He then got up and closed his office door, revealing a big Texas map that was mounted on the wall behind it.

He handed me the darts and said, "Since you have nothing to lose, throw the darts and out of the three places they land let's decide on your new destination."

My first throw hit Amarillo, the next pierced Lubbock, and the final dart went somewhere in South Texas. After some discussion,

Roy and I felt Lubbock was the best option because it would be a fresh start but was still close enough to my grandparents and family. I thanked Roy and went right over to my mom's desk and announced my plans, then straight home to make them happen.

I was thrilled to be able to reconnect with an old friend of mine who now lived in Lubbock and would be a familiar face in a new town. I had gone to high school with her, as well as the guy she married. They were kind enough to let me stay with them for a few nights, while I interviewed for a dental assisting job with a female dentist in Lubbock. Dr. Grace's office was significantly larger than any of the offices I had previously worked in. As part of my interview, the staff and I met for breakfast one morning—an excellent opportunity to get a better sense of each other's personalities and interact on a more personal level. Clearly, we must have clicked because just after breakfast, Dr. Grace offered me the position!

I wasted no time in finding a duplex with a rental available, and with my mom's help loaded up a moving van and drove the two hours north. The first night in my new place was lonely, even with my two dachshunds, but at least I had taken that one first step.

I started my new job immediately. Five positive things about the new dentist, Dr. Grace, presented themselves to me right away. First and foremost, she was inspirational. She was also honest, cared about her patients and staff, had an open-door policy for suggestions and concerns, and was an amazing mentor. I made a mental note to always keep her five priorities at the top of my list. I was thankful not to see any big quirks pop up. In fact, this dentist was the most selfless person I had worked with in dentistry. I was finally finding perks, not quirks! She agreed that the focus should be on patients and was very collaborative with her staff.

My life was taking a positive turn. I enjoyed my new office and felt like I fit in. Once again, I was working in a supportive family environment. It was the perfect place to unravel some of the confusion and chaos that had consumed my life in recent months. I found myself developing into a more confident person, both professionally and personally.

"Hi, welcome to Dr. Grace's practice, I am Joy," I said with a smile as I ushered a patient named Mrs. Barnes to the back operatory.

"You certainly look like a joy!" exclaimed Mrs. Barnes.

"Yes, I guess I am a joy, unless you were married to me apparently," I blurted out. *Oops, did I say that out loud?!* I quickly added, with a bit of animation, "Never mind, it's something I'm working through. How can we help you today, Mrs. Barnes?"

CHAPTER 8

———

Lubbock, Part One

Imagine waking up every day and looking forward to going to work because you are so passionate about what you do for a living. For me, teeth are my thing! I love educating people about dental homecare and giving them advice on how to save a tooth that has a huge cavity. Seeing the big picture is something I take pride in when doing my job.

Do you need a new toothbrush? Well, both manual and electric types will do the job, but an electric toothbrush can clean those hard-to-reach areas of the mouth in a more efficient manner. I'm a huge fan of electric toothbrushes now that they have timers and pressure sensors to help ensure the user isn't brushing too hard. They also vibrate, which manual brushes cannot do, giving your teeth a deeper clean more quickly. Most come with a replaceable brushing head that needs to be replaced every 3 months. That sounds like a short amount of time, huh? Look, I use my disposable razor on my legs until there's no blade left, so twelve weeks probably is more likely six months for me to replace my toothbrush head. Yes, electric toothbrushes are more expensive than manual ones, but the prices have come down a lot—and they make great Christmas gifts! Maybe instead of that fruit cake you didn't want any way for Christmas, someone can gift you an electric toothbrush.

I enjoy being a part of a dental family that is happy to see you every day and seems to really care that you are there. At Dr. Grace's dental practice in Lubbock, I found myself in just such a place.

"Good morning, Trish!" I yell over my shoulder as I enter the office. Trish, the receptionist, and I are always the first to arrive. Oftentimes, as I walk in, she is just heading downstairs to pop the popcorn that we offer our patients as a treat. Her reply cascades upward, "Good morning!"

After checking the schedule and setting up my room for the first patient, I run downstairs to chat and help her out.

"How was your evening? Do anything exciting?" I ask her.

"You know, I was so tired from our busy day yesterday that I picked up Chase from daycare, got us some fast food, and went home to my husband to have a quiet night."

She empties a bag of hot popped kernels into a big glass jar and screws on the lid as I set another bag in the microwave.

"Remember that Halloween when I made witch's hands for the patients by putting popcorn in the food handler's gloves, with candy corn in the fingertips?" I ask.

"Didn't you place spider rings on them?" she says.

"I did. I thought they turned out cute. I gave them out to the kids that came in that day, along with a cookie. What was I thinking, though, giving the kids chocolate sandwich cookies before their cleaning appointments?!?"

"The hygienists were upset about that for days!" she points out.

"Lesson learned, 'Wait until after they are done with their cleanings for a treat.' *Hey, I need to finish setting up for the day, so I'll see you upstairs."* I exit the basement which now smells of freshly popped popcorn.

On this day, Dr. Grace and I had a patient in the chair who gone against Dr. Grace's advice and traveled to Mexico for the removal of her lower teeth, despite them being healthy! She had come to our office for an exam weeks prior with the complaint of ringing in her ears and felt it was caused by her lower teeth. Our X-rays showed perfectly healthy and decay free teeth. Dr. Grace had refused to do the extractions for this reason. Most likely it was tinnitus because ringing continued after her teeth were extracted. After her trip to Mexico, where there sterilization isn't a thing, we looked in her mouth and were horrified by what we saw. The tissue looked like hamburger meat and bone spicules (fragments) were littered throughout the mandible. (Lower jaw). The patient had an ashen grey tone to her before she was unresponsive, prompting us to act quickly. With urgency, we tilted her back in the dental chair and placed her on oxygen. The Dr. immediately called a "code RED" and other team members sprang into action, putting their CPR training into practice. Through the collective efforts of our team, we were miraculously able to revive her. When the ambulance arrived, she was adamant about not going to the hospital, but was thankful to have had our office there for her.

Since that situation took place, I have always suggested running through a patient in the dental chair emergency scenario once a quarter. It gives muscle memory to the staff if an emergency arises.

———

The Lubbock office had an incredible atmosphere; everyone was, for the most part, warm and welcoming. I mean we had our days; it was an office full of women, after all. Once, I threw away an empty box that had held prophy angles (low-speed handpiece heads with a rotating cup at the tip that are used to polish teeth with prophy paste during a cleaning) while restocking the hygienist's upper cabinet, and that hygienist flipped out like I'd tossed away her wedding ring. She could have calmly explained that she kept a ginormous bag of the prophy angles in her lower cabinet, from which she continually refilled that smaller box (the one I threw away) to have them easily assessable. I dug the box out of the trash, and we went on with our lives. Although not every single person got along perfectly, most of us formed a friendly rapport which enabled us to provide even better care for our patients. I was glad to have friendships with some of the staff outside of the office. I went over to Trish's house often with my niece that was the same age as her son. I babysat Dr. Grace's twins and often had lunch or after work cocktails with other girls in the office.

Dr. Grace was a great leader. She was kind and gentle with her patients and had an excellent reputation for being extremely ethical when it came to her work. Let me tell you how difficult that that can be, finding a dentist you trust! On top of that she was incredibly talented; from simple fillings to complicated root canals she could handle them all with ease. She took her time and explained her procedures thoroughly, answering her patients' every question. Her passion for dentistry shined through with each patient she saw. I checked five good things off my list almost from day one and always felt rewarded for my hard work.

To help broaden my horizons as an assistant, one day Dr. Grace asked if I wanted to accompany her to an autopsy. She was the dentist on call if a deceased person needed to be identified via their teeth remains. I took her up on that offer and went on to join her on several autopsies. I was absolutely fascinated by the process.

I kept all the supplies and protective gear we needed to help the medical team in a plastic container in my trunk. I always hoped I wouldn't get pulled over for anything, because I had some very odd things in that container!

The first time I was in the morgue, the odors were overwhelming. The smell of charred flesh and chemicals were intense, almost too much to bear. To cope with the odors and avoid passing out, I put some orange solvent in my mask to cover the smell. (Orange solvent has been used in dental offices for many decades to remove anything that may have splashed onto a patient's face during dental procedures. It is a mild solution that is safe to use on the face, lips, and hands. Its light citrus smell helps to mask some of the more pungent odors.) When we arrived at the morgue, there were two bodies that had been recovered from a small-plane crash and were needing to be identified. The plane, which had been fueled up before the flight, had taken off with the wind instead of against it and they went down. Both victims had been burned beyond recognition. One of the victims was my age. Dr. Grace and I recorded existing fillings, missing teeth, crowns, and bridges. Next, we set out to track down dental X-rays and hopefully confirm a match. This just goes to show you how important it is to keep accurate dental and medical records throughout your life. These records can be so crucial if the unthinkable happens, and for this reason I have always made it a point to keep my patient's records completely up to date.

After participating in that plane-crash autopsy, the smell and taste of barbeque became a complete no-go for me for many months. Anything that even remotely reminded me of it made me nauseous. This made my weekend job as a server in the food line of a cafeteria-style barbeque place a bit tricky—wearing a face mask spiked with orange solvent was definitely not an option. I had to just grit my teeth (yikes!) and persevere through the smell every weekend!

Quirk List for Dr. Grace (Very tolerable. I loved my job!):

1. Large staff. There were days where we got on each other's last nerve.
2. At times I was spread too thin while trying to take care of all the dental assistant duties.
3. Hard to be single and make ends meet on a dental assistant's income (thus, my part time job at the BBQ place).

But I loved my job, my work family, and the patients . . . this quirk list was short and tolerable and the perk list was long!

CHAPTER 9

Lubbock, Part Two

"Mr. Land? I will take you back," I say, as I escort one of my afternoon patients back to the operatory. "Good afternoon. We will be in room two today for your filling."

After seating Mr. Land in the dental chair, I place a plastic-backed paper bib around his neck. Next, I bring his digital X-ray, taken during a previous visit, up on the computer monitor.

"I just want to show you again which tooth we will be working on today."

A tooth can have decay in three different areas. Root cavities occur on the surface over the roots. Occlusal or pit and fissure cavities occur on the chewing surfaces. (Dental sealants, a thin coating painted on the chewing surface of back teeth can help block out germs and food) Smooth surface cavities occur on the inner (near your tongue) or outer (near your cheek) sides of your teeth. If you are not a flosser, you may also develop an interproximal smooth surface the in-between cavity between your teeth, which will share decay with the tooth adjacent to it and now you have two big old cavities. Floss is your friend!

"Joy, what's your title? You do such a good job!" says Mr. Land.

"I answer to 'Your Highness' or 'Your Majesty,'" I say with a laugh, "or you could just call me, 'Outstanding Dental Assistant Joy.'"

I was with Dr. Grace for three years and enjoyed learning about dentistry through her. Our office was the first in the region to get an intraoral camera, which is a little pen-like wand with a camera on its tip that can take very close-range pictures of individual teeth. The local paper even did a story on us and the new camera. Images from the camera are sent to the computer monitor, so a patient can see a fracture in a filling or whatever issue the tooth has that needs fixing. I'm a huge fan of using one to show patients that the dentist isn't just trying to push them to have dental work they don't need. I often get asked if the dentist is making up treatment needs to fund a new car or buy a bigger house! Ummm . . . no. That would be unethical. The office has equipment to pay for, staff doesn't work for free and dental products are stupid expensive. Those lights shining above you and having a nice warm office uses electricity. It all adds up.

One cold day in December, the staff was told to clear our schedules for an entire Friday. We were typically off on Fridays or worked half a day at the most. We were to assemble at Doctor's house and meet with her and the other dentist in the practice, to discuss goals for the upcoming year. The Doctors provided a nice breakfast, and we sat around early that morning, discussing ways to improve patient care. I was eyeing the clock about two hours into the meeting, along with my coworkers, wishing we had the day off as usual. Then the dry erase board came out and on it was an outline of the remaining topics we would cover that day. The list went on and on. *We're going to be here for hours?!?* we all thought, after taking one look at the many items written on the board. Next, we were each handed a big packet and asked to just hold onto them. Doctor announced that we would all open them at the same time. She was all business. One . . . two . . . three . . . we opened our packets expecting to find worksheets and papers to help us tackle the long meeting day, but instead we each found an envelope filled with cash! As we stared at it in shock, the dentists explained that we had three hours to go shopping and spend the money in the envelope on ourselves. When the time was up we were to meet at a designated spot to show off our treasures while enjoying appetizers and a drink. In an instant this dreary, tedious day had become the best staff meeting ever!

I quickly teamed up with a coworker that wanted to go with me to the mall. Off we went to spend our windfall. Even though the rules stated that we were to spend the money on ourselves, I used mine to buy Christmas gifts for my family members. I was single with a limited income, so this was my chance to give my grandma a new electric blanket and to find something special for my mom. No one knew I was secretly buying gifts for others. I was strategic and passed everything off as something I bought for myself. Everyone knew how practical I was, so they didn't bat an eye. One hygienist went to an expensive undergarment store and quickly spent her money on frilly things. She refused to show us exactly what she bought, and we poked fun at her for not following the rules. *(We're all supposed to show what we bought!! Let's see!! No secrets!!)* The coworker who went to the mall with me bought herself a pair of cowboy boots. I was happy to see her find something she loved.

I worked at the dental office four and a half days during the week and at the barbeque place most weekends. My family lived within a few hours' drive, and I found an amazing church that I enjoyed attending. Best of all, I made great friends in Lubbock. I even dated a little (well, a lot). In those pre-Match.com days, the norm was to put an ad in the local newspaper. ("Single young female seeks single young male for long walks on the beach and quiet dinners . . .") My dating life from that time could make a book of its own, a novel with hundreds of quirky things that guys do and say in pursuit of a date and while on one. The fellow who placed the waitress' tip on the table in one-dollar bills and then snapped his fingers to demand the bill, removing a dollar for every minute she didn't comply. To the guy who hugged me tightly sooo many times on our first date, inhaling deeply into my hair because he liked the smell. (P.S. I'm not a hugger!) The one who needed a screwdriver to start his car and one day, in a fit of anger, tried to stab me with it! Oh, and the guy who used a key on his keychain to dig his ear wax out. That's solid marriage material there. After a while I became exhausted from it all and was happy to just spend time with friends and family. I really felt like I was where I was meant to be and that I fit in (even if I hadn't yet found that special someone).

One summer day while Dr. Grace and I were working on a patient, she started talking to me about me taking a week off.

"Joy, you've been here for three years and haven't taken any vacation days. You need to get away."

"I know, but my family lives close enough to see on weekends, and I can't think of anywhere would I want to go." I often spent one weekend a month at my parents' house back in Odessa. Sometimes I would drive the five hours round trip, on a Saturday to bring my little niece back with me. Stopping to get ice cream to dip our French fries in on the way back from Odessa. I would take her back the next day but enjoyed keeping the little stinker for the short time. I also saw my grandparents often. Life was good.

Oddly though, a guy friend from my Washington days had recently contacted me. He was Mr. Oklahoma's friend and had come along to events at my house a few times (after my divorce, before I left Washington). Back in December I had sent him a Christmas card because he was in my address book. It took until July for his thank you call, but we had been talking off and on since then. He was still in the Navy and had recently been stationed in Florida. On our next phone call, I threw out the idea of me coming for a weeklong visit, since my boss wanted me to get away. He liked the sound of that, so I started making plans. I flew into New Orleans, and we spent a night there. He was very caring from the first moment. We wandered through the French Quarter, but instead of trying to find spicy Cajun or Creole food, he searched high and low to find something bland for me to eat because I was a queasy from my very bumpy flight. While we were roaming the streets, a random stranger stopped us to say how in love and happy we looked. I had never thought of him in that way. The next day, we drove three hours to a town in Florida where he had recently bought a little house. We spent our days going to the beach, trying out new foods, and talking. He was a quiet person but talked for hours with me, sharing all his hopes and dreams. The military was his career, and he would be on shore duty for the next five years. He was looking forward to being in one place for a long period of time. He had previously been married; however, military life and being out to sea for most of the year had caused his marriage to fail. I knew just what he had gone through. Now, I was at a place in my life where I truly loved my job, respected my boss, had lead acting roles in community theater, had found an uplifting church home, and enjoyed living fairly close to my family. But I was so very lonely. And he was so different from the guys I was dating in Texas.

At the end of that incredible, emotional, whirlwind of a week, we spontaneously decided to get married. Yes, married! And yes, I broke my self-imposed rule about not marrying back into the military life. I am far from a spontaneous person, but it felt so right in the moment. His best friend's wife dropped everything and ran to the courthouse with us to be our witness.

I flew back home the day after we tied the knot, tired and wondering what I had done. I couldn't possibly tell my family or friends because I hadn't even dated the guy. Our plan was for him to come for a visit in a few months, at Christmas time, meet my family, and we would decide what was next from there. Well . . . that's not how it worked out. I ended up telling both my family and friends, as well as my boss, soon after I returned home. His biological mom was completely taken back with the news and quickly reached out to me to size me up. Dr. Grace, like everyone else, was very surprised. I soon found myself giving her my notice and making plans to move to Florida . . . I would leave within the month.

To say the least, it was very awkward to move in with a guy I barely knew, in a new town that was way different than Texas. I was so uncomfortable that, in the beginning, I went to the guest bathroom to pee because I didn't want him to hear me! My dogs just stared at him and didn't know what to think. They had lost their normal routine and everything they knew that was familiar (just like me). To top it off, they had been staying with my stepdad, and he had taken to feeding them the last bit of his ice cream if he had some at night. They were now pudgy and wanted their sweets, but their "new daddy" was not the type to indulge them.

Everything seemed off balance. Life with my new husband wasn't anything like I might have pictured it if we had taken more time to plan things out. But sometimes you just have to take the bull by the horns and deal with the outcome. I wanted to make a home for us and do things as a couple, but he had his friends over until late almost every night—working on car projects with him, or just hanging out. People were coming and going from the house and helping themselves to anything in the refrigerator, as if they lived there too. Since this was his first house, he wanted his friends to feel welcome at any time. We quickly began to argue over every little thing. At one point, one of his ex-girlfriends stopped by and told me she was the one who had initially organized the kitchen. Well, that was all I needed to hear. I set about rearranging every pot, pan, glass, plate, bowl, fork, knife, and everything in the pantry. I didn't know how long I would be the Mrs., but I would make sure that house knew "Joy was here!"

To add to the stress, although I was looking, I couldn't find a dental assistant job. I looked around at my life and felt a deep wave of regret wash over me. Everywhere I turned something seemed to be going wrong and one of the biggest issues was my lack of work. I just wanted to throw in the towel. My options seemed limited as I called my stepdad and said, "I messed up," and asked him what I should do.

"I agree you made a quick decision," he said. "But to give your new husband and you a chance, I suggest that you both set a date and see if by Christmas time you can work it out, see if the relationship can work. If by that time you both agree it isn't something that will work, then we will move you back home."

I went back to my new husband, and we sat down and had a talk. We both agreed that we would give our relationship a chance, and if it wasn't something we thought was going to work out, we would move me back to Texas. It was a very stressful time to say the least. There was no trace of the magic we felt that week when I first visited.

My new husband and I also came to an agreement about ex's. We agreed ex's dropping by the house or keeping in touch in any way was not allowed! Oh, and his friends were limited to how often they could come over for scheduled visits.

CHAPTER 10

Juggling Act

Now, wouldn't you like to tell young Joy about the perils of impulsively marrying someone and moving hundreds of miles away from her family on a moment's whim? Well, she wouldn't have listened. I come from a long line of head strong, stubborn women.

So, now I had a new life and needed a new job. The holiday season was quickly approaching and very few dental assisting jobs were available. I had no savings, a car payment, and the possibility of needing money to move back to Texas. I also needed to get certified to take radiographs and assist in the state of Florida.

This would be the point in the movie when the music crescendos, causing your heart to beat rapidly as you wonder what the outcome will be now that the leading lady has gotten herself into a sticky situation. Especially when her new husband's parents show up unannounced in their RV to park in the driveway for weeks, and then more weeks. I'm fine. Everything's fine. FINE! Why do you ask?

I spent a month interviewing with a few dental offices but had no luck and even less hope.

One interview was with a root canal specialist. The thought of sitting chairside, mindlessly doing the same procedure all day was less than thrilling, but I needed a job. I made it through the meet-and-greet interview and was scheduled for a one-day working interview. During that day, I followed his current assistant around as she showed me the ropes. She was careful about talking to me though and pointed out that Doctor didn't like his staff to interact. We couldn't chat about patients or our personal lives or anything. The staff even had staggered lunch hours to keep them from spending time together. What the heck?!? "Dr. Paranoid" (as I dubbed him in my head), thought this would keep a lid on any office drama. The quirks were adding up quickly, and by the end of the day the needle jumped off the chart when I accidentally overheard him yelling at his wife, who worked in the front office. He was telling her she was worthless over a billing error she inadvertently made. If he treated her like that, I knew it was safe to assume that he would lose his patience with me sooner or later and possibly yell at me. Hard pass.

Top Five Quirks (Dr. Paranoid)

1. Paranoid that processor solution would be flicked, dripped, or splashed on the carpet when I (or anyone) hand dipped an X-ray. (*OK, you told me. You don't have to hover over me every time I process a film.*)
2. Yells at staff (including his wife).
3. Staff not allowed to interact.
4. Sending me home on *DAY ONE* with three books on root canals, to read and study in preparation for a verbal test to be given by the end of the week.
5. Constantly criticizing my methods and skills (as well as those of his other staff).

After dodging that bullet, I soon headed out for an interview with a dental office in an area I was not too familiar with (not that I was overly familiar with any part of my new town yet). I drove up to what I thought was the address only to realize it was a strip club—and a very run-down strip club, at that. *I am not quite that bad off!* I thought to myself, quickly turning my car around and driving away. For a second, I worried that I had answered a fake ad, but after double-checking the address, I saw that I had pulled into the wrong place. I still managed to arrive early for my interview (at the *correct* address) and entered the office just as the dentist was finishing up her day. She was friendly and chatty as she pulled me into an operatory in the back to discuss the dental assisting position. I noticed that we didn't really touch on my resume, but instead covered some other unusual topics.

"I have a young daughter and the funniest thing happened today. She emptied the cat's water bowl and urinated in it!" she blurted out. "Isn't that hysterical?"

Ummm, no, I think that's pretty gross. [Insert nervous laughter.]

I did not really ask many questions about the position, because I desperately needed to work. It would have been a good idea to ask how many patients per day, on average, she had on the schedule. I would soon find out this was an HMO practice, which means the dentist is assigned on average, ten thousand patients. Each patient was paying a monthly fee into their insurance to get coverage. That meant that regardless of how many patients actually came in for treatment during that time, the dentist was still guaranteed to make a certain amount of money. Of course, larger dental procedures made the dentist more money since patients paid out-of-pocket fees depending on the complexity of their procedures. "Dr. HMO" had a flair for adding on fees, called "ancillary services," that the patient would pay: a needle disposal fee here, a dental chair sterilization fee there, a fee for using certain dental materials. The fees were usually very small in comparison to the dental work they were receiving, however, it all added up to a nice amount of extra income for the dentist.

I was to start the next week and would be working two days a week with her dental associate, let's call her "Dr. Doright." Dr. D., though I hadn't met her, she had an incredible reputation for providing excellent patient and dental care, the hygienist informed me. I was confident that she was going to be a great person to work with and I looked forward to assisting her chairside. The other two days, I would assist Dr. HMO. Despite the fact it was a very busy office, my new boss adamantly stressed to me that I would be the only assistant at this dental practice. I needed a job, so I accepted the position. My quirk meter was off the charts, dinging loudly, but I chose to ignore it for the sake of having an income.

Quirks Identified BEFORE Day One (Dr. HMO)

1. No discussion of my professional experience during my interview.
2. Also, during my interview, Doctor sat *in* the dental chair and suddenly pulled the overhead light to her face, turned it on, grabbed a mirror and tweezers, and PLUCKED her chin hair. (I wish I was kidding.)
3. Used interview time to tell me about her daughter's urination habits.
4. Very low pay with no benefits. (She would be giving me a few paid holidays, though.)
5. Located in a very seedy area of town. (A thriving area for panhandling and crime.) At times Doctor would give them my lunch from the refrigerator, that's if

she hadn't already stolen my sandwich, because she couldn't *help* herself.

The following week I arrived at my new "home away from home," only to find an unwelcome thickness in the air. The associate dentist, Dr. Doright, was a little put out that she didn't have a say in my hiring (and I don't blame her), as she would be the main one working with me. Awkward!! Then at lunch everyone went out to eat together, but they didn't invite me. I sat in my car and watched them load up and go. It hurt my feelings to not be included because it felt like they were rejecting me before even giving me a chance. They could have at least asked if I wanted to join them; it would have made me feel welcome instead of like an outcast.

Holy cow! This dental practice turned out to be the busiest one I had ever worked for, then or since. Thankfully, Dr. Doright and I became fast friends, which was a relief after that rocky first morning. I worked head-to-head with her for over three years in that busy practice. Some twenty-seven years later, she and I still see each other often, talk on the phone, and do volunteer clinics together. I quickly learned that she had a heart of gold and would use her dental skills to help the needy at the drop of a hat. We still to this day, function as a well-oiled machine when we volunteer our services, putting our skills to use for those who can't easily get dental treatment—giving each patient as much care as possible while they are in the chair.

It wasn't but a week after I first started that Dr. Doright invited me to join her for lunch. I don't why this was a big deal to me, but it was. It's the little things in life.

"Joy, the patient in room three needs bitewing X-rays and if you would use prophy paste and polish her teeth, I'll come in and scale them to save her from coming back for a cleaning appointment."

"Ok, I'll head that way."

"Oh, and Joy, I have a coupon for BOGO on a sandwich at the deli if you want to grab lunch out today." [Insert smiling face emoji.] My heart was happy! Just to be thought of for lunch, to be invited to share a coupon, to be invited at all . . . as I said before, it's the little things!

I truly cherished the friendship I was able to build with Dr. Doright over the next several years. She eventually moved to a dental practice closer to home, but we remained friends and colleagues. It gave me a special kind of comfort to know she appreciated me. Having someone acknowledge my contributions and talents made me feel respected and valued as an employee. That's something we should all strive for no matter what field we are in. In those few short years, we developed a personal bond and felt comfortable enough to discuss our lives outside of work. That's why I still call her or drive over to her house when my day is a train wreck and I need advice. And at least once a month, we carve out time in our busy lives for lunch or to walk around a craft fair or other event—and we are always in touch by phone.

Working in a busy dental office is a juggling act—only the balls are patient appointments—and my job is to keep everything running smoothly and on time. I am admittedly a very structured and focused person. I really have to dig in the back of my brain to recall the more mundane things. If you ask me what I had for breakfast, I gotta really stop the gears from turning and flip through the hundreds of things I've done since breakfast to remember what I ate or if I ate at all. I am busy from the minute I walk into the dental office until I leave. When I am not directly giving patient care, there are supplies to order and restock, phone calls to return, rooms to set up, lab cases to coordinate, and the list goes on and on.

First thing one morning, as I was getting set up in the back, Dr. HMO called to me from the front of the office, saying, "Joy, my mother-in-law is here in the waiting room. She has a hair appointment next door in an hour. I'm going to run an errand. Be right back." And she left to run her errand as the workday was about to start.

If you don't make eye contact with me as you tell me something, there's a high chance that I won't hear you. This is important to know if you are, let's say, thinking of leaving your mother-in-law in my care while I am doing my morning routines—especially if your loved one has dementia.

A moment later I was putting information into the front computer. I looked up and smiled at the mother-in-law, who was standing at the narrow window in the waiting room. Then I returned to the back office and continued to set up my day. I typically run two rooms and if dental procedures aren't preset for each treatment and patient, then the day runs behind. You wouldn't believe how fifteen minutes can throw you off schedule and then patients start to get cranky about waiting.

After a bit, I decided to go back up front and check on Dr. HMO's mother-in-law. She wasn't in the waiting room or restroom. I thought maybe she walked next door to her hair appointment, even though she would have been early, so I went over to see if she was there. She wasn't there. A few minutes later Doctor returned, and we frantically began searching for her mother-in-law. We called law enforcement to help. As they were interviewing me, they asked what she was wearing, her hair color, shoes . . . anything that I could recall. I couldn't recall anything. When I saw her from the front computer, most of her outfit was blocked from my view.

I had smiled at her, and we made eye contact, but I was focused on setting up for a full workday.

The dental office was located on a very busy main street. We eventually discovered that Dr. HMO's mother-in-law had caught a ride with a kind stranger to a town where she had lived many years ago. She was found safe and returned to her family, so thankfully the situation ended well. I tried after that to be more aware of my surroundings, but I just don't have the brain capacity. It's pretty cluttered in my head with trying to remember animals, work things, church events, grocery lists, chores, yard work, and everything else under the sun.

Years later I took a job at another dental practice as a receptionist, eventually becoming the office manager. It was quite overwhelming! I had to juggle the usual duties of running a dental office with the added skills of balancing insurance claims, knowing how much to write off for each patient if there was insurance coverage, patient payments, phone calls, presenting treatment plans, calling insurance companies but being placed on a long hold, then getting rerouted through the "say the member id" spill all over again, filing with secondary insurances and on and on! Just a few daily challenges. Oh, and selling amber jewelry that one of the patients made, which is the oddest thing to have in a dental office! I'm known for being quite focused when it comes to my job, to say the least. I have always asked coworkers and bosses to make eye contact with me when they say something important that needs my full attention. With so many areas of the business to keep track of in that office manager position, some days I just needed to step away and take a mental break. I would gather the office trash and take it down to the dumpster—just a short walk across the parking lot—which allowed me to take a ten-minute breather and keep my sanity intact!

The office was located next to several other offices in a business complex. Through the walls, you would hear people shutting doors, or sliding chairs, or other typical office noises. I grew accustomed to the sounds and never gave them another thought. Then one day while I was in the office alone, catching up on paperwork, I decided to take a break and get away from my desk. I gathered up the garbage to take to the dumpster and have a nice brisk walk. I stepped out the front door and passed a couple of men loading a moving van. One was up inside the back of the van, and the other was standing outside the van handing things to him. The guy on the ground made eye contact with me and said something about the weather. I smiled at him and continued to the dumpster, thinking about the cloudless sky and counting the hours until I could leave the office. On my way back, the van was still there but the men had gone back into the building, I assumed to get their next load.

When law enforcement showed up the next day to tell me I was the only witness to the office next door being robbed, I was not only shocked, but worthless in my ability to recall anything about the two men.

CHAPTER 11

The Dance

I stayed with the HMO practice for thirteen years, until I just couldn't take one more day. By the end of my time there I understood why the women you see in true-life dramas are too afraid to speak up about workplace harassment or inappropriate behavior from their employers. That's the thing about needing a job. You stay quiet and put up with behaviors you know aren't right, because you are worried you won't be hired anywhere else. Dr. HMO was always hugging me and kissing me, and just being inappropriate in general. I would jokingly tell her to stop, trying to make light of her actions, especially if she leaned over a patient during treatment to kiss me on the cheek. She was often putting me and her patients in uncomfortable situations. She openly discussed sex—as a matter of fact that was her favorite topic. Many of the male patients seemed to enjoy it when she placed her breasts in their face while she was giving them a shot. At a dental convention out of town, she thought it was so funny when she pressed her naked breasts against a glass door while I was on the other side. The list of her questionable and unacceptable conduct would have stretched far out into the West Texas horizon. There were times when the hygienist had a patient waiting for Doctor to do a post-cleaning exam and I'd have to retrieve her from the parking lot, as the day's schedule fell way behind. I knew she was out there with the guy she was dating. As I approached his vehicle it would be clear they were in the middle of having sex in the back seat. Other times she would duck out of the office to sit in his car with him and smoke pot. When she came back in to treat patients, the odor of patchouli oil (which is known to cover the smell of weed) would fill the air.

If you don't like where you are,
MOVE. You are not a tree.

This was my work life for more than a dozen years and by the end of it I was completely burned out. I was responsible for twenty-plus patients a day in my chair, far more than a non-HMO dental office that might see six to ten patients in each dental chair per day. By now my only ally, Dr. Doright, was long gone and I was subjected full time to the whims of Dr. HMO. As the stress of her erratic behavior mounted in the office, Doctor made the hasty decision of marrying a convicted felon, who was her yard guy. I mean, he did bring her flowers once and they did date for a few months. And while I tried desperately to manage the stressful and chaotic situations at work, my personal life was unraveling at home. My marriage, which had been a struggle ever since our impulsive decision to tie the knot, was spiraling due to my husband's increased drinking and apathy toward our relationship. I'm not trying to be overly dramatic; it's not like he ever physically abused me—he was a good person, and we had some happy years—but he had an addiction he couldn't overcome, and he just wasn't present in our relationship. By now I was the mom of a young child and going through a divorce. I tried for many years to save my husband—I really did. I am a caregiver. It hurts me to see someone broken who needs fixing, but I just could not help him as he descended deeper and deeper, succumbing to his demons despite having a wife and child who loved him.

We went through so many years of infertility treatment in our wish to start a family, that alone will put stress on any relationship. I wanted to be a mom so much that my focus was consumed by my hormone levels, ultrasounds, and the timing of getting pregnant. My son is truly the most wanted human on Earth. I'll admit that once I had a child, I put my marriage last and directed all my attention toward raising this precious little redheaded baby I had birthed. Meanwhile, my husband got stationed overseas and chose to go alone. I spent the next year as a single parent. As the time slipped by and my little guy was losing his baby teeth and starting school, my husband was living in a foreign country and falling faster and faster into depression and alcoholism. When he finally returned from his overseas duty, we gave our marriage another half-hearted attempt. One night we hired a babysitter and went out for a date night, only to end up driving around and around because we had so little in common that we could not find anything we both wanted to do. His workday ended earlier than mine, and many days while our child was in daycare and I was still at work, he would stop at a bar for a drink. But it was never just one drink. Many a night I would not know where he was until I got a call from him in the late hours, telling me he was not able to drive home. To top it off, because he did not want me to come looking for him when my workday ended, he would go to random bars all over town. By the time he called me for a ride home I would have to quiz him and try to piece together his location. Babbling into the phone with slurred speech, he would give fuzzy descriptions of landmarks and try to tell me where he was, but I wasn't that familiar with certain areas of the town where we lived. My life primarily revolved around work, daycare, grocery store, and home—maybe an occasional jaunt over to the pediatrician's office. Out of desperation I would call a mutual friend of ours, a guy who knew the town better than me. He would selflessly come over, no matter the hour. I would get my son out of bed, and we would pile into my car and go find my husband—the friend helping me navigate and figure out where he might be. Then our friend would help get my husband into my car and drive my husband's vehicle back to our house. What a thing to ask someone to do time and time again, and so embarrassing to have them witness our family troubles.

Our marriage ended soon after my husband retired from the military. He took our savings to start a business, but still couldn't find a reason to make it through his days and it failed. Being in a marriage with someone who is indifferent and shows no feelings whatsoever is not a relationship. He begged me for a divorce saying he just did not want to care for anyone else, since he was having a difficult time caring for himself. I leaned on his biological mom, with her I found an ally. She understood his struggle. He moved into a travel trailer at a nearby campground, and into a life where he did not have to worry about caring for a family. I would still cook dinner and have him over after he left because I felt sorry for him. I would do his laundry and bake cookies for him to take with him to his little secluded home. I was hurt that he could not fight his mental illness and choose his family over alcohol and depression. I felt like I had tried for our entire married life to battle this unseen monster and, dammit, he let it win.

---

*You never know someone
until you divorce them.*

Mean and hurtful words can be used with the intent of caus-ing damage. I tried not to be the one to throw verbal daggers back at an emotionally unstable person. I found a church with an excellent divorce recovery group and joined it to gain support and direction for both my son and me. One piece of advice I re-ceived from that group still resonates with me today. They called it the glass jar analogy. The counselor who spoke on this evening placed three glass jars on a table before her. One was filled with cotton balls, another with candy, and the last was empty. She held up the jar with the cotton balls and asked the group what we would call the container. We all agreed it was a jar holding cotton balls. So, she named it the cotton ball jar. We did the same with the candy jar.

"And what about this jar?" the counselor asked us, holding up the empty jar. "Is it just a jar? We defined these other two jars by their contents. Is that how every jar should be defined? Is it the only way to define them? What if one of them becomes empty or someday holds something else? Will that change the kind of jar it is?" She then set the empty jar down and placed her hands over all three jars, leaning in to make her point. "The contents of these jars doesn't define them, just like being married or not married doesn't define you. You are not less just because you are no longer married. We are not defined by our contents. We all have worth and pur-pose, even when our lives and contents change."

Such strong words for when you feel beat down and are look-ing for worth.

For many years I struggled with Dr. HMO's office, and with her immoral and illegal behaviors in the workplace. Where do you draw the line? My homelife was chaotic and unpredictable and I was desperate to provide a stable life for my son. Going to work was just as stressful as being at home. Finally, I endured a series of incidents at work that pushed me to leave, once and for all. One of these happened when a patient's husband came in to argue his wife's dental bill. I was standing alone at the front desk at the time. The man started yelling at me, saying he did not authorize his wife's dental treatment and wanted his money back. I was trying to calmly have a conversation with him when he called me fat and spit on me. Dr. HMO, aware of what was going on, but not wanting to deal with this type of conflict, stayed hidden in the back office. As the man's anger escalated, a patient from the waiting room stepped up to escort him outside. Dr. HMO did not even acknowledge that I had been spat on, yelled at, insulted, or humiliated, and in the end she gave the man his money back. It really irked me that she didn't stand up for me while I was being berated in front of our other patients.

Dr. HMO had quickly married her felon boyfriend, who was newly released from prison, and soon let him have free reign over her office. He started making financial decisions and even dictating what I did after work hours. He took away the bonus money that I had come to depend on since my wages were so low. Doctor started placing more and more responsibilities on me with no increase in pay or benefits. Then she insisted on placing upsell charges on her patients' dental bills, which involved me bending the truth in ways I was not comfortable with. In addition, patients would come in for a quick bite adjustment and she would tell me to pick up the high-speed hand piece and adjust a filling or crown, typically a skill only the dentist would perform. If the hygienist was running behind, Doctor would place the patient into my chair and order me to scale and polish their teeth. Dental assistants are not licensed to scale under the gumline. Dr. HMO wasn't just blurring the lines between staff duties and dentist responsibility, she was violating her licensure guidelines, and my limited dental assistant duties! She had no respect for her profession or herself and saw no problem with imposing improprieties on her staff and patients.

As a single parent to a six-year-old, I couldn't be without a job. One day I stumbled across an ad for a practice that I wasn't familiar with, despite living in the area for many years and knowing many of the local dental offices. The in-person interview with the female dentist was short, and she pressured me to take the job right then and there. She mentioned that she had a newborn baby and was juggling a lot. If I didn't accept the job right then, she indicated, I would not be considered for the position. I needed to escape Dr HMO, and the idea of interviewing for weeks or months without an income was just too risky, so I accepted. This job would put me in the front office as a receptionist. I didn't know it yet, but as far as quirky workplaces, this one would surpass my out-of-control previous employer quicker than a chicken on a June bug.

Here we go again, I thought, as I made my way into the new office. I sensed tension in air right away. Throughout the day, I noticed staff members huddling close together, quietly chatting among themselves in hushed whispers. It seemed like something was going on but kept my head down and focused on learning the ropes of the new job. There was a new computer system to learn, not to mention a jewelry case in the waiting room filled with beautiful handmade amber jewelry, crafted by one of the patients, that I had to sell. Super odd for a dental office, but whatever. The female dentist who owned the practice was quite of fan of awards, particularly the ones she bought for herself, and I was told to make sure they were polished. She would often point out that while she may not have actually won an award for OUTSTANDING DENTIST OF THE YEAR or BEST COSMETIC DENTIST, she could still enjoy these accolades by simply purchasing and displaying generic awards. Taking a page from her book, I did the same when I stumbled across a WORLD'S BEST MOTHER figurine at a thrift shop. The moment I saw it, I knew it was meant for me, so I snatched it right up! This little trinket now proudly stands on my desk at home as a reminder of who truly is the world's best mom—ME! Hey, I have an award to prove it.

Another unique requirement of my new job was to freshly brew coffee, place it on a serving tray with mugs, creamer, and sugar, and run it up a narrow stairway to where Doctor and her husband (who sort of helped to run the practice) had their private office. *Just what the heck have I gotten myself into this time?!?* I wondered. *Am I a dental receptionist, a maid, or a waitress?!?* The list of nondental-related tasks that would be asked of me in this job grew and grew. So much so, that by the end of that first day I had secretly dubbed my new boss, "Dr. Megaquirks."

Early one morning, a few days after I was hired, I quietly opened the back door with my key and started to step in. Just then I saw the office manager, who looked hastily thrown together, coming down the back stairs while buttoning up her shirt and patting her hair into place—with Dr. Megaquirks' husband following behind her! I silently backed out of the entrance, knowing they hadn't seen me, and waited a few minutes before reentering. While I waited, I looked around the parking lot for Doctor's car, but saw only the husband's and office manager's cars. Gulp. Unsure of what to make of this suspicious scene I had stumbled upon, I just I kept it to myself. Could it be that Dr. Megaquirks' husband was having an affair with the office manager? The last thing I wanted after my years with Dr. HMO was another dental office full of drama! I was already starting to wonder about my new workplace, because the day before the dental assistant had kindly pointed out to me all the cameras and voice monitors littered throughout the office, through which Doctor and her husband kept an eye (and ear) on the staff. Another quirk for sure. I only hoped the husband wouldn't "replay the tape" and see me stepping into that awkward moment when he and the office manager had come down the stairs.

A few days after that, the office manager either abruptly quit or was fired (all I know is I never saw her again). That same day, before anyone arrived at the office, Doctor's husband swept through and removed the computer server that ran the entire office dental program, as well as several other major pieces of equipment that were needed to run the practice. And with that, he left his wife. Dr. Megaquirks tried to downplay that her husband cleaned out her dental office. This was not an amicable split by any means. When I arrived to work that day, I was told I would now be the office manager and my position change was nonnegotiable and would not include a pay increase. Doctor told me I would have to start from scratch to figure out passwords and how to run the entire dental practice. We never spoke another word about the former office manager. I just assumed her office duties and that was that. It became apparent that "Husband" (he did not have, nor does he deserve, any further name or title) had not been paying the bills for some time. Many bills were way past due, and the dental supply company Doctor used had frozen her accounts. It was a mess to say the least! I got to work on finding another supply company that would allow her to order dental products. To be honest, I am very proud of how quickly I was able to figure out insurance passwords, billing, staff, and the overall navigation of my new position.

Overnight I went from being support staff to supporting the staff. I had been friends with the assistants and hygienist, now I was their manager. I held morning huddles, helping to map out our day, and addressing the daily or weekly challenges. Thankfully, our morning meetings didn't always include Doctor because she had a newborn baby, so some days it took her longer to get to the office. When she was present the meeting always started with her asking, "Who looks better today? Me, or Joy?" (Quirk!) The staff always gave the same answer to make her happy, "Of course, you look the best, Doctor!" Seriously, it wasn't a beauty pageant.

———————

As the months went by, more and more menial tasks were expected of me. Doctor's coffee was now to be brewed fresh three times a day. She would buzz me on the intercom to bring her cup after cup, made just the way she liked it. Some days a bite of chocolate was to be included on the tray. If I was busy with patients and forgot to make the coffee for the afternoon, she would buzz me on the intercom and say, "Joy, Doctor does not like old coffee, she needs a fresh pot." *Yes, Dr. Megaquirks,* I would think to myself, as I set aside my work to go and brew her coffee. My quirk list was growing by leaps and bounds.

Soon Doctor started adding more to my daily tasks (to make her burdens lighter). I was often asked to run errands on my personal time. Some days she would have me come in early or stay late. I was not allowed to clock in and was doing this as a "favor," she would tell me. The tasks she would assign to me ranged from mundane things such as going to the post office or dry cleaners, to more time-consuming errands like grocery shopping. For one such trip to the grocery store, Doctor instructed me to buy high-protein frozen meals, as she was trying to lose baby weight. I hauled the groceries up the stairs to her office, placing the bags on the counter that ran along the far wall. I crossed the room to throw something away as Doctor looked through the bags. She picked up one of the frozen meals and read the ingredients. When she saw that it contained rice—a starch—she quickly pointed out that was not what she asked for and threw the box at me!

"I specifically asked for protein only!" Doctor snapped.

What in the actual hell had just happened?!? I asked myself. Quirky, annoying, and downright hurtful! But I apologized and promised to be more mindful next time.

Walking up those stairs to her office became increasingly nerve racking for me. Dr. Megaquirks made more and more requests, even for tasks I wasn't knowledgeable about and struggled to learn. And if the result wasn't up to par in her eyes, she would yell at me. Nothing seems good enough for her. One day, she called me up to her office for a meeting, saying she heard one of the assistants in the office talking about her on the monitor and now she wanted me to fire the assistant. This put me in a difficult position because I was friends with that assistant, I had just had her daughter over to my house to play with my son. The assistant, of course, felt I stabbed her in the back. But what could I do? Florida is an At-Will Employment state. In other words, an employer in Florida can legally fire you for any reason. Now, Dr. Megaquirks, being the EMPLOYER, should have done the firing herself, but no, she preferred to force me to drop the axe. There were so many times that Dr. Megaquirks and I would sit alone in her office, while she verbally abused and berated me. Nothing would please her. I would take notes on how I could do better and fulfill her requirements. The quirks and eccentricities were off the charts, but I just kept my head down and soldiered on because I needed the job to care for my son.

My divorce took quite a while to fully finalize and was a long and difficult journey. I was both surprised and disappointed when my ex-husband ended up being awarded our home in the settlement agreement. This meant that my son and I had to find a new place to live, so we moved to the opposite side of town, to a more family-oriented neighborhood with better educational opportunities. I did get to keep the relationship with my now former mother-in-law. My son and I attended divorce recovery classes at a nearby church over the course of the next year, where I sought to help him make sense of what was happening and understand that although his parents chose different paths, he was still loved unconditionally. My little guy and I spoke openly about the entire divorce process. At times my ex-husband would take him for a weekend visitation, but not often, and never midweek. I never pressed because I knew how heavily he was drinking. When he started to date a much, much older lady with grandkids the same age as my son, those kids were often at his place along with my son. When that was the case, the elderly girlfriend would not allow my son to eat the same food or take part in the same activities as her grandchildren. Little by little, my ex-husband became less and less involved and then stopped taking his weekend visitations altogether. I hated to think what this abandonment might to do to him; at the same time, I couldn't help but feel a sense of relief as I noticed on several occasions when he arrived to pick him up, he had an open beer in the vehicle cup holder. For my son's safety, I tried to report this to law enforcement, but they were not the least bit concerned.

After that year of divorce recovery classes I started dating again, but very cautiously. I did not want random people coming in and out of my son's life. The one person who was a constant throughout the divorce, my job issues, hurricanes, and even times when my child was sick, was the guy who had always been available when my now ex-husband needed picking up from a bar. In fact, this guy had become my best friend, my rock. One day as we were walking around downtown, he asked me if I would be interested in becoming more than friends. I told him to give me some time to weigh it out in my head. For years he had been the glue that held me together. If being more than friends did not work out, I would lose his friendship and support. He had taught my son how to ride a bike without training wheels, listened for hours while I talked about work and life, switched meals with me in a restaurant if I thought his was better, and tutored my son with his schoolwork. He was always patient, always there, never asking anything of me. After careful reflection, I realized that I had been developing feelings for him without even realizing it. He was everything a partner *should* be, and I could finally see that maybe I was worth having a good person to walk with through life. I decided that he and I deserved a chance at true happiness, so we started dating.

———————

Meanwhile, at work, I was still the office manager—in charge of everything and every type of chaos that came along. One recurring theme was that we could not get an assistant to stay with the practice for more than a few months.

The office staff and patients were under surveillance via voice monitors and cameras, so Dr. Megaquirks could watch and listen to the staff from a computer in her office. I was constantly called upstairs to go over something the staff had just said, or that Doctor found disturbing as she watched on her computer screen. It was a struggle to be friends with the staff and execute what Doctor wanted us all to comply with day in and day out. The staff saw her as a friendly boss and had no idea that for years, in that upstairs room, they were being watched so closely in so many areas of the office and I was taking verbal lashings.

One day Doctor called me upstairs and surprised me with the news that her husband was going to start coming in and taking over some of the office duties again. I was to treat him with respect, she instructed. He was a belligerent drunk who kept a coffee mug filled with alcohol in his hand most of the time, even at the office. *Oh, yippy skippy, I get to deal with someone else with an alcohol problem!* I thought. He was at no loss for the number of tasks he wanted me to do. I wrote everything down in my notebook and tried to get it all done. I had daily meetings with both now, Doctor and Husband, in which they made a point of letting me know I was not living up to their expectations. One day, Husband opened the closet where I kept my purse and lunch bag. I watched in disbelief as he pulled a letter from my purse and began to read it. When I questioned him, he smugly put the letter down and said that anything that came into the office was his property and he had a right to go through it. What an arrogant jerk! That was the last time I brought in my purse for quite a while.

As the quirks on my list mounted, one day I was hit with a whopper: Dr. Megaquirks suddenly informed me that I was to throw her a baby shower. I had no idea she was even pregnant! She hadn't told any of the staff, including me, and had hidden her pregnancy under bulky clothes. It had crossed my mind that she was gaining weight, and obviously her husband was back, but her pregnancy came as a shock. Doctor wanted me to use my own money for the shower and make it nice for her. I was at a loss on how to throw a shower on a single parent's income, but I did the best I could. My mind quickly raced with ideas for the perfect celebration, but also with keeping my budget in check. I included the staff and the new female dentist that had recently been hired.

After all my efforts, however, Doctor said that she was disappointed—accusing me of a lack of caring—and said that I could have done better.

Before long, Dr. Megaquirks had her baby and took a maternity leave. A dentist was hired to fill in for two months. It was nice to be at to work without the stress of her constant monitoring of the staff and yelling at me the end of each day. Husband stayed completely away as well. During her leave, however, Doctor had me stopping by her townhouse regularly, to get instructions on the things she wanted me to do at the office and to drop off groceries. I did all of this outside of work hours, without any compensation for my time. Thankfully, she did pay for the groceries. Being in her house just felt odd, and I remember being genuinely taken aback by the sheer amount of coffee mugs that were present in each area of her house; they seemed to be everywhere! Whether they were hers or Husband's I couldn't say, but I had a suspicion those mugs carried more than coffee.

Upon her return, the upstairs meetings occurred more often and became more intense. I always carried my own notebook with me to write down every demanded task, prioritizing the things she stressed were most important. These meetings always left me shaken up. When Husband was present, he would get right up into my face to belittle me and tell me how worthless I was. Doctor would sit there and watch it all and then agree with him, nodding as he shouted profanity in my face. It was all I could do to not cry during these meetings as the most fowl curse words flew out of Husband's mouth. They both told me repeatedly that I wasn't measuring up as their office manager.

With Husband back, my plate was piled high with both office manager and dental assisting duties. We still couldn't keep a dental assistant for longer than a few weeks. I was always stepping in to assist on a patient. Finally, a candidate came along who had a great resume, so I was hopeful she would work out. But then. . . . Early one morning Dr. Megaquirks called on her way to work and asked me to have the assistant duplicate a waxed-up model of some teeth for an appointment that day. Typically, this involves taking an impression of the model using alginate, a type of molding material used in dentistry that has a unique property that allows it to set at room temperature; it can be easily molded around and then from removed a waxed-up model without damaging it. Once the alginate impression is made, a new model is "poured up in stone" to make an exact duplication of the original waxed-up model. So, *DEAR HEAVENLY FATHER*, when I heard the sound of the machine that was used for heating up plastic, I raced to the lab just as the assistant was placing heated, soft plastic on the waxed-up model—thinking she could mold it around the model to get the impression. Heat on wax . . . no, no, NO!! She completely melted the original. Doctor had paid $900 dollars for a dental lab to create that waxed up model, and the assistant had ruined it. I called Dr. Megaquirks immediately to explain the error, all the while bracing myself for her inevitable yelling and cursing. She wanted me to fire the assistant and fix the model. I tried to explain that I had no experience with waxing up a model.

"FIX IT!!!" she screamed and hung up.

I could not fix it or even remotely come close to what the lab had created, and by then the patient for whom the model had been made arrived. Doctor fudged through the error by showing the patient pictures of what the outcome of treatment would be (instead of using the models), all the while loudly blaming me for the mess up.

But wait, there's more! One day, Husband called in all the players of a local hockey team, saying we would make them custom mouth guards. He wanted the free advertising for the office. There was an assistant working with me to take impressions, then I would pour them up in a two-part process and follow the steps to make each mouthpiece. We were at the office late into the night, almost to the next day. Husband was mighty proud of himself when he provided cheap fast-food tacos as a meal, which I passed on. The next day was Friday, so no patients would be scheduled, and I thought I would have the day off, but Husband had other plans. When I was finally dismissed, he made sure to point out there would be no special treatment for me. I was expected to be back in a few hours for my normal workday. My typical Friday consisted of answering phones, submitting insurance claims, and catching up on overflow from the week. It was a long, grueling day and the work really could have waited, just that one time.

After two years that felt like twenty, I knew my time at this office had to come to an end, so little by little, I started to take my personal items home with me. I wasn't sure how I would provide for myself and my young son, but I couldn't take any more of that terrible work environment. It was not that I could not do the jobs I had been given, it was the many additional tasks that Dr. *and Mr.* Megaquirks constantly threw at me—up to and including being ordered to create a discount services dental flyer in *Russian!* I pointed out that I did not speak or read Russian, nor did I have software that would convert the flyer copy for me. When I made a lame attempt and presented it to Husband, he balled the paper up and threw it at me, telling me to get out of his sight. My heart just could not take much more of their abuse. I knew I had to quit as soon as possible, so I started looking for another job.

A week later, on what would turn out to be my last day at that office, things really hit the fan. It was a regular workday, with dental patients on the dentists' side and cleaning patients on the hygiene side. Late in the day I was told we would have a meeting upstairs before I was allowed to go home. I was always quick to comply with their demands because I needed to get home to my son, but thankfully my boyfriend would get him if I ran late. At this point, he was in elementary school and attended an aftercare program. Are you curious about my love life at this point? It's going well. My best friend had become my boyfriend and the love of my life. [Applause please]

Husband came to get me for the meeting, grabbing his keys and locking the front door of the office because we were now closed for the day. He then demanded that I follow him upstairs for the meeting. I grabbed my notebook and went up the stairs to where Doctor was waiting. Once I was in the room, Husband used his key to lock the office door which had a key lock on both sides, then sloppily threw the lanyard with the keys down on the floor. I sat down and put my Blackberry phone in my lap, with my boyfriend muted on speaker, so he could hear what I had been tolerating for months. He would later tell me that he only heard yelling and muffled noises but started driving to the office, worried about what might be happening. My hands were shaking as Husband started off the meeting by telling me I was worthless and not doing my job. In my head I was trying to keep from crying, so I all I could think of was *You can't treat me like the celery on a hot wing plate!* As he shouted out the things I had fallen short on for the week, I tried to write them down, but my hands were shaking so badly that my handwriting was illegible. He leaned in close to my face as he shouted at me, so close that I could smell the alcohol on his breath. He spat out that he had heard me say (via the monitoring system) that I was offended by his cussing. Then he leaned in even closer and shouted even louder, using the most vulgar profanity, saying that was *TOO BAD*, because he could and would cuss at me anytime he wanted because it was *HIS OFFICE*. I was writing his words down as he spewed them out of his drunken mouth. Doctor sat across from me with a sick smile on her face, allowing him to rage and verbally abuse me. She appeared fine with it.

I am not sure how long this went on, but at some point, I stood up to leave, knowing that I would have to get past the locked door. As I stepped away from my chair, Husband suddenly jumped up and said, "Now give me the notebook."

My heart pounded in my chest and a feeling of fear swept through me. This meeting was far worse than any I had endured in the past. The anger in the room was reaching a new level, and I could feel my instincts screaming at me, telling me that I needed to get out of there as quickly as possible. Holding my notebook tightly against my chest, I said,

"This is my personal property. I bought it with my own money."

This of course only served to infuriate him even more; his face contorted with rage until it was almost unrecognizable. He was wild with anger. My entire body began to shake and everything around me seemed to move in slow motion as I reached down for the keys on the floor and hurriedly unlock the door so I could escape those two and that miserable office. *Just get down the stairs,* I told myself. I felt like I was in a bad horror movie where the girl has only a few seconds to escape before the chainsaw-wielding maniac gets to her.

PAUSE. Are you wondering why I didn't just give him the darn notebook? Well, it's quite simple. I hate to be bullied. It wasn't just that the notebook was mine or that I had written something incriminating in my notes that day. Actually, my notes from that meeting weren't even legible. But this was about feeling bullied, feeling terrified, being made to feel like I was in danger, being made to feel like the other two people in the room were about to bring harm to me.

UNPAUSE. Somehow, I managed to unlock that door and flee down the stairs, moving as fast as I could with Husband close behind me, still shouting profanity and "GIVE ME THAT NOTEBOOK!" over and over.

He chased me to the front office with Doctor right behind him as we circled my reception desk that sat in the middle of the room. I just wanted to get close enough to my purse, which was on the desk, to grab it and leave. *Why, oh why, did I start to bring a purse again?!?* I thought. Still clutching my notebook, around the desk we went, his anger escalating, with Doctor standing frozen just a short distance away. It almost felt like a dance—a most sickening and frighteningly choreographed dance. Was he really chasing me round and round a desk, trying to grab my little notebook?!? His eyes were psychotic. What the heck did he think I wrote down that was worth this? I honestly thought he would hurt me if he caught me. I took a chance and reached for my purse, but that gave him time to catch up to me. He now stood directly in front of me, shouting and demanding my notebook as he lunged for my throat with his hands. He barely got them around my neck when Doctor finally stepped in, shouting at him to stop and throwing her arm across us, allowing me to escape. I ran down the hall and straight out the back door, leaving that nightmare of an office forever.

Outside I found my boyfriend waiting anxiously by my car. He had driven over out of fear for me when he heard the raised voices and commotion on the phone. I was crying and hysterical as I tried to tell him what happened. He wanted to call law enforcement, but I just wanted to get my son and go home.

I faxed my resignation the following day and filed a restraining order against Husband, worried that he still might try to come after me. They quickly hired a lawyer to get me to drop the restraining order, saying it limited Husband's flight status. (He flew cargo for a major airline company when he wasn't torturing me at the dental office.) In filing my order of restraint, I was shocked to discover the past restraining orders that Dr. Megaquirks had filed against him. He had beaten her, and once she hid with her baby in a closet to escape him. Her face unrecognizable in the photos. My goodness what a way to live life. Their lawyer claimed that they had camera footage from my last day in the office, and it did not show any of the events I alleged in my restraining order application. But I knew his claim was false because the cameras hadn't been working properly for over a week leading up to that awful day. I recalled hearing Husband yelling about the cameras that week. Therefore, no footage whatsoever existed from the day of our altercation in the reception area. The lawyer also stated in a letter that my resignation was never received, and that I had abandoned my job. When the case went to court, the judge dropped the restraining order after Husband gave his word to never come near me again.

Quirks (Dr. Megaquirks and Husband)
1. Too many to list here!

Life Lesson: I know who I
am and what I deserve.

CHAPTER 12

Fluffing of Feathers

The average person changes jobs about twelve times in their life, changing careers three to seven times. I was on my way to job number six at the age of thirty-seven. I decided this would be a good time to continue with my education and enrolled in an in-person full-time program while I searched for work. I thought about changing careers and moving into the medical field as I continued to work on my degree. Even though I had a full course load, I managed to work two flexible jobs. I fell back on babysitting (*I know!*) and cleaning houses because they allowed me to make my own hours around the demands of school.

During this time, I also got engaged to my best friend turned boyfriend and we made plans for a simple beach wedding. He has always been my biggest cheerleader and an outstanding dad to my son. He is a gentleman, always opening doors for me, because that's how his daddy raised him to treat a lady. Even in the pouring rain, standing without an umbrella, he opens the car or restaurant door to whisk me out of the elements. I fuss, telling him he is getting soaked. But he won't listen. He raised the child he calls son to have the same respect for women. He accepts my flaws, celebrates my accomplishments, and loves me unconditionally. He snores and works long hours. When he doesn't snore, I wake him up to make sure he is all right. When he gets too engrossed with work, sitting in front of his computer, I make him a sandwich cut up into bite size pieces so he can take a phone call and have a bite between comments.

His dating profile would never say he likes long walks on the beach or raw oysters, but for me he will endure a nice stroll along the water. Early on in our dating life, to impress me, he threw back some raw oysters. Never again he says! He's always up for an adventure, going along with my planned activities list so we can make every moment count. After an eventful trip to Nashville, he is adamant about "not drinking where's there's country music, because you might make me dance." When I tell him he has big juicy lips like a tomato worm, he knows that's a compliment. He knows I am a handful but, as he says, that's why he's got two hands. We never drive around town at a loss for something in common to do because we are too busy kayaking, fishing, binge watching some show he thinks I will like, hiking, having late night talks by a fire pit, or any of the dozens of other things we do.

*Sometimes it's the things you don't plan
for that bring you the most happiness.*

Dropping off resumes in person was the way to job hunt in the early 2000s. I would pick a day and bring along a stack of resumes. Door to door, office to office, I would hand out my resume in hopes that the perfect place would hire me. I walked medical complexes and filled out lengthy applications in any office that would let me. In my car, before venturing into yet another mystery office, I would say a silent prayer that someone inside would take a chance on me.

Not one office called, not even one. Six months went by. Then one day my phone buzzed. It was a friend of mine . . .

"Joy! I was at my dentist's office and his assistant is leaving. You *must* go drop off your resume. I told him all about you!"

After she described where the office was located and the dentist's name, I told her that I dropped off a resume there some weeks ago. I remembered handing it to a youngish gal with a curly ponytail.

"Do me a favor," she persisted, "and just go back and give them another resume."

I did just that. This time handing my resume to a sweet older lady. She kindly said she would give the resume to the dentist, and she thought he might just be in touch.

I was ecstatic when I received the call that I had been invited for an in-person interview with Dr. Huntington, a local prosthodontist. Upon arriving the next day, I was shown into his operatory and he did lab work while we chatted, and he explained how his practice worked. I watched in amazement as he meticulously set denture teeth in wax on a model at his lab bench. His precise techniques and detailed approach to this delicate art demonstrated his skill. Dr. Huntington explained every aspect of the job clearly, and what would be expected of me.

He appeared to be an honest, laid back, kind individual with a natural gift for dentistry. I caught myself feeling that I could trust him—something I had not felt for an employer since my days with Dr. Grace and Dr. Albright. His careful listening showed that he was paying close attention to everything I said, and I could tell immediately that his knowledge and expertise far surpassed anything

I had experienced in the field of dentistry. After our discussion, he suggested that I start work the following week, and I readily agreed.

"Are you planning on staying in college full time?"

"No, no!" I quickly answered, "my last exam is next week." I decided right then and there that having a stable full-time position was more desirable and predictable than babysitting kids, cleaning houses, and juggling schoolwork—not to mention the years it would take to finish school and start over in a new profession. It was better to take the job I was being offered.

My first week was a challenge to say the least. I had entered yet another strange new world and my head was still spinning from the mania of the last two offices. In fact, I felt like I had once again landed on the moon or some distant planet. It's amazing how alien a new environment can seem, even if you are still within your chosen field: new faces, new voices, new routines, new quirks. Your list of five things, good or bad, starts over and you try to keep your head above water amidst all these changes. I kept expecting something wildly inappropriate to happen, but I reminded myself that not every dental office would be as dysfunctional as the ones run by Dr. HMO or Dr. Megaquirks. *Maybe this time,* I thought, *I'll find that family environment I've been searching for—like I had with Dr. Albright in Washington and Dr. Grace in Lubbock.* I had enjoyed interviewing with my new boss very much, and was feeling quite comfortable assisting him, but his small office was populated by several women who were far from welcoming (not including the receptionist, Doris, who was precious). Despite being in my late thirties by this time, I was still a spring chicken in this office. The hygienist, right away, lorded over me like she was my queen.

Women working in dental offices can be vicious territorial beasts, circling their prey with razor-sharp claws. I have yet to work in an office that was peace, love, and sunshine right away. You need a thick skin, quick wit and inner strength to endure the adjustment period. In my opinion, having a male dentist present may help to balance out the high levels of estrogen flying around. But these women are masters of their craft and will find subtle ways to express their animosity when the doctor is not around. It's a "Joy Fact" that it takes a year to finally be comfortable in a new office—an intimidating task that feels like trying to fit an elephant into a mouse hole!

Penny, the assistant who was leaving, was tasked with training me for a week before she moved away. Every dentist has their own preferences when it comes to certain instruments, dental materials used, and how they prefer to perform each dental procedure. Five things. Every dentist has five things that are important to them. I had no idea at the time, but Penny was deliberately teaching me the *WRONG* way to do things! In fact, she and the hygienist had ganged up to sabotage me, hoping I would fail so that Doctor would fire me and hire a friend of theirs instead.

I had a fresh, new notebook handy at all times, and jotted down steps to the procedures, preferred dental products, and everything else Penny shared that I thought would be helpful in my new position.

"Don't set the room up until the patient is seated in the waiting room," Penny pointed out. "You don't want to take the time to set it all up and the patient doesn't show." *Hmmmm ... I* thought, *that was super bad advice, that goes against every dental office I've ever worked in ...*

I found it odd that this office would have patients that didn't show up after waiting months for an appointment, and it seemed ill prepared not have a room set up, but I dutifully jotted down her advice.

"He likes to put his own injection syringe together. So, don't put the needle or carpule in the syringe."

"Don't take the trashes out, his lazy wife can do that when she's cleaning the office." *Oh? How do you really feel about his wife, Penny?*

"Don't get too comfortable here," Penny said on day two. "I will be moving back in three years and taking back my job." In terms of being an invaluable employee, she appeared to have set the bar rather low, so I felt certain I could easily exceed her accomplishments with my own work ethic and skill set.

P.S. I overheard the conversation three years later and he wished her well but wasn't hiring. [Insert smug emoji.]

As I took over the assisting work, she took the week to relax and nap, laying her head on the desk where she was supposed to be working. This was out of Doctor's line of sight, so she was safe. The hygienist would fly past me and make snarky comments throughout the day, to make sure I knew I wasn't welcome in "her" office and that Penny was her friend. *Hmmm . . . birds of a feather flock together*, I thought. This behavior made my blood boil every time and reminded me of how much I loathe people who try to intimidate others through hateful words and mean actions.

Dr. Huntington was a specialist and although assisting was, of course, very familiar to me, the procedures and level of care he performed were as if I was stepping foot on a different planet unlike anything I had ever experienced! I found myself forging into uncharted territory on my very first day, but rather than feel overly worried (which I have been known to do), I was excited by his work manner. Plus, I'm a quick learner. On day two, I seated a patient to do a soft reline in an upper denture. Using a dental product that starts out as a liquid, you place it in the denture and then into the patient's mouth until it reaches a bubble-gum-like consistency. After five minutes you remove it from the patient's mouth and trim the excess off. I had trimmed it with the heating knife and wanted to get Doctor's approval before giving it to the patient and dismissing them. I stepped out of the room to look for my new boss, leaving the upper denture on a sterile tray on the lab bench behind the patient. When I returned with the dentist, I was shocked to see that upper denture looking not at all as I had left it. The material inside the denture had been gouged out and it had deep holes in its surface. Someone had sabotaged my upper denture! Dr. Huntington just shook his head in dismay, and of course he said I needed to redo the liner. Just then, Penny breezed past the room with an arrogant smirk on her face, as if she was proud of her mischief making. *Oh Penny*, I thought, *I'm a firm believer in karma.*

Friday finally arrived with no patients scheduled, it was the day to clean the office and do lab work for a few hours. I was relieved to have the short day, because one of the houses I cleaned had begged me to keep working for them. I would spend three hours, two Fridays a month, for the next six years (until they moved away) cleaning that home, this after a six-hour workday. On this Friday, the end of my very first week with Dr. Huntington, Penny was to train me one on one, but called Doctor to say she had an emergency and couldn't come in. I ran into her at the grocery store later that day and she quickly blurted out that her dishwasher wasn't working. *That was your emergency?!?* Personally, I had been relieved to be in the office, doing my lab work and cleaning, without her or the hygienist to bother me. When Doctor and his wife stopped in that morning, I was diligently going about my dental lab work and other tasks, following my notes and trying to make sure I did everything correctly according to my notes. I remember feeling so overwhelmed by the new protocols, but also proud of myself for writing everything down so I could learn the ropes of my new position. However, Doctor stopped me several times, his kindness tinged with a bit of frustration, as he explained that literally everything I touched was being done wrong. Again and again this happened. After finishing a few more tasks and having him point out even more errors, the frustration caught up with me and I started to cry. What can I say? I'm a crier, it's what I do. I mean, yes it was awkward for my new boss to see a grown woman with tears streaming down her face as if I were a toddler, having a meltdown.

I pride myself on learning to do new things quickly and correctly, so I just couldn't understand what was happening, especially since I had written Penny's every detail in my notebook.

"Dr. Huntington, I have no idea what's going on, but I am doing things the way Penny told me to!" I blurted out, tears still streaming down my face. I took out my notebook and showed Doctor my notes. As he held his finger against his lips, he scanned my notes before looking back up at me.

"I think Penny might have been giving you incorrect information. It seems like she's been telling you the exact opposite of what I expect from my dental assistants."

I just stood there a moment, staring at Doctor, as his words slowly sunk in. I couldn't believe it, I had entered a jungle where the vicious beast circle their prey.

After that challenging and emotional morning, my new boss and his wife, Joann, decided we should end the day early. They very kindly took me out for a sit-down lunch before I headed to my house-cleaning job. (Oh, happy day!) I remember Joann being matter of fact about how the other two staff members were treating me, telling me to hang in there.

"Don't let them intimidate you," Joann advised. "Fluff your feathers!"

"Ummm, what?"

"Birds fluff their feathers to keep predators away."

They were both kind and understanding as we discussed the office dynamics. Even with this little hiccup, I had a feeling I was going to like working for Dr. Huntington.

In the wild, an animal may defend its territory by fighting off an invader. Others will give a warning such as a piercing sound, a foul odor, or a visual threat (example: fluffing of feathers).

CHAPTER 13

Nomenclature

No matter how bad you think your mouth is, I've seen worse—decayed teeth, abscesses from infected teeth so painful that even a gentle breeze can push them over the edge, meth mouth, black hairy tongue (it's a real thing) that causes unsightly black filaments to grow on the surface of your tongue), gum disease so severe it can leave your breath smelling like a cross between a sewage drain and a rotting carcass. You name it, I've seen it.

I want to let you in on a little secret that makes all dental professionals dry heave: ladies who are drenched in perfume or men who have gone to town with the cologne or body spray. We are right next to you for goodness sake. If we can smell you in the waiting room, you have on too much fragrance. And please, oh please, don't hug me before you go back to the operatory. One, I am *NOT* a hugger. And two, that strong fragrance clings to my clothes and hair, and I am reminded why the convenience store is not the best place to buy Mom's Christmas gift. That French onion soup you had at lunch may cause a double mask situation for me, but B.O. and strong perfume will drive us to put orange solvent in our masks or pop a peppermint into our mouths to cover the not very pleasant smell. Again, I'm right next to you, please bathe and wear deodorant (and skip the perfume). I swear the canary was alive before you came into the office!

"Mr. Richards? Come on back. I'm Joy, Dr. Huntington's assistant," I say, as I lead the patient back from the waiting area and into the first operatory. "What brings you in today?"

Mr. Richards is interested in upper and lower dentures. After his meeting with Dr. Huntington, I am asked to take an X-ray that goes all the way around his head as well as a cavity detaching full mouth series. First stop is the Panorex X-ray machine, called a *pano* for short. If you were paying attention earlier, you know the first machine of this type was one the patient sits down in. We are well past that, so now you stand VERY STILL while holding two handles on the machine, which looks kind of like a rocket ship. It even makes the noise you would assume an alien rocket ship would make as it beams you up. This digital image is taken to show the head, neck and jaw and compared with your full series of eighteen little X-rays, giving the Doctor a clear picture of which teeth need to come out (extractions), which teeth have decay but can be treated and retained, and which are free from any issues. During a new patient exam, Dr. Huntington and I speak a kind of a dental language to communicate what he finds in your mouth:

"#3 (O) resin," he will tell me.

In the dental computer program we use, I highlight the molar in the upper right (#3) and select the tooth surface (O) for "occlusal" and select "resin" or tooth colored for the type of filing Doctor has identified in the tooth. You might also have an amalgam (silver) filing, or a crown. For each tooth he calls out to me the different restorations present or, if none, it's called a virgin tooth.

Panorex X-rays are incredibly important for providing accurate information about a person's dental health like wisdom teeth placement, any bone abnormalities. For the record, most insurances typically cover one every three to five years. I also get the radiation question a lot. Honestly, there's no need to worry. With digital images you really get a very low amount of radiation. Much less than you'd receive from everyday activities like being in the sun, using your cell phone, digging in your garden, or even eating a banana!

Remember when I lived in Lubbock and my boss and I helped the forensics team to identify bodies that were burned or otherwise unidentifiable? If, God forbid, the only thing left of you after a fire is your mandible (lower jaw) with your teeth, tracking down the X-ray that shows a match with a filling in tooth #31, and any other dental work that can be noted, could be the only clue that identifies you.

Now, with Mr. Richards in the chair, Dr. Huntington mutters something to me from behind his mask as he leaves the room. (This will be an issue for the next ten years). As a new employee you don't want to say, "Huh? Speak up!" to the boss. That comes years later. After spending awhile going through the possibilities in my head of what he may have said, I come up with nothing. By now too much time had gone by, and I don't feel I can go to him and say I didn't hear him. *Why didn't I just ask him to repeat what he said right away?*

"Mr. Richards, did you catch what the Dr. said?" I ask.

"No," he replies.

"Well, I guess we will just chat until he comes back and then he will point out what I haven't done, and we'll go from there. It's my first day here and I hate to tell him I didn't hear him."

I learn that Mr. Richards miraculously cheated death when, despite all odds, he survived a car accident, something that he remembers vividly. This eye-opening experience paved the way for him to truly appreciate and treasure every moment he gets to spend with his beloved wife, and to cherish and value life like he never did before. As I intently listen to his story, I sense the profound impact it had on him—and he cherishes each day.

When Dr. Huntington returns to the room, he looks at me and asks, "Did you take upper and lower impressions?"

Ahhhhh…first impressions!!! That's what he said! Before I have the chance to say no, Mr. Richards jumps in with, "She was about to take the impressions and I asked her to wait a minute and explain some things to me." *Thanks for covering for me, Mr. Richards!*

As the weeks fly by, I come to cherish spending time with Mr. Richards during his many long dental appointments. He soon becomes someone very dear to my heart. Dr. Huntington tells me that as long as I don't have pressing lab work, I can be in the operatory talking to patients while he methodically sets teeth in wax or does other lab work for the patient's to have a wax try in for their custom dentures.

"Wait!" I exclaimed in disbelief. "You want me to TALK all day?!? So, let me get this straight. You are going to PAY me to do this?" Was it possible I had stumbled into a dream job? From chatting with random strangers while shopping at the grocery store, to exchanging small talk in an elevator. You know I have always been up for a conversation!

Mr. Richards and I spend many hours together throughout the course of his dental treatment. I learn of his hardships and how he overcame them. He never has to "cover" for me again because it turns out that Dr. Huntington isn't the type of dentist who overreacts to things not being done immediately. However, I appreciated what Mr. Richards did for me on my very first day. By the time his dental treatment comes to an end, Mr. Richards has the most beautiful set of dentures, which allow him to have a nice smile for his remaining years. When he passed away his wife called to tell me. It always feels like a brick has been dropped on my heart when a dear patient passes away.

Keep in mind, however, that even after many months of working in this specialty field, I was still struggling with my newfound position on the moon. It was like everything I had learned in my previous dental life didn't exist. Everything is done to the nth degree in dental prosthodontics: the procedures use dental tools and instruments that general dentists typically don't use, and the steps for procedures are more intense and thorough. I was still writing things down to review at home, months later. I have always excelled at my job, and I would say I am a quick learner. Learning dental prosthodontics, however, was slowing me down. At every turn there seemed to be an obstacle or a new challenge.

Here's a good example: Doctor and I were about to take what I call a "fancy impression." This type of impression is more expensive than the regular alginate used in most offices because it delivers very accurate results. Typically, we only use it when an appliance needs to fit very super-duper close to the teeth. To prepare for this task, I set out supplies for Dr. Huntington on his side of the counter: alginate bowl, mixing spatula, and a huge plastic syringe to hold the material. He will do the "A" and "B" steps of this process. Once Doctor's gooey mix is ready, he loads it into what looks like a huge horse syringe (no needle, though!) and carefully squirts this material on top of the patient's teeth and in the vestibule (the space between the lips and the cheeks). For my part of the process (steps "C" and "D"), I have a plastic bowl that locks onto a mixing machine that, to cut down on air bubbles in the mixture, spins in only ONE direction. After my mix is complete, I remove it from the bowl and place the now firm goo into an impression tray. I run the tray under water and then hand it to Dr. Huntington. It's an orchestrated event: *A, B, C, D.* He will also hand off his mirror that he uses to pull back the cheeks. In the other hand he will do his juggling act, throwing not one, not two, but three balls in the air! Not really, I just threw that in. The material will start to set very quickly, so timing is everything. I always give Dr. Huntington a little head start, so that he will have just finished with his big syringe as I am handing him my impression tray. The first time we had a patient in need of a fancy impression, I set everything up so the process would go as planned. I'm a very organized and methodical person.

"Joy, give me a thirty-second head start and then add the water to your mix and press the button that makes the machine rotate the mixing bowl."

"Alrighty."

While I didn't actually *time* Doctor or anything, I knew when it was GO time for me. With my right hand, I poured premeasured (not too hot, not too cold) water into my bowl that already held my powder. Then, using my right pointer finger, held down the button to start the bowl spinning and off it went. In my left hand I held the mixing spatula that I would lower into the mix to help the alginate smoothly incorporate. But we overlooked one tiny detail: I'm left-handed. Why would this matter you ask? Well, this spinning machine is meant for the mixing spatula to be lowered in from the right side, NOT the left side (the spatula even has finger indentations for a right-handed person) and rotates as if you have the mixing spatula in your right hand. It's a right hander's world after all. So, the second my mixing spatula hit the mixture:

Splat! Splat!!! SPLAT!!!

My goopy material went soaring right out of the bowl and splattered all over Dr. Huntington—there was goo everywhere!

His scrubs, his face—every part of him that was facing me was completely a goopy mess. I stood there with my finger still on the mixer button, stunned. Now, you would think that my brain might react faster and order me to take my finger off that button— you know, to *stop* the material from splattering all over him—but you would be wrong. Luckily, he and the patient were laughing, and this is how I discovered that Dr. Huntington is a kindhearted person and can handle any situation with good humor.

Welcome to the moon. In lieu of
any ordinary activities, your visit
will include carelessly slopping your
boss with flying dental materials.
We hope you will enjoy your stay!

This new dental office had tons of lab work that was associated with absolutely everything. Every new patient got a very comprehensive work up, starting with preliminary or "first" impressions. That's the oozy pink stuff we put in those trays you think are too large for your mouth, to take upper and lower alginate impressions. Now, it's not the most comfortable thing in the world, I know. And trust me, after doing this procedure for years now, I've gotten pretty fast at it. Note, if you bite down on my fingers after I have asked you to keep your mouth open, we will have to redo the impression and that will not make either of us happy. I like to keep your mind off the gooey grossness by telling funny stories while I have the trays in your mouth, which usually does the trick!

Now, quick set alginate is your friend (only a 1–2 minute set time). The powder is mixed with premeasured water that is on the warm side. Careful there, Skippy. If your water is hot, it will set before you place it in the patient's mouth. Here is my easy alginate impression cheat sheet:

1. Explain what is about to happen to the patient. Stress that it will help to breathe in and out slowly through the nose, and that the impression only takes a minute.

2. No need to overfill the tray to get your landmarks. Let's talk about the upper impression: After you've tried empty trays in the patient's mouth, and selected a tray size, mix the alginate. Squish that stuff in the tray till the material is coming out of the holes—this locks it into the tray. Then run the impression under water and run your finger in the shape of the arc to get a little trench. You can use the extra material in the palate, just swipe it up there quickly and place the tray in the patient's mouth. Gently pull the patient's cheeks up and over the tray to let the material get into the vestibule.

3. Meanwhile, as you are lightly holding the tray in place with two fingers, use your forearm behind the patient's head to lean them forward—so the material doesn't run down the back of their throat. And NEVER EVER, say the word *gag* before, during, or after the procedure (or you may just cause that to happen as this is a mind-over-matter experience for the patient).

4. If the patient's eyes are showing signs of stress, or if they grab your arm (a huge pet peeve of mine, because I'm trying to help them stay in position so the

impression will be a success), or they start making choking sounds, have them raise their right leg . . . then their left leg. This will shift their focus from the impression tray to their legs as they concentrate on following your directions, which will help them to stay calm and pass the time.

5. An impression takes one to two minutes tops, and this includes the forty-five seconds of mix time. When taking the tray out of the mouth, use your finger to break the suction along the cheek and remove the impression with the tray, pulling down in one solid move. Wrap it immediately with a wet paper towel so it doesn't distort. Pour it up within thirty minutes or refrigerate to limit the distortion.

The next step is to pour up the impression in stone. Think of it like this, I have taken a negative mold of your mouth and I am pouring material into that impression to make a positive model. This is how we can see your teeth outside of your head. After the upper and lower models of your teeth are set up and trimmed, I mount them on an articulator. This is a frame that holds the models and can be manipulated to imitate jaw movements. This is a lengthy process which has some room for error if the teeth are not in proper alignment. Using bite registration material, I have already seen how your teeth come together and use this when mounting the models. After a series of steps that include plaster setting up and the models being polished, Dr. Huntington uses the model to do a treatment work up.

For each patient, this was a typical work up, in addition to the photographs I would take of your profile and inside your mouth to get the clearest look at your teeth. And some patients even required extra steps, such as a custom tray made just for your mouth! Don't worry, we make those on the model! Another process with many different steps. Soft blue material is molded over the model of your teeth with a barrier to create space (thick wax with foil over it), then the material is trimmed so the final product won't be bulky. The tray on the model with the uncured material is then placed in the "cooker" to cure. The cooker is actually called a dental oven. In it, things set up pretty quick. "Oven" is just a weird term to me—like I'm baking cookies at work—so, I call it the cooker. Then there are a thousand steps to getting a custom tray ready to go in the patient's mouth. Dr. Huntington loves custom trays. I do as well, wink wink.

"Good morning, Mrs. Wilson! How are you today?" I say with a smile.

It's always nice to have patients that are friendly and happy to see you. It takes years to build trust in people and form a special bond.

"Let me take your dentures and put them in the shaker with some cleaner, before Dr. Huntington does your exam."

The shaker is an ultrasonic cleaner. It's a bigger version of the type of machine a jeweler uses to clean your jewelry. It uses ultrasound that creates sound waves to agitate the fluid inside to clean deep into pores and surfaces. But the name "ultrasonic cleaner" is such a mouthful, I just can't say it all day.

"I'm putting your removable dentures in an ultrasonic dental appliance cleaner."

Nah.

"I'm putting your teeth in the shaker." That has a much friendlier ring to it, don't you think?

———————

A few months into my extended stay on the moon, Doctor set up a meeting between he and I—to take place at the end of the workday—to go over the things I was doing well and discuss areas where there could be improvement.

I'm standing at his desk while he has "the talk" with me. "Blah, blah . . . the patients like you . . . you seem to be catching on . . . blah . . . blah . . ." He mentions that he would like for me to work on my nomenclature.

Huh?

"Yes, of course, sir," I say.

In my head, I'm thinking, *You've got to be kidding me. What the heck is nomenclature?!? I am trying to keep my head above water and now I have this nomenclature thing to deal with. Is that some-thing I can take a class for online?* Well, my moto is fake it till you make it, so I smile and tell him I will work on it.

When I get home, I ask my husband where or how I can work on my nomenclature. He laughs and says, "Ahhh, nomenclature, huh? That's gonna take some work for you."

What the heck?!? Really?? Well, it's something that is import-ant to Dr. Huntington, so just point me in the right direction.

My husband then tells me the definition. Nomenclature is knowing and using the proper names for things, particularly in areas of science (and in my case, dentistry).

Fast forward to nine years later:

> Joy to Dr. Huntington: "How many snappy hats
> do we need for the lower thingy?"
> *(Translation: How many implant locators do we
> need for the lower overdenture reline?)*

Dr. Huntington to Joy: "Joy, place this thingam-ajig in the shaker for a spell, please."
(Translation: Place this denture in the ultrasonic cleaner with tartar cleaning solution for the five minutes as suggested on the bottle.)

Dr. Huntington to Joy: "Let's cook this for another minute."
(Translation: Place a prosthesis with added acrylic in the lab curing oven, to harden the material that starts out pliable.)

Dr. Huntington: "Joy, hand me the periosteal elevator, please."
Joy: "What? You mean this sharp, pointy thingy?"
Dr. Huntington: "Yes."
Joy: "Then why be all fancy? Call it what it is . . . geez!"

It took a few years, but I did train Dr. Huntington on "Joy" nomenclature.

And just like that, there was sun on the moon.

CHAPTER 14

Larry, Ken, and Dave

I fell into a career that has allowed me to meet new people daily, and some of these people are forever woven into the tapestry of my life.

Take Larry, for instance, who was an older man with a big personality. Larry could talk to a bar of soap. He was especially eager to talk about his mama or give you parenting advice. Larry and I developed a relationship full of kind teasing and quick wit. I always had to lengthen his appointments to include some "Larry Talk Time." He enjoyed visiting the casino, where he spent his time gambling and picking up some young "womens." I would tease him about the age of his "womens" knowing they were many years younger than him. Larry admittedly couldn't keep a lady around long because most of them wanted commitment or honestly couldn't carry on a conversation with him. He was full of wisdom and bursting at the seams to share his years of knowledge. When he arrived for his dental appointment, he would come in and loudly announce, "Where's my Joy?" I would try to drop what I was doing to go greet him. He would be laughing and always say to me, "You may not be joy to the world, but you are the joy in my world!" Larry was an incredible patient to have, he always came in with a joke, a funny story, and life advice. It's amazing that Dr. Huntington got any dental work done on him, because he and I could talk for hours!

"Larry," I would say, "Fermer la bouche!" In French that is *close your mouth* or stop talking. And the only reason I remember this phrase may be because the French teacher said it over and over to me.

Typically, the patients who came to Dr. Huntington and I for dental work were in a higher socio-economic bracket and looking for more specialized care. Being a specialty office allowed for more fine tuning of each patient's treatment, thus costing more of the doctor's time and skills. There were, however, patients whose treatment was covered by workers' compensation or similar programs. This brought us one especially wild patient, Ken, who likely would have never set foot in our world had his treatment not been covered by workers' comp.

From the first day that Ken meandered into our office for a new patient exam, he had us enthralled and entertained with his hillbilly charm. He had hitched a ride with a female companion, much younger than himself, he pointed out, to make his appointment. At well over seventy years of age, he made sure to inform me that she was not related to him in any way to ease any misconceptions. He volunteered that she "came around often," an implication that suggested a greater involvement than merely that of acquaintances. *To each their own is my motto!* He was dressed in old worn blue jeans, a plaid flannel shirt that was faded from years of wear, and boots that had seen many miles. There was no need for Ken to worry about food getting stuck between his teeth because there weren't that many left anyways which is how he found himself in Dr. Huntington's office.

"Good morning, Ken. I'm Joy, Dr. Huntington's assistant. What brings you in to see us today?"

"I need some teeth; it's getting harder and harder to eat squirrel and I ain't been having luck catching anything else," Ken said with a big toothless grin.

Thinking this gentleman was pulling my leg, I asked, "You really eat squirrel?"

"Yep, I live out yonder in the woods. I eat whatever comes around."

"Well, I for one am not eating anything with tire marks on it or that doesn't come from the store," I said with a laugh.

He was a character! As I got to know Ken, I found out he really did eat things that would be considered out of the ordinary for most people. I enjoyed picking on him and his simple country ways and he loved teasing me back. He had a kind heart, loved dogs, and shacked up with whatever female would have him. Ken touched my heart so much that over my lunch hour one day, I accompanied him to the local hospital to help him navigate the large facilities.

Ken had been involved in a car accident in the 1970s and had full medical and dental coverage for life. His insurance wanted him to have teeth that would require the least amount of ongoing care, and he was a good candidate for upper and lower all-on-four implant-retained fixed teeth. This type of dental restoration involves the placement of four implants in each arch of the upper and lower jaw, and then affixing a set of permanent false teeth to the implants with a titanium bar in the substructure. You can still clean under them, but only a dentist can remove them. The process is time consuming as the implants (that look like screws) have to be left in the jawbone, to allow for integration, for six to nine months before they can securely hold a set of permanent false teeth. While the implants are fully integrating, a temporary acrylic supported prosthesis is held in place using the implants. See the words *temporary* and *acrylic*? It is very important to not put stress on the implants while they are integrating, as this could cause one to "fail" and we wouldn't have the support of all four of the needed implants. During this temporary period, Ken faced a challenge due to his diet being mainly compromised of animals he trapped and cooked. The weak material of the temporary denture could not withstand the stress caused by crunchy or tough foods, so the false teeth would break off or the acrylic would fracture. I worked him into the schedule for lengthy repairs quite often during that period.

Every time I saw a possum, I would think how lucky that little guy was not to be in Ken's yard. Ken was definitely one of our more memorable patients!

Doctor, Doris, and I loved reminiscing about our patients and their widely varied stories. We would jog our memories and try to remember the many patients we had treated and even made a game out of it. Sometimes over lunch in the break room Doctor and I would play, "I wonder what happened to . . ."

Doctor: "I wonder what happened to the guy who came in wearing an upper full denture that was held in with frosting?"

Me: "Really that was genius because it was sticky, so it held in the teeth, but also tasty."

Doctor: "But because of the sugar it would quickly dissipate."

"You mean it would 'wear out' of the denture fast?" I say, laughing while making air quotes with my fingers. "And for the record, that was your one biggish word for the day!"

"I wonder what happened to the guy who was a psychiatrist, who went for years without teeth, and then we made him a full set of dentures and he never came back?" Doctor ponders.

"I wasn't a fan of him, to say the least," I say. "Remember I was in the room making small talk with him and he made kind of a rude comment, so I flippantly said, 'I love you, too.' After that he began to analyze our entire conversation and said that I was trying to subdue my real feelings for him and was actually in love with him. The whole conversation was completely ridiculous since I genuinely couldn't stand him. After that I limited our conversation time as much as possible."

"He was very particular about his title and wanted us to not call him a psychiatrist, but a psychotherapist. He worked in a mental institution," Doctor adds, but then he switches gears. "I wonder what happened to the sky diving granny?"

"I remember her! She was ninety years old and for her birthday she went sky diving. She brought in a picture showing herself in the air doing a tandem fall. She ended up fracturing her arm during the landing."

Dr. Huntington thinks for a minute and then, pulling from the back of his memory bank, remembers her exact treatment, "It comes to mind that we did a bridge on her upper right posterior teeth, and we never saw her again."

My turn. "I wonder what happened to that rude lady who had a physician as a husband—the one that made us stay late nights working on her?"

"She was a difficult case and wanted to dictate treatment. I presented a long-term plan for her, and she wanted to approach it with her timeline, her way," Doctor recalls.

This jogs my memory: "I remember she came over from another specialty office after having some teeth out and gum surgery, and it was already late in the day. After you prepped the teeth for her temporary, you told her I would make her long-span provisional and left the room. I explained the process again to her and started placing the temporary material in the stint and getting it ready to put in her mouth. She grabbed my arm as I was about to place the stint, and you know how I *love* when patients grab my arm and said loudly that I was not going to put anything in her mouth, because I would "infect her mucosa." I assured her that I was taking the needed precautions and listened as she stressed that she only wanted *you* to make her temporary teeth."

"I ended up doing her provisional and explaining to her we weren't doing anything to compromise her soft tissue," he says as he busts out laughing (in our dental world, this is a knee slapper).

Doctor has another one: "I wonder what happened to Dave, the guy who had the biggest dental phobia ever? He has the older son that his world revolves around..."

"I actually think he's on the schedule next month for a cleaning," I say.

"When he first came to me; he wouldn't sit down in the waiting room; he was so nervous."

"I know," I add. "He was nervous because he had been through so much dental work and had a bad experience. I think he was amazed that when he acted like a smarty pants, I gave it right back to him."

"He had so much bone loss on the upper anterior teeth and was going to lose a tooth. I sent him to see the periodontist to be evaluated for an implant and he wasn't the best candidate, but..."

I cut in, "After we did that whole work up, I explained he would need to travel from the periodontist's office up the street, two traffic lights, to our office without a front tooth. He was a mess over that."

"A mess is putting it delicately," Dr. Huntington says. "He had to be prescribed a valium to get through treatment."

"I explained to him over and over he would go from one office directly to the other office a few blocks down. After having his front tooth out, his son would drive him two lights down to our office and we would make a temporary bridge to fill in the space. No one would know. 'Just don't smile at anyone on the way here,' I told him."

"Didn't he arrive and sit in our waiting room and laugh it up with the others out there?" Doctor asks.

"Yes!" I say. "And he kept telling the same joke over and over, but it didn't make sense. He thought it was so funny and kept laughing. He also asked for paper and a pencil so he could draw me a picture. He had an idea. The picture was a piece of art, he told me, over and over."

I saved the picture for his follow up visit and made him sign it just in case he became a famous artist and forever teased him about losing his fear of having anyone see him without a front tooth. A little valium and it was, "Hi! My name's Dave! Can I tell you a joke?"

CHAPTER 15

Hey, Bear!

It's a well-known fact that I scare easily. I'm sure I've mentioned this before, but it's worth pointing out again. I've always told Dr. Huntington that he needs to put bells on his shoes so I can keep track of him. One day I was chatting with Ada, a patient, while Doctor went to the back-office lab to polish her denture. I was talking away, still able to hear the loud polishing machine rumbling, so in my mind I knew where Doctor was and what he was doing, when he suddenly popped back into the room. He probably didn't pop in so much as quietly walk in, but in my mind, he wasn't there and then, BAM, he was. So, I screamed. It was the kind of scream you'd expect to hear in a horror movie when someone is being chased down by an insane person wielding a chainsaw. I had Ada in stitches; she thought this was absolutely hysterical.

Fast forward to me in a clothing store at the mall. I was just walking around the clothes racks checking out the latest sales, not that I needed any more clothes, when out of the freaking blue a person jack-in-the-box jumps at me from inside a nearby rack, scaring me to pieces. It was Ada! I shrieked even louder than my chainsaw-wielding scream. I let out a full-throated, blood-curdling scream—then I added:

"JESUS!!!!!"

An older lady standing near me grabbed her purse, clutched it to her chest and ran away as fast as she could.

Ada had tears running down her cheeks from laughing so hard. My heart was beating a mile a minute.

When the fright turned into laughter, the older lady came back to get her shopping cart.

"I am so sorry I screamed and scared you," I said to her.

"That's all right, Dear. I just didn't know if the Lord was coming back and you saw Him, so I grabbed my purse and prepared to meet the Maker!"

———————

For the many years I worked beside Dr. Huntington, he always treated me with respect and was a fair boss. He spent endless hours puttering around at his dental lab bench, setting teeth in wax to see if the placement was perfect for his patient's custom dentures. To me it was like watching someone untangle Christmas lights. He, however, had the patience of a saint.

He would pop in a DVD on the little TV/DVD combo near his bench and be all set for a day of lab work with his hunting shows. Sometimes I would sneak up on him and whisper like the guys in the video, in my best Elmer Fudd voice,

"Shhhh . . . I'm hunting bunny wabbits. Whisper, whisper."

The funny part is, the guys in the videos don't talk because they are stalking their prey, which is why I always tell Dr. Huntington that I can't imagine watching anything more boring.

I could never wait silently in the bushes for a prized animal to step into my scope, mainly because I talk too much.

"It's an instructional video, they have to be quiet, or they would scare off what they are hunting."

"Oh! Do you know what they should do if they run across a bear? I do!"

That gets a laugh because he knows I haven't run across a bear before.

"Well, tell me, what should they do if they run across a bear?"

"You know how I scare easily? Well, if you wouldn't sneak up on me, I wouldn't scream. When you spot a bear in the woods you yell out, 'HEY, BEAR!' and they typically go the other way and mind their business."

"I'm going to see if that's true."

---

*And this, my friends, is how
Dr. Huntington started saying
"HEY, BEAR" to avoid scaring
me around the office.*

P.S. It worked! I haven't screamed since!

CHAPTER 16

You're So Pretty

I absolutely love having older people as dental patients; they have so many fascinating stories to tell and bring a wealth of life experiences that I truly enjoy hearing about. Their recollections can even take you back in time and provide insight into events in history.

An older man might tell a tale of going into battle in his youth and the things he did without fear. I can't imagine the level of courage and bravery that requires. But I've noticed when I put a bib and protective eyewear on the same elderly gentleman he shakes like a leaf. In my dental career I have found that men are typically more anxious than women when it comes to having dental work performed. This nervousness is often rooted in previous dental treatment, sometimes traumatic, they may have endured while serving in the military. They might not have had access to numbing agents, for instance, while out in the field. Most folks who have experienced a traumatic dental procedure in the past start out gripping the arms of the dental chair, waiting for something painful to happen. Dental procedures today are far more advanced than they used to be, with modern technology allowing the dentist to perform much more delicate procedures without causing any discomfort whatsoever. As a matter of fact, when Dr. Huntington gives you an injection (shot), most patients tell me they didn't feel a thing and I can attest to that! His technique is to go very slow, so the anesthetic has time to work its way through the tissue. I could knit a sweater in the time it takes Doctor to give you a shot.

With that being said, I like to take a patient's mind off what the dentist is doing, and I like to talk.

I like to talk. There, I said it again! I come from a long line of annoying chatterboxes. Shout out to my grandma (Rest in Peace) and my mom. I've had many patients who let me know that they enjoyed my stories and chatter during their procedures. You can only look at light fixtures for so long while the dentist and I pry your mouth open. Have you ever wondered why the dentist puts his hands in your mouth and then asks you a question? It's the same reason a waitress who has not been around the entire meal will suddenly appear when you have a mouth full of food and ask how everything is. I never really knew if Dr. Huntington listened to my stories—he was usually focused on the task at hand—but he was the perfect wingman, asking me just the right questions here and there. At times I knew he was keeping a light banter going with me to buy him some time while he figured out his next step in a procedure that wasn't moving along as planned—or maybe to kill five minutes while we were waiting for the local anesthetic to numb the area. Doctor and I were very confident in our skills, so chatting while we worked and being aware of a patient's level of calm came as second nature to us. Over many years, I have learned to read body language and try to head off a patient who is starting to appear overly anxious. I try never to cross personal boundaries—and I know which patients are not comfortable with someone touching them—but for the most part everyone appreciates a hand to squeeze when they are getting numb, or my chatter as I slide a tray of gooey impression material into their mouth (while instructing them to focus on a tree outside the window so they do not gag). And I remember to never, *ever* say the word gag, or the patient may come to associate the word with the procedure!

Have I told you about my golden retriever? Stay with me a minute, here. Her name is Aspen, and she is a typical golden except she doesn't retrieve. She also doesn't love water. I always tell her she's defective because she doesn't do or like the two things her breed is most known for. Throw a ball and she will walk over to where it lands and stare at it, then return to your side for some affection. Aspen isn't the only dog in our practice to have fibbed on her resume. Dr. Huntington invested a lot of money, training, and time on his beautiful French Brittany Spaniel, expecting her to become a skilled hunting dog and guess what? *That dog don't hunt.* As we say in Texas, "She's gun shy."

Aspen, my sweet pup, smiles when she is getting attention and follows commands like an honor student. When I take her outside to do her business, she is trained to come back to my side if we see someone approaching who is out for a walk. This is so she won't run up to an unsuspecting person, tail wagging, and try to go on a walk with them. She's very opportunistic about attention. "Velcro Dog" is her nickname.

I try to comb her daily because golden retrievers shed like an unwatered Christmas tree. She won't let me near her hind quarters, so she will pretend to hear a noise and head off to investigate something. I'm on to her, but I won't let her know. When I get to her head, I always comb it and pet her smiling puppy dog face and coo to her that she's pretty.

Me: "You're so pretty! You have such a pretty face."

Aspen: Big dog smile with an excited tail wag.

Me (as I stroke her hair and repeat over and over): "You're SO pretty."

Aspen: Bigger dog smile and . . . thump . . . thump . . . thump . . . goes her tail on the hardwood floor. If she was a peacock her tail feathers would surely be fanned out on display.

One day Dr. Huntington spent hours placing a full upper denture for an older gentleman. Onery old coot. This patient spent the entire appointment telling me how these teeth were probably funding something very extravagant for Doctor.

"I don't know why everything is so expensive nowadays! I guess Dr. Huntington needs a new boat," Mr. Gene says.

"Mr. Gene, he doesn't even own a boat. The Doctor must pay me, you know, and the office bills!" I say, laughing.

"Well, I guess I'm making his truck payment then," Mr. Gene states matter-of-factly.

"Nope, he drives a 2003 truck that has some history on it," I reply. And then I add, "You are paying for his many years of knowledge since finishing dental school, and all the training he continues to gain in order to make you the most bestest denture ever!"

The final moment arrives and it's time to grab a mirror and let Mr. Gene see his new teeth and all the Doctor's hard work. I love seeing how excited a patient gets over having their smile back.

"Mr. Gene! You look amazing!" I excitedly say.

I look into the mirror with him and say, "You are SO pretty!"

"Men can't be pretty!" he laughs.

"Oh, but you can be, and you are SO pretty with those fancy new teeth!"

Mr. Gene beams at me with his big smile, showing off his new teeth. I think if he had a tail, it would be wagging. Mr. Gene shakes

Doctor's hand on the way out the door and I'm pretty sure at that moment you couldn't slap the smile off his face.

When Dr. Huntington delivered a new set of dentures or crowns on front teeth, both nerve wracking experiences, I would hand the patient a mirror to show them their new smile and encourage them with a heartfelt, "You're so pretty!" You could see them immediately peacocking—you know, throwing up their colorful feathers and strutting around, finally feeling proud about a part of themselves they had been ashamed of for a very long time. It made my heart happy to know that we had done something to make a person feel more confident.

CHAPTER 17

This Is for the Birds

He was an older man from the country, a good drive from our office. A simple man, really—didn't want a cell phone or have many needs. He was peculiar, but also rather interesting. One of the many colorful characters, all so different from each other, who would come in for cleanings or dental work and keep us from ever getting bored. And so, on this fine day . . . enter . . . Mr. David. He needed a dental specialist to help him with something that was troubling him. After filling out the new patient paperwork and taking the needed X-rays, he was ready for his exam.

I read his forms and quizzed him.

"Do you have any teeth bothering you today?" I asked.

"No, not bothering me. Just bothering my chickens," he said without missing a beat.

"Bothering your chickens? In what way?" I asked, thinking, *Chickens?!?*

"Well, I sleep with my chickens, and they have a very keen sense of hearing," he began. "At night I grind my teeth and my chickens wake up and have a hard time settling back down."

I just stared at Mr. David for a minute, making sure to keep my expression pleasant. I could see that he was absolutely and completely serious.

"I see," I said, thinking, *only in the South would you sleep with poultry.*

He continued, "I need Dr. Huntington's advice on how to stop grinding my teeth, so my chickens and I can get a peaceful night of sleep."

Well, that was his issue, and it was clearly causing him distress. So off I went to share this story with Dr. Huntington. We could certainly help him with his teeth grinding . . . chickens or no chickens.

We made him a laboratory processed upper night guard to wear over his teeth while he slept. This hard, plastic splint would allow him to grind quietly on the plastic material and not on the enamel of his teeth. A few weeks later, Mr. David returned for a follow-up appointment. He was happy to report that the splint did the job. He and his chickens were now sleeping beautifully!

So many patients, so many memories.

Mrs. Willes came in every so often with a repeated issue. She would just need a quick appointment whenever a pea got lodged between the very overgrown tori under her tongue and she couldn't remove it on her own. Torus or Tori (plural) are an overgrowth of healthy bone that can be caused by excessive teeth grinding, or clenching. It's your body's way of buttressing or protecting the bone to preserve it. Tori most frequently form on the lower jaw, near the tongue, but can also appear on the cheek side as well. In extreme cases, such as "The Pea Lady," the tori were so dense and thick she could not even fit a toothpick between them to help in her pea battle. Dr. Huntington and I were always happy to assist. By the way, using a mouth guard during nighttime grinding helps reduce or stop the growth rate of a tori.

And then there was the widow, Mrs. Hofner. She was a German woman with a big personality. She always wore pink because "Pink! Pink makes the boys wink!" She enjoyed bringing us specialty treats ordered from Germany when she came in for a dental appointment.

Now, don't get me wrong, we weren't always showered with love. We also had those patients that thought every step in our treatment was making their spit toxic, from the moment they sat in the dental chair.

Snap . . . snap, the patient would signal us by raising a hand and snapping their fingers, excitedly pointing to their mouthful of spit.

"I need suction!" they would struggle to say without swallowing anything that was in their mouth. Ummm . . . you literally just sat in the chair. You swallow your spit all day long but suddenly you can't when you are in my chair. Never mind, you can DIY: here's the baby suction and this little switch turns it off and on.

I know the anesthetic leaves a lot to be desired with its bitter taste. I do try to rinse it out, really, I do! But come on, there isn't anything we put in your mouth that can't be swallowed in small quantities. I may even over rinse your mouth because I don't want little chunky particles counting as your daily fiber. You're welcome.

CHAPTER 18

Patients Are Like Family

While I was so grateful to have found another "forever office," every day at Dr. Huntington's wasn't always rainbows and sunshine. The hygienist and I were professional to each other, but she was often passive aggressive in her behavior toward me for as long as we worked together. I tried to let her actions roll off my back. I even found it in my heart to overlook the evening she followed me after work. I had an appointment with a personal trainer to discuss my workout plan, not that it was any of her business. She saw him give me a quick hug when I arrived for our meeting and quickly ran back to Dr. Huntington with a story that I was having an affair!

But aside from that one bad apple, Dr. Huntington, his wife, and Doris became like part of my family. I also grew quite close with so many patients who passed through the office. You wouldn't believe the amount of tasty homemade treats our wonderful patients brought in. Of course, we always brushed after enjoying them! My phone contacts were full of patients who had become friends and often called just to chat. When my son graduated high school one dear patient spent days printing out and even handwriting copies of her best and most treasured recipes. She kindly gave me these, along with several samples of her famous desserts. She shared that these were the treats that people in her church were known to go back for seconds and even thirds of because they were simply that good! Each and every sweet treat was truly delicious and made with love. She wanted me to have these prized recipes so I could make them for my guests during my son's graduation festivities. And I did indeed make them! Everyone at the graduation celebration raved about the desserts!

Another very dear elderly patient was always bringing us holiday gifts—and I mean for *every* holiday, big or small. When I started working at the office, she was in her late 80s and would create the cutest little treasures for us. One year she even surprised the entire office with hand-knitted scarves. She was in her 90s by then. I still have and cherish the one she made for me.

We were very appreciative of anything we were gifted from other dentists or patients. Sweet Doris, the receptionist, would promptly have us all sign a thank you card to be mailed the next day. When patients treated us like family, it was our pleasure to treat them as family right back.

When I'm out and about, I regularly come across people who are connected to me in some way. It's a small enough town, so between church, my son's schooling, Mardi gras celebrations, dental committees, and the offices I've substituted in, I often hear my name being called when I least expect it.

One fine day at the grocery store I made an attempt to just run in, get butter, and run out. I had on my gardening clothes with my well-worn yard shoes and no makeup. I was on a mission: dash in, grab butter, dash out. I was almost to the cashier when I heard, "Joy, is that you?"

Gasp!

"It's not me!" I blurted out, laughing, "I don't look like this!"

"I would recognize those blue eyes anywhere," he said. "You talked me into saving a rotten tooth of mine ten years ago. It is still hanging in there."

"Hallelujah! Let's not talk about it or it will start acting up!"

When I cross paths with a familiar face my mind goes through a sea of "profile photos" to try and figure out if I have worked in their mouth, prayed for their soul, coordinated a lacrosse fundraiser with them, treated them at the volunteer dental clinic, or where on earth I know them from.

Shopping in a big wholesale club one afternoon, while still in my scrubs, I heard a familiar voice.

"Joy! Joy!" her voice rang out.

I knew her from Dr. Huntington's office and anticipated that she would pump me for dental information, as she had done in the past. I really don't mind giving dental advice when people are in need, but I wanted to get my shopping done and get home. But I like to talk, so I pushed my cart over to her.

"Hey Lydia, how are you?"

"I'm so glad I ran into you; I have a question."

I knew it. But I'm secretly flattered that she trusts my opinion on dentistry.

"Okay, ask away."

"Last time I was in here, I bought an off-brand laundry detergent to save money. My husband got a rash from it, and I do love the way the old detergent smells. I just don't know what to do."

"Oh, ummm, okay," I did not see that coming, "I think you should switch back to the old laundry detergent prior to the off-brand one. Sure, it may cost a bit more, but it will keep your husband from itching, you smelling great, and you will live happily ever after!"

"Oh, that's a good idea! I knew you would know what to do! You are so smart! Thank you!"

See, I'm full of good advice.

Our practice brought in people from all walks of life. They were all treated the same. You could be a ditch digger or a television executive but at the end of the day, we are all cut from the same cloth.

"Mr. Pelman?" I asked, as I looked over the few people seated in the waiting room.

"Please, call me Bob," said a man, covering his mouth with his hand as he spoke to me. He quickly got up to follow me to the back.

"Hello Bob! How are you today?"

"I'm fine," he replied quietly.

"Bob, did you know your name is a palindrome? B-O-B. It's the same forwards or backwards," I told him, amusing myself, "and now I have used my one big word of the day." Bob looked at me like I had just fallen off a turnip truck.

Do you know why I remember meeting Bob that first time? Aside from the look he gave me when I made my B-O-B joke, that is. Bob was a good example of a quiet, gentle soul—one who would endure my picking on him and come back for more, because he enjoyed his dental appointments. Sometimes we laughed so much that tears rolled down our cheeks. After a few dental appointments he started calling me "Ellie Mae" after the character on the TV show *The Beverly Hillbillies*. Prior to Dr. Huntington retiring, Bob joked that he got a dental appointment with entertainment, which he would pick over dinner and a movie any day.

On his first visit, Bob's paperwork revealed some health issues he was dealing with, so I made a point to ask him more questions about his health. As we were going over the specifics, he explained in his soft-spoken voice what his issues were and how he was being treated. As he spoke, he kept his hand over his mouth, ashamed to show the state of his smile. He needed some extensive dental work; in fact, he was missing some teeth and a few showed signs of decay. Nothing super exciting, by any means. I guess I felt immediately comfortable picking on Bob because he had recently married another favorite patient of mine, "Thunder Cloud" (her own nickname not mine!) who had referred him to our office. I was confident that Dr. Huntington had the expertise to give Bob a stunning new smile. After taking the needed radiographs, I excused myself to get Doctor and share Bob's information with him in his private office.

Minutes later, Doctor entered the operatory. "Good afternoon, Bob! I'm Dr. Huntington, it's nice to meet you," said Dr. H., already sensitive to Bob's habit of putting his hand over his mouth to hide his teeth. Within seconds he had Bob feeling very comfortable and willing to drop his hand and let his mouth be seen when he spoke and for an exam. Dr. Huntington's caring, nonjudgmental manner always put patients at ease, which was so important for a prosthodontist who saw mouths in need of the most extensive care every day. The appointment ended with Doctor explaining the need for a records appointment with me to get additional information to be used to map out Bob's ideal dental treatment.

"Lucky for you, Bob, my dance card has a slot open next week and it's all yours." I said.

"Well, I wouldn't want you to have a dance card that isn't full."
Bob's quick answer got him a gold star in my book right away.

After an initial appointment, Dr. Huntington would have me schedule a records visit with the patient, to collect additional information for a full treatment plan work up. Photos, impressions, and bite registration, oh my! It would all start with those first impressions, taken using the gooey alginate material to record the patient's teeth in their current state. After that, I would mount the case, print out the digital X-rays, and print out the digital photos to get a big visual picture. Dr. Huntington would use all this information to map out the steps for an ideal treatment plan for the patient. Meanwhile, we would also get the patient scheduled with my favorite oral surgeon, Dr. Extraction, for an evaluation to determine how best to replace any missing teeth (often with implants). Dr. E. would do a CT bone scan, which is an imaging test used to assess whether the patient has sufficient bone to hold an implant. There are other factors involved in being a suitable candidate for an implant, such as not smoking, and having healthy bone and gum tissue. Without the proper amount of strong and healthy bone, the implant can become loose over time.

Major cases, such as Bob's, can take about a year or two to complete. At the start of extensive dental treatment, the appointments can be quite lengthy, often requiring a full morning or a full day. The focus for each appointment is usually one quadrant of the mouth, doing treatment on the upper and lower right side of the mouth perhaps. This allows us to ensure your occlusion (the way your teeth come together when you bite down) is ideal. To do this, Doctor might prep or shape the teeth that will hold a temporary resin bridge in place after a tooth has been extracted (removed) but before implants can be placed. Additionally, some patients may also need to be fitted with a temporary flipper (fake teeth that are held in the mouth by a plastic removable appliance and are for looks, not chowing down on pork skins!). Temporaries provide patients with the ability to eat and speak properly during the extended period it takes for an implant or socket to heal from the tooth removal. It takes between three and six months alone for (here's a big word) osseointegration to occur, or bone to grow around the implant screw that is placed in your jaw—all in preparation for the final restoration that Dr. Huntington will place.

After many months of visiting the office, Bob started to relax and even smile at my corny jokes. He continued to dub me Ellie Mae and we laughed at hillbilly jokes every dental appointment. I enjoyed getting the inside scoop on Thunder Cloud's crazy life (Bob's wife). You know when a TV ad says "... but WAIT, there's more!" She had faced an epic amount of struggles throughout her life, but there was always more to the story! An incredible plot twist that you could hardly believe. Even now, I always end up laughing when she calls to catch up, because the things that befall her, you just can't make up. She and Bob would both mark off the days on the calendar until their next visits because we all had so much fun. I got a kick out of trying to make Bob laugh by picking on him. After only a few visits he stopped covering his mouth with his hand because he now had a temporary removable partial and felt more confident talking and smiling. This removeable appliance gave him beautiful teeth while we worked toward completing his fixed teeth. A flipper is not always the best fitting thing and can even be annoying, but they fill in the gaps so no one in talking distance knows you are missing teeth.

One day Doris came into the treatment room while I was seating Bob and said, "Dr. Pelman, I tried confirming your appointment yesterday, but your voicemail inbox was full. I just wanted to let you know."

I was taken aback and looked at straight at Bob and asked, "Wait, YOU are a doctor?"

He smiled up at me and said, "Yes, I am."

"Like a REAL doctor?"

He smiled and slowly nodded his head.

"Nooooo . . . *you? You are a real doctor?!?*"

I looked at Doris, the receptionist, and asked, "You knew he was a doctor?"

"Well, not until I tried to call him yesterday to confirm his appointment."

"What did you think I do for work?" Bob asked me.

Thinking for a minute, I said, "I was envisioning an archivist, an accountant, or an assistant manager at a rent-to-own store."

"So, any job that starts with an 'A'?"

"Well, I guess you could be *A* doctor," I teased.

"Well, I am *A* doctor," chuckled Bob. "I work in hospice care and have for ten years. I am on call for hospice nurses when they need to change a medication, to ensure their patients can be as comfortable as possible."

"Oh my gosh," I said. "That's a pretty heavy thing to carry on your shoulders."

He truly had the kindest soul, so I could imagine him as a quiet, compassionate, and calm-under-pressure doctor. He used his dental appointments to put that part of his life on hold and enjoy our humorous banter. Not that I would have treated him any differently because of a title, but this was just another testament to how soft spoken and mild-mannered Bob was. As the months progressed, he found the confidence to speak and let other see his teeth and smile. I teased him about being a model and needing to grow his hair out so he could have it blowing in the wind in a photo shoot. Maybe, I teased, he would end up on the cover of a cheesy romance novel—like the hunks with rippling muscles and flowing locks of long blonde hair . . . and, of course, a great smile!

His wife, Thunder Cloud, continues to be one of my favorite people. Her life truly was a series of unfortunate events, then she met the good doctor, Bob, when she was a hospice nurse. During the time she was our patient, she was attending college to become a rock star nurse practitioner, while still working nights in hospice. She was and is a duck on water and always took pride in her job caring for those at the end of their lives. I could see how she and Bob made the perfect team. She was always honest with me, filling in the blanks when Bob suddenly had to cancel a dental appointment. He had been diagnosed with bladder cancer. He and I never spoke of it, just as we never spoke of his work life. He used our appointments to escape, if only for a few hours.

Many years have passed now, but Thundercloud and I still chat on the phone, and I can hear Bob in the background shouting hello to his "Ellie Mae" while his wife tries to hush him. She says he no longer uses his hand to cover his mouth when he speaks. I've never called him "Dr. Pelman" because that would be weird. To me he is B-O-B, Bob. I send up daily prayers for his health because I hate when bad things happen to good people, thankfully he's doing okay. Overjoyed, he was recently promoted to Grandpa. His wife texted me a picture of him with his big, ol' cheesy smile, as proud as can be, wearing a shirt with Grandpa spelled out on the front.

CHAPTER 19

Rest in Peace

Our dental office was a special place, and it showed through every interaction we had with our patients. We were able take the time and connect with them and their families. There is a certain amount of trust when working in people's mouths. This was not lost on Dr. Huntington or me. I would spend hours chairside hearing stories from patients who trusted me with their personal experiences—stories that helped me feel connected to each of them and understand their happiness or heartaches. When one of our patients or their family member had a celebration, we celebrated as well. If a patient died, we usually got a phone call from the family to let us know, even if we hadn't treated their loved one in years. Like clockwork, Doris would have us sign a condolence card, to let the family know they weren't alone in that difficult time and mailed it right out. She was always so delicate in the way she came to the back of the office to share the news of a loss with us. There were days when I needed a moment to get past the sadness. These patients weren't just a mouth to work on, they were family.

Thankfully on January 26, 2017, we were working on a patient of many years who was dear to my heart.

I can vividly recall every detail of that morning, the smell of the room disinfectant, the soft hum of the dental drill, the sound of the high-volume suction. Dr. Huntington and I were doing a lower front bridge prep on a woman who had been a long-time patient. Her husband was in the waiting room and would peek in and check on her every so often, knowing the appointment was scheduled for three hours. We were about an hour into the procedure when my cell phone vibrated in my scrub pocket indicating a call. Gloved up and unable to reach my phone, I checked my smart watch on my right wrist, and it showed that my only nephew was calling. He lived in West Texas and would be at work at that time of day, so it was odd that he was calling me. I have a mental snapshot of the time "10:10 a.m." which was the time of the call. Ten minutes later, I received a text message that turned my world upside down: <u>Dad had a heart attack,</u> it read. My brother. I saw the text on my watch, but I just couldn't believe it. I told Dr. Huntington and the patient that I needed a minute and had Doris take over assisting for me. When I was able to gather myself, I explained the situation to everyone: My brother was being placed on life support after suffering a cardiac arrest at a job site. Dr. Huntington and I stepped out of the operatory for a moment to talk. He was willing to let me leave so I could prepare myself and go to West Texas, but I told him I felt like I could finish the procedure. At this point, all I knew was that my brother would be placed in a medically induced coma for the coming days. While we were out of the room, the patient, whom I had always been fond of, spoke to her husband and they offered to drive me to Texas that afternoon. She had a plan mapped out on her phone and was sending her husband home to pack and be ready to go in a few hours. This is what it means to have patients who are like family, who would drop everything to come through in an emergency. Their offer was so kind, but in the end my husband drove me to Texas.

We left that afternoon. Our son stayed behind to care for all the things that needed attention—pets, house, schooling, a lacrosse game he was scheduled to start in, and the list went on and on. Suddenly, nothing was as I had expected it to be. I had just been texting with my brother the night before. We were joking about him shoving a can of beer up a whole chicken and putting it on the grill. You cannot be walking the earth one minute at age forty-seven, joking with your sister, and then just be gone, I reasoned. He had left a message on my phone just a few days earlier: "Hey Sis, it's me. Call me back." I had teased him for that, saying that he did not need to leave me a message, I would see that I had missed a call from him and return it. Plus, who leaves a message saying, "Call me back"? I had asked him. But now I was so grateful to have that message, to have his voice on my phone.

The sun was still shining, and the earth was still spinning. *He cannot not be gone,* I kept thinking over and over.

By now I had more details of my brother's very grave condition. As we drove through the late night and into the early morning, I asked God for a sign to let me know if he was meant to stay in heaven with Him. I knew that he had been on life support since the previous day, but in my heart I was hopeful. As I stared at the sky, lost in thought, the sign I needed appeared. The clouds in the sky that my eyes were resting upon were formed into a perfect cross.

As a family, we all took a few days to say goodbye to him before he was taken off life support. It shattered my mom's heart to see her only son laying unresponsive in a hospital bed. It crippled my nephew to see as his dad and best friend attached to machines, one breathing for him. I stayed in the room as much as possible, at one point even picking on him in a sisterly way because I knew if he were able, he wouldn't let me have the last word. I begged him to wake up! We had an agreement, darn it! He had promised to build new cabinets in my house and take care of mom when she gets old.

Later that evening, when the heaviness of losing him was weighing on us all, we met to discuss funeral arrangements. We chose a date a week away. With this decided, my husband and I left for our eighteen-hour drive home to get our son. I had been in contact with my dental office and Dr. Huntington told me to take the time I needed, so the plan was to arrive back in Texas with our son the day before the service. But hours before we arrived home in Florida, I learned that the funeral had been moved up. This did not leave me enough time to travel back to Texas, and as a result, I was not at my brother's funeral. It still breaks my heart that someone other than myself read aloud the eulogy I wrote for him. I was able to listen to the service on my phone, thankfully. My nephew had his phone on speaker at the funeral, so my husband and I could hear the service.

My brother—may he rest in peace—was indeed welcomed to Heaven that day.

CHAPTER 20

The Wag

Throughout my dental career, I have enjoyed meeting new patients and the comradery I've formed with existing patients. My favorite patients know I pick on them to show that I like them. This has become a battle of the wits at times, many giving me a run for my money. Larry, Bob, I'm talking about you!

Working for a dental specialty office, we rarely see patients that are "run of the mill." As I've said before, we're the last train out of town when it comes to hoping your smile can be restored. That being said, there are many who know how well-trained Dr. Huntington is and want his expertise, even on a simple restoration. But most often, patients come to us once they have exhausted every other option.

Walking out into the waiting room to call back a new patient is always a spin of the wheel. What will we have today? Do you have one single, rotten tooth holding in a nine-unit bridge, and you think it just needs re-cementing? Do you have a laundry list of dental issues, years in the making, and you want a pretty smile by next week?

Peeking at the schedule for today, I see we are starting off with a new patient. By her birthdate I know that she's elderly, so mentally I note that she will probably take longer to welcome and get settled.

I open the door to the waiting room and greet her.

"Welcome to our practice Mrs. Wagnowski. My name is Joy, I am Dr. Huntington's assistant. I'll take your medical history and have the dentist review it before I take you back."

With our first exchange of words, I know that Mrs. Wagnowski will need extra care. What, you ask, was my first indication? Well, here's what she said to me . . .

"Hello, Joy. I have brought my brother David with me. Father David is a catholic priest. He will be with me for my dental appointment today, watching over you and the dentist."

"It's nice to meet you, Father, so you are Mrs. Wagnowski's brother," I say, as I am introduced to Father David in his full black clergy attire. He would wear the clerical collar for each appointment he attended with her. He was not at all intimidating, but rather, very quiet and kind.

Mrs. W. asks if I will allow her brother to pray over me before we start our appointment, as I am the helping hands of the dentist.

"I will always take all the prayers I can get, and most certainly you may pray over me," I say. I take a seat next to them in the waiting room, and the priest prays for my hands to help Dr. Huntington help his cherished sister.

"The Wag," as she became known to me (in my mind and later to Dr. H.), has an extraordinarily dry mouth. As we age and medications are introduced to us to correct one problem or another, many of us experience this common side effect. Most older patients are on numerous medications, so dry mouth is common in our older population. This is a concern because saliva helps with lubrication, keeping food particles off teeth. Decay, or a cavity in these teeth can be the outcome of a dry mouth. We've also treated patients with Sjogren's syndrome, an autoimmune disease that can cause your mouth to be as dry as the Sahara Desert. Using fluoride in trays daily at home is one way to arrest the cavities that these conditions can cause.

Starting from that first day, the Wag followed the same ritual every time she came to the office. She would push her walker down the hall to use the restroom and wash her hands. Then she would slowly make her way to the dental chair, but before she sat down, she would lift the seat attachment of her walker to get to a few things she kept in the storage compartment. First, she would use hand sanitizer, then place it back in the compartment. Next, she would unscrew the lid of her mini bottle of water and take a drink, then put the bottle back in its place. Finally, she would carefully ease herself down into the dental chair, using her walker for support, and when settled she would ask for a tissue.

"Joy, will you please place my walker in the corner? But, not too far, I like to be able to get items out of my purse."

Periodically, she would ask for something out of her purse, and I would wheel her walker, with her purse sitting on it, back to her after sitting her up in the dental chair, so she could retrieve the item and wait patiently while she did her little ritual. Sip of water, swish, another sip of water . . . screw the lid on, a dash of hand sanitizer. The Wag was about 85 years old. She was a *germaphobe*. She also had a ritual for her at-home mouth care. A total of twenty-two minutes to floss, brush, and use an interdental pick three times a day. I picked on her mercilessly. It was all in good fun, and she enjoyed being at the office and having her "little sister" tease her. So many patients I have known over the years really spark happiness in my heart, and she is one of them. The sound of her laughter when I teased her really was priceless.

Through her years of dental treatment, I was able to spend many hours getting to know her. And yes, she drove me crazy every appointment with her demands. I jokingly made it known that she drove me nuts.

"I think God put you in my path to slow me down, because you are so methodical in your routine!"

"Wait! Are you saying I'm slow?"

We would be working away, and she would often ask for a break. Off she went to do her restroom routine all over again—many, many times if it was a long procedure. As often as possible we scheduled most of the morning for her appointments, to give her the time and attention she needed.

She was apprehensive (in the dental world we never say scared or afraid) about having the oral surgeon do some needed dental surgery on her. She was a candidate for an implant, but prior to the placement she needed a sinus lift. She had looked up the term "Maxillary Sinus Floor Augmentation" on the internet and gotten herself worked up. The name, in and of itself, can be nerve wracking, but the procedure is quite routine with a high success rate. The amount of bone is increased through elevating the sinus membrane. Increased bone helps to hold an implant in place.

I told the Wag that if she was scheduled on a day I could be there, I would be present for her oral surgery; and how exciting for me, the oral surgeon also allowed me in the room—gloved and masked—to observe the procedure. I had never seen the sinus membrane prior to her surgery, so it was a learning opportunity for me. As he inspected the Wag's sinus membrane, the oral surgeon pointed out that she wasn't a smoker, and that the membrane was healthy; then he packed bone in the area under the membrane and sutured her back up.

Watching dental procedures that are new to my eyes always amazes me. I marvel at how complicated the human body is and that there are doctors who have the talent to make surgeries and other treatments look easy.

Several months after her oral surgery, the Wag went back to the oral surgeon to have the implant placed in the tooth #6 (canine). This type of surgery is a relatively simple procedure that doesn't cause much discomfort because nerves aren't present in the bone. You will be sore from the injection site where you were numbed up, but after the procedure you can usually go about your daily routine or job—unless your job is jackhammering asphalt. I wouldn't go back to work and do that job; I think your head should remain somewhat still just for that one day.

Do you remember from a few chapters back the process of integration of an implant? There's going to be a pop quiz, so I hope you paid attention. The answer is: it usually takes between three and six months for an implant to integrate, during which time bone has to form around the implant or "screw" embedded in the jawbone.

After several years of treatment by Dr. Huntington, the Wag's mouth was fully restored, and she was on routine maintenance. It's always bittersweet to me after seeing a patient almost weekly or monthly, and then one day they finish their dental treatment, and I don't get to spend as much time with them anymore. I may see them in passing as they come and go from the hygienist's room every six months, but only if I'm in the waiting room at the right time. If I have the opportunity, I go back and say hello, but it's not the same. Of course, I'm always happy to see them get their smile back, but I'm sad to not have them in our chair where I can easily joke around with them and keep up on the events in their lives.

The Wag ended up moving to a care facility in a town three hours away. I teased her that her days would be filled with bingo and soft food. I told her she would have to be nice to the older people that were playing cards with her because sometimes they cheat, and I wouldn't want her to get in a fist fight and compromise her teeth. When I last spoke to her daughter, she informed me that the Wag was thriving in her new home and not playing bingo at all.

CHAPTER 21

Bushy

"Mrs. Remi? Good morning. We are ready for you."

Dr. Huntington, like most dentists, prefers big, time-consuming cases to take place first thing in the morning. I agree that you are at your sharpest and do the best work before the day wears you down. The best days for major dental work are Tuesdays or Wednesdays because on Mondays the staff is tired from the weekend, plus we return phone calls from the weekend's emergencies first thing, which can clog up an already overbooked schedule. By Thursday, everyone is looking forward to the weekend and focusing on their packing list for the beach picnic they have planned.

I bought my vehicle based on this days-of-the-week theory. She is over twenty years old and in great shape. I showed up to the dealership in town to walk the lot, looking at the sticker inside the driver's doors to see where and when each vehicle was made. I found the color and featured I wanted on a vehicle that was made in Texas on a Wednesday. Ding, Ding, Ding! We have a WINNER! The car salesman seemed confused when I proclaimed she was the one. He told me to take her for a quick test drive or look at some of his higher-end models. He couldn't believe that just looking at that sticker was a way to make an informed decision on such a large purchase. I jokingly kicked the tires and said, "Yep, they have air in them, should drive good!"

Turning to Ms. Remi, I direct her to the back, "You will be in here most of the morning, for your lower bridge prep."

I try to always state the procedure we will be doing on a patient and, using a mirror, point out which teeth we will be working on. If you are imagining a small filling and we have you scheduled for a crown prep, then it tends to shake things up. It's also an opening for the patient to ask me questions about the procedure.

"I have a few preliminary impressions to do, then Dr. Huntington will be in to get you numb," I say. I place the dental bib around her neck as Mrs. Remi is sits down in the dental chair quietly.

It is not easy to trust someone to work on your mouth. Even the strongest and bravest of men can be intimidated by the sight of the dental chair. But I'm here to make you feel comfortable and relaxed during your visit. I like to tell stories to put anxious patients at ease and let you know that I can relate to what you are going through.

"My goodness it is so hot today! It reminds me of growing up in West Texas and going out to help pick the garden with my grandparents . . ."

And this is how my day of storytelling starts. Maybe it will turn out that you've traveled through Texas. Or maybe you enjoy gardening. Now we're chatting and your stress-o-meter is starting to go from "frazzled kitty" to "snoozy retriever."

I know you don't want to be seated in a dental chair with two masked faces staring down at you. And of course, I'm not discounting that your mind may have envisioned the needle to be a foot long with an injection that sends excruciating pain straight into your brain. I will admit that in my career of watching injections, Dr. Huntington gets the biggest trophy and a statue erected in his honor for BEST DENTAL SHOT. He takes F . . . O . . . R . . . E . . . V . . . E . . . R to give a shot. He slowly presses down on the plunger of the anesthetic syringe, letting the anesthetic travel through the tissue so gently that patients don't feel the pressure of the liquid traveling into the injection site.

Before we start any dental work, I do our standard blood pressure and pulse check as I explain the procedure steps and continue chatting with Mrs. Remi—stopping between my tales to ask questions and make sure she understands the procedure.

As I continue to chat, I place different impression trays in her mouth to make sure the tray I use will be the right size to get all the landmarks needed for a good impression. After years of taking alginate impressions, I can get them done in a matter of minutes without much discomfort to the patient. I personally have a sensitive gag reflex, so I am very conscience of what it takes to get these wet and goopy impressions without causing a patient to choke.

I'm always glad when a patient trusts us and feels comfortable, so we can all joke and share some laughs during their long appointments. At times, though, the pressure is on, and we must be serious (no joking around). For example, if Dr. Huntington is trying to retrieve an implant screw (think of a micro mini version of a carpenter's screw) that has been damaged from another dentist drilling into the head of the screw while trying to remove the access filling. Maybe the implant crown was loose, and the dentist was hoping to replace the screw . . . but went a skosh too far. Retrieving a tiny implant screw that you can't get with the usual wrench means Doctor will use a tap set—a specialized tool with various sized jaws to grip the implant screw—that will allow him to back the screw out once it's engaged. Talk about finding a needle in a haystack. (Not sure why you would have a needle by a haystack, but anyway . . .) This is not a time for chatting or stories. Talking during an implant screw retrieval is like being on a game show and hearing that annoying music just as you are trying to solve the million-dollar puzzle. Shhhh . . . I can't think! Voila! When he has it backed out, we replace the little screw with a sterilized new one and celebrate as balloons drop from the ceiling!

We have heard countless amusing and fascinating stories over the years from our patients; but some people, especially once they're numb and know all that's left to do is wait for their treatment to be finished, tend to just drift off to sleep. One patient in particular stands out, an airline pilot who had a knack for getting into in the chair and immediately falling asleep. Full blown snoring. He was that relaxed! I would just pop a rubber bite block between his teeth to keep mouth open and Doctor and I would carry on with our work while he was snoozed away. On the flip side, though, if his wife needed any dental work whatsoever she was prescribed a light sedative just to get her in our front doors. Even then we literally had to scrape her off the ceiling in order to treat her. I understand, I ziplined in a dark cave above razor sharp stalagmites once. Dark cave, heights, and the possibility of death is truly as daunting as dental work. I was a wreck, but I did it. And I, like most other dental professionals, am a horrible patient and liken the experience of getting in the chair to ziplining in that dark cave. Heck, when Dr. Extraction had to remove my #30 (a molar), because I fractured it grinding my teeth, I raised my hand as he was coming at me with the dental forcep and pleaded. . . "Don't hurt me!"

No pressure, right?

Mrs. Remi hadn't been in America for very long. She came over from Asia after marrying an American. The English language was a challenge for her so she would often struggle to find the right word as we talked. She would ask me, "What's the word for . . ." and then we would play charades until we figured out what she was trying to say. She quickly felt right at home in our office and shared stories of the crowded open-air food market in Thailand where she had lived. She recalled fondly the many vendors and their tempting dishes, like crunchy fried chicken feet, and how she would select the best ones to snack on while making her way to another vendor that had the best hot-and-sour soup.

We had many lengthy appointments with Mrs. Remi, which allowed us to learn a lot about her life in Thailand. She beamed with joy and laughter as she reminisced about her culture. She was also incredibly talented in the art of origami. She could take a sheet of colored paper and fold it into intricate little animals. One day she presented me with the most beautiful, tiny, pink origami swan.

Since her dental appointments often went on for hours, we had plenty of time to joke around about our different cultures.

"Why do Americans say, 'How are you doing?' When you meet someone, first thing you say is, 'How are you doing?' But I want to say how I am doing, and no one cares."

"You are right. I think it's just a greeting. I do that! I say to everyone, 'Hi, how are you?' but I don't wait for the answer. "

She was reclining in the dental chair with her dark, protective eyewear on, mouth slack from the local anesthetic, and telling us stories of the food she was missing from Thailand. I would try to interpret the type of food she was talking about, since it varied so much from typical American food.

"In my country we walk open-air markets to choose a bite of food for mealtime, going from vendor to vendor. There are many meats of grilled pork, roasted chicken, squid, and fish. Noodles, Pad Thai, curry dishes, crickets, and so many flavorful things," she reminisces.

"Interesting that you would walk up and chose a fried cricket," I say to Ms. Remi.

"Crickets and chicken feet are a treat in my country," says Ms. Remi. "Chicken feet are marinated in a sauce of rice vinegar and other seasonings. Cooked properly they are not; how do you say . . ." motioning with her fingers up and down.

"Chewy?"

"Yes! Like a boot rubber," she replies.

"Have you tried to find a restaurant here in America that makes authentic Thai food?" I ask.

"I have! I went to the one place on the east side of town, and it was BUSHY!" she replies.

"Bushy?" I ask.

Dr. Huntington, meanwhile, pauses from organizing the burs he needs for the next part of her procedure to join in with the "What is She Trying to Say?" game.

"Butcher?" Dr. Huntington throws out there.

She replies again, with gusto, "No, it was BUSHY!"

"I'm not sure, what you are saying . . . bushy?" Doctor asks.

"Bushy, bushy, BUSHY!" Mrs. Remi says.

"Are you saying BULLSHIT?!?" I suddenly ask.

"Yes! Bullshit!!" she says. Finally, we have found the right word! Dr. Huntington and I laugh until we have tears in our eyes.

Since that day, when things don't seem to be adding up for Dr. Huntington and myself, one of us will state that something is *BUSHY.* And the other will say, "For sure, BUSHY," as we laugh and fondly remember Mrs. Remi.

CHAPTER 22

Princess

From my operatory window I watch as a large, luxurious SUV pulls into the parking lot. The man who gets out is in his early seventies, with greying hair, wearing a nice suit and tie. He kindly opens the door for his companion, letting her have his arm for support, and escorts her into our office waiting room. She appears frazzled from the drive. Once inside, she loudly remarks that her husband is an awful driver and asks Doris where she might find the powder room, her voice reverberating through the entire office. The husband's face shows that he is used to her mannerisms, and he patiently waits while she marches into the restroom.

I look at the time and know she will run us behind for the morning because she is already late for her appointment and still has paperwork to fill out. I poke my head into Dr. Huntington's office, where he is seated at his desk.

"Dr. Huntington, our next patient is a referral from a colleague. Did he indicate what type of dental work she needs?"

"No. Just that she lives two hours away and it is his wife's distant relative twice removed."

One thing I have noted over the years, is that people who think they are privileged due to having money don't like filling out paperwork. I understand it's a hassle and appreciate that it takes precious time to check so many boxes and write out important health information. Knowing your medications, allergies and medical history can help us anticipate any potential issues that may come up during a procedure. For instance, if you are taking a blood thinner and require a tooth extraction, we need to be prepared in the event of excessive bleeding.

Princess, as I quickly nickname her in my head, seems to have no idea that the world has other people in it, and on days when she does see others around her, she is annoyed that they are breathing her air.

"Dee Dee?" I announce, as I open the door to escort her back from the waiting room. I've got the clipboard in hand and I'm reviewing her medical history. She throws her hand in the air with a gesture that screams, "Just a minute, girl!" Her hands show her age even if her face does not. I would have pegged her for sixty with a face lift, but her date of birth puts her at sixty-eight.

Standing up, she gathers her purse, then a bag she brought in with her, and looks around for anything else she may have left behind. She seems flustered and hot, giving her husband snippy directions to "Sit there and don't move!" and proceeds to follow me like I'm the help.

"My name is Joy. I'm Dr. Huntington's assistant and I will be asking a few questions and taking a few X-rays. We will be in this first room to the left."

"Oh, I don't need X-rays," Princess flatly informs me. "I had them the last time I went to the dentist."

"Okay, let me check to see if they were sent to us or we need additional images," I say, as I search through her records. "What date were you last at your dentist?"

"It was a few years back," she says.

Patients typically don't understand the need for dental X-rays. They often feel they are just a money maker for the dentist. X-rays show us what the naked eye can't see. It's like having a roadmap before you set off on your journey. It's nice to see landmarks and get the lay of the land before you head off into a direction that might be a dead end. "A few years back" is not up to date enough for a dental specialist.

"Is this going to take long?" Princess asks. "I left my housekeeper with some tasks, and she will need me to look at her work before she leaves. I have a heavy wooden dining table with intricate woodwork that I am having her use cotton swabs to clean in the grooves. She tries to cut corners, but I am on to her. Last week I had her polish the silver," she continues. "I found a short cut where you put a large pot of water on the stove with a foil ball and some baking soda. I think you might add a touch of salt . . ." She pulls out her phone to google the steps for me.

Ugh. Rich people problems.

I don't have silver to polish, so the polishing information isn't something I can use, but I act as if I'm interested. I'm trying to find a tactful way to navigate our conversation back to dentistry, but it's a futile attempt. She just wants a magic wand waved to make her dental issues go away—she is a busy woman. The longer I stay alone with her in the room the more she talks about her own life issues instead of the dental topics I need to cover. She's a talker. My best option, to save time, is to get Dr. Huntington in the room so he can navigate the conversation back to the needed dental issues. Before he comes in, I'll tell him to initiate a "need for X-rays" conversation with me, in front of her, to convince her that X-rays are indeed needed today, so that he can diagnose her dental needs.

Over the course of treatment, she is always quite a character. Animated and full of demands. I remain very attentive to her needs. Especially on one day that is etched in my mind. Dr. Huntington and I accompanied her to the specialist, Dr. Extraction, who would be taking out some teeth and placing immediate implants. We worked closely over the years with Dr. E., so he was very accommodating about us joining him at his office for dental procedures with mutual patients. It benefited us to be present and observe the surgery, for ideal implant placement and to take a quick preliminary impression immediately following placement to use in the initial phase of restoring her prosthesis back at our office.

Princess had taken prescribed medication to make her loopy ahead of the oral surgeon starting the procedure. An IV had been started, and I was alone in the room with her when she suddenly announced that she needed to use the restroom. Since she couldn't maneuver the IV stand on her own, I helped her up and wheeled the IV alongside as she wobbled her way to the only restroom I was aware of, the one reserved for office staff.

"Hold the door open for me so I can get this IV pole through," she ordered. "You are coming in with me! I can't possibly get my pants down by myself."

Well, I hadn't planned on that as being part of the deal, but we had come this far. After I wriggled her pants down, and her undies, she plopped down on the toilet.

"Ok, now wipe me."

"I'm sorry Dee Dee, that's not any part of my job description and I'm going with a solid 'no' on that, you are just going to have to drip dry," I said, as I helped her stand up and get dressed.

We made our way safely back to the surgery room, where the procedure went as planned. Dr. Huntington and I took the needed impressions, and we left to head back to our office.

"I think I deserve a special reward for today," I said to Dr. Huntington with a sly smile as we climbed into his truck to head back to the office. "Maybe lunch out next week? Or maybe a little bonus? Going above and beyond should come with some sort of incentive. Don't you agree?"

"How's that?" he asked, looking amused and anxious to hear a good story.

I recounted dear Princess's antics, and I think I saw him turn about three shades of red with a dash of purple as I relayed a part of the day he had not been privy to.

Doctor was quiet for a moment after I finished my tale, followed by a simple reply:

"So where would you like to go for lunch?"

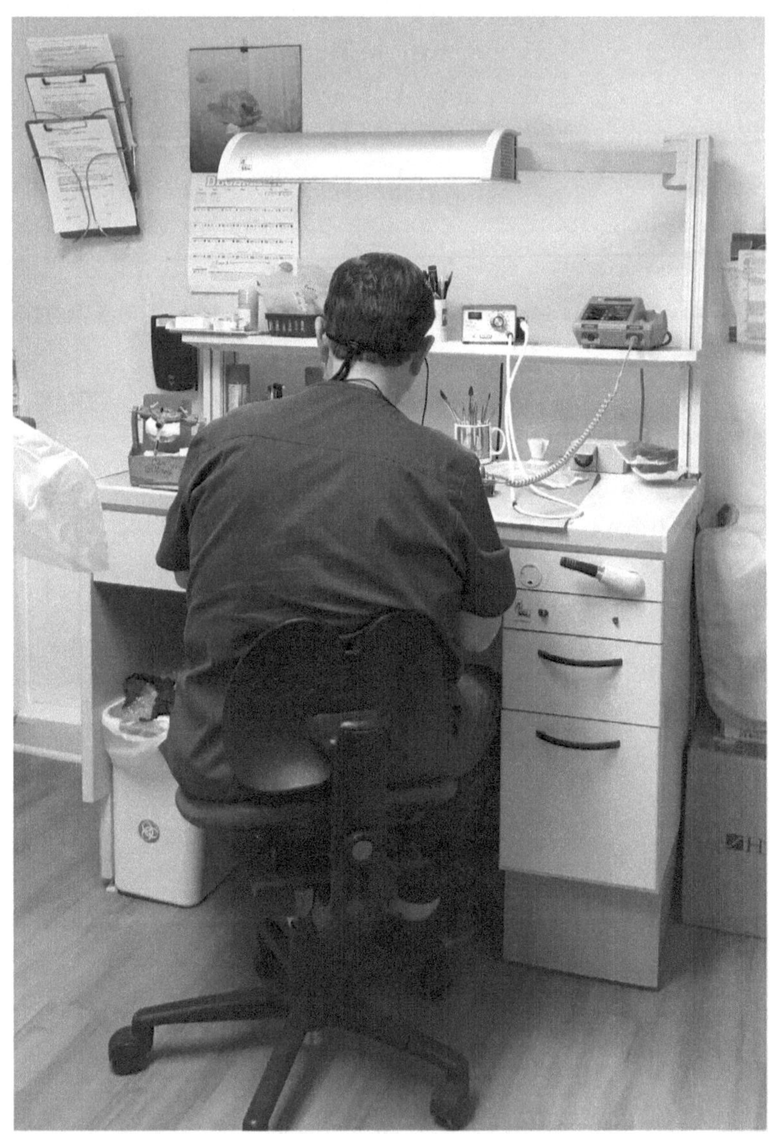

CHAPTER 23

FIRE!

Over the course of all my years working in the dental field, I have had extensive and ongoing training in CPR and First Aid. I have been trained in a variety of different techniques and in several states across the US. In the early 1990's, for example, CPR was all about the ABC's: Airway, Breathing, and Compression. If you encounter a person who is having a known or suspected heart attack, in addition to calling or designating someone to call 911, you follow certain steps. First, you assess the scene. Then, you check the airway and, if they are not breathing, tip the head back and give two breathes. Then, in the middle of the chest with your hands interlocked, you begin compressions. We would practice until we were winded, doing the steps again and again until they became second nature. Because in an emergency, every second counts to save a life.

Early in my career, CPR recertification was a yearly event for the office. The entire office took the on-site class with a CPR certified instructor to prevent our certifications from expiring. If a certification lapses you are required to take a much more extensive course, the whole enchilada, not just the refresher course. One year, Dr. HMO and I got entirely too close to our expiration dates, so she signed us up for the soonest available class. She neglected to tell me that it was a healthcare-provider-level CPR recertification at a local hospital.

On the way to the class she asked, "Did you have time to look over the book for today's course?"

"The book? You never told me about a book or gave me a book!" I said in a panic.

"Probably because I misplaced it," she quipped.

There are a couple of things I have learned in my life about testing. The first is that if the teacher kindly says that you will be allowed to have an index card with anything you want written on it for the test, you are in deep trouble. What this really means is that there is NO WAY you are going to pass the test and you should just put your name on your test paper, turn it in, and call it a day. The second is that when you are asked to review a book or a handout prior to class, this means you *might* stand a chance of passing and getting your recertification, but only *if* you have studied said book and prepared in advance.

I was, at this time, huge pregnant with my son. When we arrived, I noticed physicians, nurses, and other healthcare providers all reviewing the book that I had not been given. This was a little bit worrisome since the people present save lives daily and they were studying the information to be covered in the class and on the test! When the instructor started asking which chambers of the heart do what jobs, I knew I was screwed. I had learned human anatomy, of course, in school—many, many years ago. Then she started on veins and blood flow. There are a lot of veins in your body. I can't remember the name of the cereal I had for breakfast much less the scientific names for veins and muscles. *Remember my chapter on nomenclature?!?* Now, there are times when I like being surrounded by overachievers. They are so eager to answer questions that you can typically hide behind their ego and willingness to display their knowledge. Today was definitely one of those days, and it was all I could do to resist the temptation to pipe up and ask if I had enough time "just really quick" to run home and get my medical degree.

When it came time for the one-on-one instructor testing, I was not in any way looking forward to being on the floor with my big pregnant belly. The instructor had no mercy on me as I bent over to demonstrate my skills. She would bark out the scenario and you had to react. Leaning over a big belly while trying to blow into someone's mouth wasn't easy, and neither was reaching over to do compressions after dragging the manikin to the floor. I grew tired quickly. Meanwhile the instructor threw questions out at me, which I answered, all the while doing the necessary compressions and breaths into the dummy. Somehow, I passed and have kept that certification card to this day—I definitely earned it!

Early on in my training in Washington state, all healthcare providers were required to take First Aid along with CPR. This was to ensure that if an earthquake happened, there would be plenty of people to cover wounds and delivery babies. We even had to wear lace-up shoes in those days in case we had to deliver a baby and tie off the umbilical cord.

In my mind, I am a ninja in a crisis, ready to pounce into action at the drop of a hat if the situation calls for it. Over the years, I've had to preform CPR on multiple patients while they were in the dental chair. I've also had to react quickly to prevent a patient from swallowing a crown or a tiny implant screw—no small feat! I have warded off someone almost vomiting with an impression tray in their mouth, or as I am taking it out, hundreds of times.

So, fast forward to some twenty years later. It was a quiet day in the office. Dr. Huntington was doing lab work at his dental bench. I was milling about doing catch-up work. Doctor and I use the lab bench in an operatory to do tasks like wax ups or mounting dental models because the tools we need are handy and we can use the counter as our work surface. Air, a little alcohol torch, waxing tools, and burs for the handheld handpiece. Dr. Huntington was carefully placing plastic teeth into a warm layer of wax on a mounted model, a painstaking process that often takes several hours to complete by hand. He had the alcohol torch in one hand and the block of wax on the bench top, just working away. I was restocking the operatory when he picked up the alcohol torch pumping the little button on the alcohol torch to produce a stronger flame. This helps to remelt wax that may have cooled and started to harden. In a split second, a few drops of the alcohol dripped out of the torch and down his scrubs, setting his pant leg on fire. There was fire . . . my boss's pant leg was on fire. *Ninja time, Joy . . . let's go . . .*

Tick tock . . .

Tick tock . . .

Okay, if you're picturing me "ninja-style" dashing the short distance down the hall to get the bright red fire extinguisher, you are wrong! I tell patients a dozen times a day to *turn by the fire extinguisher* to get to the restroom. Instead, I just stood there and stared at the little line of fire slowly climbing up the leg of his scrub pants. It was all happening in slow motion. In my head, I was trying to remember the steps you follow when a person is on fire. *Is it stop, drop, and roll? How do I make him drop? Should I tackle him off the chair and make him roll on the floor? Should I go for the fire extinguisher? How do I operate it? Do I have to pull a tab? Should I call the fire department?*

Tick tock . . .

Tick tock . . .

Doctor, being the calm, stoic person he is, simply picked up a towel that was laying nearby and patted out his leg fire. All the while, I stood frozen to the floor.

Thankfully, the outcome was nothing more than ruined scrub pants. Doctor was fine and we laugh now about my lack of ninja-lifesaving action when he was on fire, and *Dang it!* I blew my chance to use the fire extinguisher!

PART III
SET ADRIFT

CHAPTER 24

The Merge

They say all good things must come to an end. If you are fortunate enough, you get to gear down before the end happens. Retirement. I had been working with Dr. Huntington for nine years when he sold his practice to another dentist and closed the location we had been working out of, to merge our patients with his. I hesitantly agreed to follow him to the new office. Our receptionist, Doris, decided that it was finally her time to retire after dedicating so much of her life to the office and its patients. She wanted to stay home and care for her husband who was struggling with health issues. The cranky, passive-aggressive hygienist had previously been relieved of her duties (or lack thereof), and the part-time hygienist currently working in our office simply left us to increase her hours at another dental office where she also worked. The merge plan was for Doctor and me to work full-time in the new dentist's office for one year—to finish up long cases and hand off patients to the new dentist for continued care. When our year was up, Dr. Huntington would fully retire and had plans to move away. I would stay and work for the dentist who bought Dr.

Huntington's practice. Combining two dental offices is no easy feat. Imagine your divorced parents each remarrying and creating a bigger family unit with even more children, and then you all live together under one roof. Knowing that the situation might very well start out a bit rocky, I decided to make an effort to meet the new staff we would soon be joining. I stopped by the office with a platter of homemade treats. My motto is, *"Food is love."* As soon as I walked in, I was met with warm greetings by the two receptionist at the front desk. One of them hopped up and offered to show me around the office, which was a sight to behold. There was plenty of natural light coming through the large picture window that ran the length of the office, so the patients could look out at a tranquil pond full of beautiful goldfish and lush, green plants. In fact, there didn't seem to be an operatory in this open concept plan with a bad view. The dental hygienists were also incredibly friendly and welcoming, further raising my spirits about the impending merge. Unfortunately, my high hopes were quickly dashed once I met Gwen. We didn't so much "meet" as I was hit with the barrage of very abrasive words she hurled in my direction. I had simply walked past the operatory where she and the dentist who would soon by my boss were treating a patient, to say hi and introduce myself. After all, she would be one of my fellow dental assistants. But rather than receiving a warm welcome, I got:

"Hey, YOU! I am OVER working with this jerk!" Meaning the dentist and owner of the practice sitting right next to her, working on a patient. "I can't wait to switch and start working with the new dentist, I heard he doesn't suck!" (She was referring to Dr. Huntington!)

She blurted all this out as the dentist just kept drilling away in the mouth of the patient in the chair. I would later find out that Gwen and that young dentist threw barbs like this at each other all day, and many were so epically inappropriate it caused my elderly patients to cringe. Gwen seemed to have a tendency to be brash and candid, rudely speaking her mind with the other staff members who, unlike me, were unfazed by her comments. She had no filter when it came to verbalizing her opinions, regardless of who she was talking to.

This dental office was designed in an open-concept plan, which allowed for very little privacy. The operatories were separated only by X-ray cabinets, so Gwen's comments were heard loud and clear by everyone in the office.

"Don't get too comfortable here, we run people off," she wickedly laughed. "And don't think about putting your stuff anywhere near my things. Especially in the lab. I've been here since he opened the place!" As she continued throwing out comments my head started spinning and I pictured the wicked witch in *The Wizard of Oz* saying . . . "I'll get you, my pretty, and your little dog, too!"

My biggest fear leading up to the merge was that my working environment would be drastically altered. Working closely with Dr. Huntington for years, I had become comfortable in our relationship and had grown accustomed to his expectations as well as the way I ran his lab and office space. I am, above all else, very efficient and my organized workspace is the key to my sanity. I had agreed to take part in the merger under two conditions: I would continue to be Dr. Huntington's assistant and would organize my lab space and rooms just as I had been doing for years. And now, this rude woman had blown up both of my conditions, leaving me feeling anxious and uncertain about this new venture. Her harsh words struck a nerve and made me fearful of what the future might bring in terms of changes in my environment, workload, or responsibilities.

I started to cry. Yep, standing in the middle of this new office. Big ole teardrops started streaming down my face. The receptionist handed me some tissues and tried to give me some words of comfort . . .

Remember when I said women are territorial? Here we go again. Suddenly I felt I had no control, no say in how this blended office would run. I was accustomed to my own processes for organizing and working efficiently in the lab, which would require me to be set up in a designated space, just as I was now. Was this not going to be the case? Would I instead be assisting this young-gun dentist who hadn't even looked up as Gwen berated me (and him) in front of a patient? Would I not be working with my kind, polite boss of nine years?!? Was I not going to get my own lab space? If I could have peaked into a crystal ball at that moment, I would have seen that Gwen's thorny demeanor was foreshadowing my whole year to come. I sensed that she felt threatened by my presence and wanted to establish her dominance over me; however, I knew the knowledge, skill, and value I brought to Dr. Huntington, our established patients, and even the new patients. After the initial shock of her hostile greeting passed and I stopped the tears, I knew I could not allow myself to be intimidated by her. I knew I had to remain confident. This was not my first rodeo, but I had been working in such a respectful environment for so long that it would take me a minute to get ready for our new place. *Time to fluff my feathers again,* I thought. Honestly, to greet me with "we run people off" in front of her boss AND a patient was an eye opener, and it was only the beginning!

Weeks later, just before Doctor and I moved into the new place, the new dentist asked me to come by on my day off to meet with him and Gwen. I stepped into the staff break room and found him sitting at the head of a dining table, speaking on the phone. I cautiously advanced toward the table and smiled politely, even though I felt like running away. He had seen me enter—I could tell by the way his gaze briefly shifted to meet mine—but he was otherwise unresponsive and still engrossed in his phone call. It was irritating that he didn't even bother to give me a simple nod of acknowledge.

I sat down at the opposite end of the table and waited for him to end his call. I caught the end of the conversation. My grandma would have said he was "putting on airs" (pretending to be a very important person). He finally wrapped up his call and then turned to me and without missing a beat, said:

"Just so you know, I will never (insert rude word rhyming with truck) you, because I don't like fat girls."

That was the first bullet. He proceeded to offer me a gym membership and inform me that I would have to go three times a week to keep it active and bring him proof of my gym visits once a month.

"Gwen is fat, too, and I hate looking at her. She'll be joining the gym as well."

I just sat there in complete shock. I could not believe what I was hearing. What a jerk! I could not believe what he was saying. Who talks like that to an employee?

He went on to tell me that Gwen was the only person that came through for him during a tragic time in his life, and he felt indebted to her. *Oh*, I thought, *so she's under an umbrella of protection. This explains her behavior.* I had heard rumors of his checkered past that involved alcohol and getting in an accident while his young children were home alone.

Then he told me that I was to go to counseling once a week on my day off in order to "keep the peace" in the office.

"I'll pay for the counseling with the same counselor I have been seeing, but I'm not paying you for your time to go." He stated this without any emotion in his voice, like he was dictating facts he had simply memorized.

"I just want to throw out there, that I don't agree with using my day off to see your counselor," I stated with conviction. I would eventually go once just to appease him and get him to stop pressuring me about it.

He wanted Gwen to go as well because, apparently, they had a very volatile office relationship. He continued to outline his list of demands, declaring that I was included in the merge contract, so therefore, he claimed, he "owned me." He then proceeded to tell me that he often referred to his female staff as "bitches and hoes," but shrugged it off as a joke and that I shouldn't take offense, because it was all in good fun. Finally, he ended with this little tidbit: If he was going to invest the next year of his life in grooming me to be his assistant, when the year was up, he would not let me quit; and if I tried to leave, he would smear my name all over town so that no one else would hire me. I knew that he was "peacocking"—the younger dentist had bought Dr. Huntington's thriving caseload—but my emotions were raw, and I couldn't find any humor in his offensive monologue. I felt belittled, judged, and insignificant. I knew other dentists in our town barely tolerated him, so his banter about "smearing my name" was meaningless. But still . . . *who says that?!?*

I just sat there, my shock deepening by the second as I absorbed the nightmare that my work life had suddenly become. Then Gwen entered the room and joined us at the table—wearing clothes you might entertain your husband in late at night. The whole thing was getting stranger from one moment to the next, and I felt completely taken aback by it all. I struggled to take in what Gwen and "Dr. Toothache" (as I now thought of him), were saying during the rest of our meeting; even now, I recall very little of it. My mind was clouded with confusion at this bizarre turn of events. I think I checked out somewhere around "bitches and hoes" and from there it all seemed like a dream. A very, very bad dream.

Needless to say, this was going to be a complete shit show, there was truly no other name for it. I knew Dr. Huntington had no idea what on earth I walked into. I really wanted his last year before retirement to be as stress free as possible because he deserved that much. However, I spent the weeks before the merge lamenting over what would be the best path for me to take in my career. My husband had always been supportive of my every endeavor, so I knew he would back my decision no matter what. I filled him in on my meeting with Dr. Toothache, and how I couldn't fathom working for him. But at the same time, I had given Dr. Huntington my word that I would go through the merge with him, and I couldn't bear the thought of leaving him and the patients we served together. I did explore other options and even had some great offers. In the end, however, I stayed true to my loyalty and commitment to Dr. Huntington and my desire to help ease him into retirement.

I decided to stay.

CHAPTER 25

The Year I Can't Get Back

I've read plenty of those motivational books full of inspirational sayings designed to teach you that you can choose to make each day a good day. As I eased into the new dental office, I started off each week with plenty of these phrases in my head—and also played motivational CDs in my car on the way to work—to pump me up and give me the courage I needed to survive in that office. Both the receptionist and the hygienist continued to form work relationships with me, and I enjoyed getting to know them. But despite my efforts, by the end of each week I would be left feeling completely beaten and exhausted. The sheer intensity of that office's atmosphere drained me of any enthusiasm I had at the beginning of the week.

Until I came along, Gwen had been the undisputed leader in the office, and she hated having her territory challenged by my presence. She begrudgingly "let me" take a small corner of the roomy dental lab; but it didn't provide nearly enough space for my extensive lab work which often required me to spread out the work I was doing in stages. After battling with the arrangement for months, I made an executive decision to use some of her lab area, and constantly had to fight to keep even that little bit of work-space. When I took some vacation time later that year, I quick-ly stopped by the office to pick something up, only to find that Gwen had completely eradicated my lab working area. Another example of territorial behavior between females!

Though I still worked head-to-head with Dr. Huntington, I was at the mercy of Dr. Toothache—it was, after all, his practice. Almost every day I would be summoned into his dark and cramped office where he would be puffing away on his electronic cigarette, filling the room with a strong scent of grape vape. GAG! Despite my coughing fits and requests for him not to vape while I was present, he continued to do so, responding only with a smirk or smart com-ment before puffing another billowing vape cloud into all four cor-ners of that small room. After so many blissful years working for Dr. Huntington, my quirk list was active again, and Dr. Toothache's quirks were so many that they filled an ever-growing list I kept in my mind. From day one he continued to pressure Gwen and me about our "mandatory" counseling sessions, saying he wanted us to grow as people. I finally agreed to attend one session, setting up a time on my day off to meet with a counselor chosen by my new boss.

When Dr. Huntington was at the office, his presence offered me a sense of security from Gwen's sometimes oppressive behav-ior. She mostly left me alone when he was there, at least in the beginning. Dr. Toothache, however, was always eager to shake things up. One Friday when I was in the office alone, finishing up some pending lab work—pouring up models, grinding them down, and articulating the casts—Dr. Toothache suddenly ar-rived, accompanied by a very young, very skinny female wearing a tight top and skintight leggings. After introducing us, he took her around the office, giving her a tour of the place before sending her off to wait for him in his car. As soon as his companion was gone, Dr. T. approached me in the lab and told me he was so tired because he had been up all night "banging her." He continued to give me the intimate details as I shooed him away, but not before he managed to ask me if I thought she was "screw worthy." (And I'm using a nicer term than he used!)

"Go away!" I said, as I covered my ears.

Oh, but wait, there's plenty more! The following week he started doing what he called "booty dances" (highly erotic, distasteful dance moves that he thought were hilarious) in areas of the office that he deemed "safe zones." When I asked him why he was referring to his dance areas as safe zones, he pointed to the various cameras mounted throughout the office and then to the corners of the office that were not being monitored. He was as proud as he could be as he tucked himself into a "no-camera zone" and danced in an offensive way, just to see the looks on the faces of his staff. They would roll their eyes and shrug him off, but I was not comfortable with his childish behavior.

Ugh. Not again! I thought. *Yet another arrogant boss who assumes he has the right to spy on his staff and "entertain" us with his vile behavior.*

Dr. Toothache's staff just laughed off his inappropriate antics, saying that's just how he was. He seemed to crave getting a rise out of his employees, especially when the office was full of patients, and we couldn't let our reactions show. He even did this whole "crucifixion" bit with arms outstretched and head hung low while sticking out his tongue.

"I'm Jesus on the cross, get it?" he would say, laughing at his own joke.

"You are going to be struck by lightning for being so disrespectful and I don't want to be anywhere near you when that happens!" I would tell him.

When I voiced my concerns to the office manager, she suggested that if I was uncomfortable with a particular type of conduct I should, whenever possible, try to remove myself from the situation. However, this often proved to be *impossible* because many times I was with a patient.

For a while I tried to win Gwen over so she would stop making snide little comments to me whenever we were near each other. To show her that I respected her opinion, when it came time for me to pick a custom shade for a tooth that was having a crown restoration, I would call her over to get her input. I didn't need her two cents, per se, because I prided myself on being able to easily shade match, but I thought this would make her feel like I valued her input. Unfortunately, my plan backfired because she took it as an opportunity to show off how much more knowledgeable she was with tooth shading than me, pointing out that I *needed* her help.

As was the norm, I dropped by the office early, before staff arrived on the day of a joint surgery with Dr. Extraction at the nearby hospital. I had carefully stored all the needed surgical supplies to take with me in a plastic bin the night before and completed the checklist. However, during the surgery it was discovered that some of the needed supplies were missing. I knew Gwen was the only one in the office after I left that evening, so it was hard to not accuse her of trying to sabotage the procedure. Honestly, if it was not one thing it was another with her. In an attempt to build a bridge between us, I decided to try sharing more of my personal life with her, telling her stories about my weekends and such. I told her about craft fairs I attended, my kayaking adventures and tried to arrange a blood donation drive. In return, she told me about her son's outstanding warrant, and colorful family drama. One day, her son stopped by the office with a clear plastic cup which she promptly grabbed from him and took into the restroom—telling me she often provided urine for his drug tests when he applied for a job. Clearly, Gwen and I were from two different worlds. She continued to verbally harass me at every turn, even when I tried to be friendly and supportive. When I brought up her bullying to Dr. Toothache his exact words were that he didn't want to talk to her about it and risk "pissing her off, because she's already a bitch to me."

Well, I thought, *I'll have plenty to talk about with that counselor this Friday!*

How did that go? Funny story. I had the strangest feeling when I received the name of the counselor, it seemed so familiar to me, but I couldn't quite place it. After a quick search online I found her and realized she was someone I knew—specifically, another parent from the board of a team sport my son had participated in during high school. Lucky me, I would be using my day off to see a certified *addiction* counselor. I couldn't help but laugh as I recalled how she abruptly quit the board after her son got caught allegedly smoking pot. Back when that happened, she had dropped all her responsibilities on me and wished me well. Now she would be presiding over a counseling session to help me cope with my very dysfunctional boss. Of course, the session was a complete waste of my time with the counselor conceding that while Dr. Toothache was abrasive, rude, and inappropriate, she didn't see that changing anytime soon. She advised that I just learn to live with his behaviors. When the hour was up, I stood to make my exit. Before I left, she informed me that since Dr. Toothache was covering the cost of our session, she would be providing him with a thorough report detailing everything we had discussed. I just sighed and shook my head, not at all surprised that she had waited until the end of the session to divulge that little tidbit of information.

Before long, Dr. Toothache decided to bring on a dentist right out of school and also hired a dental assistant to work with him. The dental office was quite large, with seven dental chairs in a big open concept room. The new dentist was given an operatory to himself as he did not yet have the patient load to warrant needing more rooms. I was told to help him if the need arose, which once again changed the working arrangement I was promised in the merge. Heck, I was busy enough juggling my patient load, lab work, and even some front desk demands. But what's another pound on an elephant's ass?

I tried to get used to working with Dr. Toothache, knowing that Dr. Huntington's retirement was eminent. But when I assisted Dr. T., I always felt on edge because he rushed everything. Dr. Huntington was slow and methodical. Dr. T.'s shaking hands as he hurried through giving an injection to numb a patient was also very concerning. Of course, money made his world go around and was always the main focus of his practice, rather than the care of his patients. After spending years in an environment that prioritized providing outstanding care and looking out for the patient's best interests, it was disheartening to witness Dr. Toothache's excessive greediness. Add a dash of no bedside manner and you have a recipe for disaster. The new dental assistant cozied up to Gwen and also quickly got swept up in Dr. T.'s escapades, thinking her new boss was just hilarious. To top things off, the two dentists enjoyed pretending to have a homosexual relationship, with Dr. Toothache chasing his protégé all around the office, grabbing him in improper places or trying to kiss him. They talked of screwing goats and taking wild ski trips with loose women. Sometimes I pointed out how juvenile they were acting, but that just egged them on. I know they were just having fun, but I worried constantly that our numerous elderly patients might hear their vulgar banter. I hated the thought of a dear older patient hearing or seeing these young dentists act so unprofessionally.

The year sped by quickly and for Dr. Huntington's last day in the office, I planned a little celebratory luncheon, decorating the break room and placing numerous pies on the table—because he loves all pies. On that special day, many people dropped by with their best wishes and gifts for him and some, as a kindness, even brought me little gifts. I was pleasantly surprised when Dr. Extraction, the oral surgeon we often collaborated with on surgeries, stepped into the break room to express his well wishes and congratulate Dr. Huntington on his milestone, a second retirement.

"Guess they will let anyone in the door!" I said as Dr. Extraction stepped into the office.

He countered my comment with, "Hey, I have a question..." (He opened every conversation with this statement, especially on our weekly consultation call.)

To which I replied, "Nope, fresh out of answers. This is a time of reflection and peace."

"Ok, I'll save it for our Wednesday call. That's still on, right?"

For about six years, Dr. Extraction and I had a standing fifteen-minute call every Wednesday morning. We would exchange information on mutual patients, confirm scheduling, discuss treatment, and toss the jokes back and forth. I really looked forward to these lighthearted weekly calls.

"Sure! I like to feel important," I teased.

Then he said, "One more thing... here," and he shoved a card and a bottle of wine into my hands.

"You went to an actual store and bought me a card?!?" I said, feigning shock.

What a kind gesture for Dr. Extraction to bring Dr. Huntington a retirement gift and also something for me. The era of our office collaborations was ending—two specialty offices headed by dentists who believed in providing exceptional care for their patients. It was truly a bittersweet day in my career.

Inside the witty card I found a nice gift certificate for what I knew was his favorite sushi restaurant. One hundred dollars was written in ink on the amount line. It was a generous and thoughtful gift. Dr. Extraction was excited for me to try this place he had told me about many times, where he ate often and knew the owner.

A few weeks later my husband and I took our son and his new girlfriend to the restaurant. We were giddy with excitement and ordered a plethora of sushi rolls and dishes. Like kids in a candy store, we had fun trying everything and could see why Dr. Extraction loved the restaurant. At the end of the meal, our bill came to just over $120.

I put down cash to cover the extra and the tip, along with the gift certificate, and handed everything to our server saying, happily, that the gift card should cover most of the bill. She returned a minute later and whispered into my ear that the gift card only had $11.22 left on it. *Pardon me?!?*

Oh my gosh! Dr. E. must have gotten his wires crossed somehow, I thought, as I shed tears of laughter. It must have been one of those moments when he had more than one gift certificate: one he was using, and one to give me, and he probably mixed them up! We chalked it up to "just one of those things" and said it was absolutely the thought that counted as we paid the full bill. I didn't tell him on our weekly call because he's getting old and maybe his mind is going. Just kidding, he's still sharp as a tack!

CHAPTER 26

Hummingbird

Like any emergency, a dental emergency can happen in the blink of an eye. A patient can even require emergency assistance during a dental treatment. The best way to prepare for these situations is to be well trained and have your muscle memory ready to take over. This is why you enact the steps of CPR over and over in the certification classes—because you will lose your mind when a patient starts to not feel well and then stops breathing, or the doctor catches himself on fire.

In dentistry we have codes or emergency safety words that stand for everything from "call 911," to "a patient is being difficult," to "someone has a weapon." We use these codes and words to inform staff of certain situations without upsetting any patients in the office. Calm handling of a situation is always best, especially if you are not yet sure the situation will turn into an actual emergency.

When Dr. Huntington's practice merged with Dr. Toothache's practice, we worked with the larger staff to incorporate our safety words with their safety words. I have a lot of years of safety words floating around in my head. At one office, "Dr. Pepper" meant an unruly patient was alone with an assistant or the hygienist and the dentist was needed to come and play sheriff. At another office, "Blue Skies" meant a patient was having a difficult time breathing, be prepared to administer oxygen. And at almost every office I have worked in, "Code Red" meant call 911.

At this office, the operatory that Dr. Huntington and I used had a large glass window that looked out over a beautiful koi pond surrounded by flowers and shrubs. The scenery year-round was just breathtaking.

One beautiful summer day, we had a patient in the chair who was having a tooth prepped for a crown. I was looking down and using the high-volume suction to rinse the patient's mouth, when Dr. Huntington suddenly said, "Hummingbird!"

I stared at him, perplexed and asked, "What?"

He repeated "Hummingbird!" with enthusiasm, but I still had no idea what on earth he was alerting me to. I started going through my mental file cabinet for the safety word "Hummingbird," but kept drawing a blank.

Let's see, I remember the one for a person with a weapon. So, that's not it. "Apple" was a code word once, but I think we got rid of that one. There's "Oklahoma," which means the good times are over, escort the patient up front . . . Hummingbird could be the patient is dizzy from sitting up too quickly, or they swallowed something (let's be honest we use some really teeny tiny instruments when working in your mouth), or low blood pressure. Patient looks fine to me . . .

I've got nothing.

Dr. Huntington noticed my confusion and raised his eyebrows with a slight twinkle in his eye.

After a few seconds, I couldn't stand it anymore. I confessed to Dr. Huntington that I had forgotten what the "Hummingbird" code meant. He just stared at me, then he started laughing out loud.

"No!" he said, pointing out the window onto the pond behind the office. "I just saw a big hummingbird!" Sure enough a beautiful hummingbird was perched on one of the branches near the water's edge.

The patient sat up as we watched it for a few moments until it flew away into the sky and disappeared from view. We shared a laugh at how funny it was that Dr. Huntington's "hummingbird" was NOT one of our secret code words!

Emergency averted.

CHAPTER 27

Pardon Me... Do You Have the Time?

There's an old saying about refusing to pay the slightest attention to someone, so you won't have to give them the time of day. I've run across many dental professionals in my career that seem to live by this adage, my current boss included. Drives me nuts.

It was six weeks and two days after Dr. Huntington and I entered the merge, that I approached Dr. Toothache in the sterilization room to ask him why he never spoke to me. He never replied to my cheery good mornings when I arrived to start the day—not even a nod—and aside from asking for an instrument when I was assisting him, he acted like I wasn't even there. Even Gwen would respond to or initiate a morning greeting. When Dr. Toothache replied to my question with a flippant, "And who are you, again?" I knew he was just being obnoxious. He never missed a chance to make a sarcastic remark, and seemed to expect I would share in his amusement. Honestly, his behavior was like that of a bratty child who demands attention and disregards those around him. Despite being the owner of the practice, he was seemingly oblivious to the impact his words and actions had on those around him.

As the year progressed, Dr. Huntington slowly reduced his schedule, leaving me to work directly with Gwen and Dr. Toothache more and more often. Some days Gwen and I had an easy, friendly banter but that didn't make up for Dr. Toothache's constant inappropriate behavior and antics. I had good relationships in the office with the young hygienists who were always very friendly to me and took fabulous care of patients. Also, the older receptionist and I had a wonderful relationship. The office manager and I, prior to her passing, built a solid relationship as well. We spent many an evening together in the office trying to merge computer systems and visions for growth for the office. I tried to picture myself in some role in that office, because I did not want to leave the patients I had built relationships with over the course of many years.

As the merge year came to a close, I sat down with Dr. Toothache and the newest dentist to discuss my role going forward. Our office manager had passed away from cancer six weeks prior to this meeting, so everyone was still reeling from the loss. We were short staffed up front during her sickness, and of course hoped that she would conquer the disease. Out of respect for her, no one would even sit in her front office chair. Well, that's not true, Gwen went through her desk when she was in hospice care and took lotions, good pens, and other things she wanted.

In the meeting with the two dentists, I stressed my concerns over continuing to work with the practice and the daily challenges with Gwen. The other assistant just plain ignored me and so I, in turn, ignored her. No harm, no foul. I discussed with both dentists the idea of me becoming the office manager because I already knew how to run the office and wanted out of the clinical side.

"That would have been a good idea," Dr. Toothache said, "but we already interviewed and hired a young gal from another office."

"Oh, I had no idea."

"She has three younger kids, but big titties, so it all balances out," Dr. Toothache rudely added.

"Does it though? She will need time off for sick kids, school events, and things I am well past with having an older, college-age son. Maybe we could co-manage the office?"

"I'll think about it, but you and Gwen seem to be in a power struggle, and I need her to not be an a-hole to me. If I put you up front, then she'll be miffed, and I'll have to live with her."

"What does she have over you that you won't make her stop being so rude?" I point blank asked him.

"Let's just say she was the only one to help me out when I f'd up."

We decided to table the discussion for the time being because we were not able to come to an agreement that made us both happy. The new front desk person started and after only few days she called me on my cell phone after work. She made it clear to me that she could hold her own but asked if Dr. Toothache was always a pompous jerk and completely out of line. I confirmed that she had pegged his personality correctly.

"He's not going to change, and the staff accepts his behavior," I followed up, wanting to add that I absolutely *did not* accept his behavior, but decided against confiding in someone I did not know well.

Dr. Huntington was now fully retired and no longer in the office. I was working at the front desk and being a "rover" or someone who goes where they are needed in the back of the office. Without him there to shield me from Gwen's hurtful behavior, I felt like I was tiptoeing through a minefield every day. I kept hoping the drama would dial down but it did not, so I gave my notice and started looking for a new job. Not surprisingly, Dr. Toothache initially threw a tantrum and then simply accepted my resignation.

Side note: That new receptionist didn't last very long.

Quirk List (Dr. Toothache):
1. Booty dances!
2. Calling the staff bitches and hoes, beyond disrespectful.
3. Gwen, the office bully!
4. Pushing dental work on patients like a salesperson and modifying fees when they could afford to pay more.
5. Pushing dental assistants to do much more than is allowed by law.

Life Lesson: Plant seeds of happiness. If they don't grow where you are . . . move to better soil.

CHAPTER 28

Let the Interviews Commence

In the dental field, it's typical to do a "working interview" as part of the whole interview process. This entails being at the office for a set amount of time—usually a half or a whole day—to see the mechanics of the practice, how the staff interacts, and how you might fit in as an employee. I updated my resume and filled my notebook with each interviewing office's information and any quirks that popped up. Several weeks after leaving Dr. Toothache, I did a working interview for a receptionist position with a root canal specialist (also known as an endodontist). I arrived at the appointed early morning hour, but things just didn't flow. The initial phone interview had been with his stepdaughter who was also the office manager. Now, I have mentioned that I can tolerate five quirky things, but I also have five absolute deal breakers:

1. Family members working in the practice
2. Low pay for a high-stress position
3. Rude or otherwise unfriendly staff
4. Working a full day on Fridays (I'll do a half) plus NO Saturdays

5. Not offering paid holiday, sick, or vacation time, or any other perks (scrub allowance). Dental offices typically offer NO medical and minimal dental benefits, so higher wages, paid time off, bonuses, or at least an annual review with the hope of some sort of acknowledgement for your hard work are good reasons to accept a position.

Now, let me emphatically reiterate #1: **NO family members working IN the office day in/day out**. Not only does this make it a challenge to poke fun at your boss, but having family members report back to dad, mom, wife, cousin, etc., can create distrust and tension between coworkers.

The stepdaughter/office manager informed me that they opened at 8:15 a.m. on Mondays and told me to come in at that time. I always arrive fifteen minutes early, so when I arrived at 8:00 a.m. the doors were locked, and the lights were off. Had I made a mistake? Were they closed on Mondays? The sign on the door confirmed 8:15 a.m. as the open time. Patients were beginning to show up and wait with me for the doors to open. We all watched the staff arrive at 8:15 a.m. on the dot. The office doors were opened shortly thereafter at 8:17 a.m. This told me that the dentist did not want to pay staff to "ride the clock" (arriving fifteen or so minutes before patients are allowed in to turn on lights, prep the rooms, and answer voice mails). Many offices I have worked in also held morning huddles, allowing us to go over our daily schedule and make sure we didn't have any questions. I think this allows staff to be better prepared and ensures that patients receive high-quality care without unnecessary hiccups due to lack of preparation. It also promotes a team mentality. This staff appeared to all clock in exactly when it was time to seat the first patient, which is a huge pet peeve of mine. I am always early. My motto is "If you are not at least fifteen minutes early you are late." I personally need a few minutes before the appointments start, to get my wits about me and make sure my operatory is set up properly, or at least get my ducks in for a row so the day will run smoothly. For patients to get a warm welcome upon their arrival, the staff should arrive early enough to not be running around like chickens with their heads cut off!

I was quickly greeted amid the flurry of activity. Patients were streaming in, and the phone continuously rang. A receptionist acknowledge me, and I was quickly introduced around as the frenzy continued. Because I was interviewing for a receptionist position, I was directed to the front desk and told to wait until the gal could catch her breath. As she sped by me, she breathlessly stated that she would get me a chair. I told her thank you and that I would use the time to visit the restroom. She stopped in her tracks at my statement . . . a beat or two passed, then off she went.

Quirk #1: Office day starts with unnecessary chaos.

As I made my way to the staff restroom, I crossed paths with the endodontist who was just grabbing his lab jacket and getting ready to start patient care. I introduced myself and commented on his nice office. He looked at me as if I had told him his baby was ugly. I was hoping for a short but civil exchange, but instead I was left with the impression that he didn't like to be interrupted, ever.

Quirk #2: Blinky, fishy eyes that refuse to acknowledge my existence.

Upon returning from the restroom, I sat in the chair provided by the person who would be training me. She quickly went through the basic office policies, starting with a correction of my use of the term "restroom." The endodontist, and owner of the practice, discouraged staff from mentioning anything personal, so instead of saying "I need to go to the restroom," we were to say we would "be in the back and returning shortly." Personal water bottles were to be kept up front but only in a certain area and in securely sealed containers. What were we, toddlers who couldn't be trusted not to spill our sippy cup? Phone etiquette requirements included over enunciating the type of specialty office it was, to ensure callers understood the speaker the first time. Calls were to be answered within two rings. If a patient wanted to veer off and talk about personal things, you were to cut them off and get down to business. What a huge change from my days with Dr. Huntington when both the patients and I were encouraged to share personal stories and interact as family. The office manager continued to tick off the policies, expecting me to internalize every detail.

Next, I was told to answer a few calls to see if my phone etiquette lined up with the office policies. It was very difficult for me to cut people off when they were obviously in discomfort. If the patient had been referred by a dentist that was not at the top of the referring list, they were given an appointment three months out. The practice operated on a "you scratch my back and I'll scratch yours" arrangement with certain dental offices in town. Oh my gosh! The patient is in pain!!

Quirk #3: Delaying patient care due to playing favorites with other offices.

During my short stint at the front desk, I had the chance to witness firsthand how the office manager, Dr. Fisheyes' daughter, seemed to micromanage the staff when she blew through the office mid-morning. I also observed how she would interrupt the front staff and correct their verbiage or give instructions on how they should better handle various situations. It was clear that this was a regular occurrence, and very stressful for the employees.

Quirk #4: The boss's daughter is a micromanager.

After three hours, I had my answer to the age-old question, "Can I work here?" Really, I knew in the first ten minutes. Though the ladies up front were friendly and helpful with answering my questions, I concluded that this wasn't a good fit for me. As I left, I thanked the front office staff, and said goodbye to the staff in the back. I told the endodontist that it had been nice to meet him and was not surprised when all I got in return was a slight nod.

A day later the office manager called to offer me the position. When I declined the job, she pressed me to tell her what her team needed to work on based on my few hours in the office. I said it just wasn't a good fit for me and I had chosen to go in a different direction, but she continued to press me. Finally, I said, "Well, since you are being so insistent, the truth is your dad wouldn't take the time to talk to me when I greeted him, and barely gave me a nod when I said goodbye. I am not a scripted person, and I just didn't have warm fuzzy feelings about being a valued employee." She was blown away with my response. Hey, I was just being honest.

I was on the hunt for a dental office where I could feel appreciated and respected. One that went beyond simply providing a paycheck for its employees. I wanted to find an office where the patients' time was respected, and the dental care was just that—care—provided with a personal touch. I had found this before. Dr. Albright, Dr. Grace, and Dr. Huntington could not be the only dentists to run their offices with integrity and politeness. I would just have to keep looking.

Quirk #5: Did I mentioned the script the staff follows for phone calls?

CHAPTER 29

My Kind of Dentist

I first met Dr. Gentle, a very kind and very professional female dentist, when I interviewed for a front-desk position at her dental office—shortly before Dr. Huntington was due to retire and leave Dr. Toothache's practice. Once Dr. Huntington was gone, I knew I wouldn't be able to endure working in Dr. T.'s toxic environment for long. Dr. Gentle was soft spoken and we chatted like friends, unlike the typical interview format. I knew right away that she was a good human. I appreciated this about her and was excited to potentially be a part of her dental team. During my interview, the office manager popped in and observed for a while from a corner of the room. Her face held a look of slight distain, as if she didn't appreciate having her day interrupted for such a menial task. Or maybe she swallowed a bug? Any input she offered was short and clipped, with an "I don't have time for this" manner; I also noticed that she was not big on eye contact. *No wonder this dentist can't keep anyone up front,* I remember thinking to myself. *This lady does NOT seem like a people person.*

At the end of the interview, Dr. Gentle shared that she needed to fill the position sooner than my availability would allow, and due to my sincere allegiance to Dr. Huntington I had to decline her offer. She promised to keep me in mind for a fill-in position in a few months when her dental assistant was due to go on maternity leave. I let her know that I would be very interested in filling in and we agreed to keep in touch via texts.

True to her word, months later I found myself preparing to start my first day as Dr. Gentle's fill-in dental assistant. I donned my black scrubs, pulled my hair back, put on my name tag, and made my way to her general dentistry office. The staff trickled in, and all were quite welcoming except one hygienist who couldn't be bothered to even say good morning. Oh well, I'd been around that block before! The day started with setting up treatment trays and stacking them in the order of patient arrival times. I pulled open the drawers I thought might hold the items I needed for the trays and was happy to find almost everything stowed in the most logical place. A very friendly, young assistant happily showed me how they did things in Dr. Gentle's office. All dentists have little idiosyncrasies, so it's nice to know what they are and plan accordingly. I started my notebook list, keeping in mind my rule of five.

Dentistry is like baking a cake: most procedures follow the same steps and require the same ingredients— but the order will vary, depending on the dentist's preference.

The morning huddle started, which is a staple of every workday in most well run dental offices, and a scene very familiar to me and akin to my years with Dr. Huntington. The staff went over the day's schedule and made comments about patient treatment and potential help that might be needed from other staff. The office manager, standing yet again in the corner with tight lips and a judgmental stare, perked up only when Dr. Gentle was present—as if she would only participate when the boss could see.

I was secretly grateful that I hadn't taken the front office job months prior. The office manager gave me the impression that she was very unapproachable would be difficult to work with. From the start I did my best to keep my interactions with her to a minimum. Whenever I had a question about patient care, she would either tell me she didn't know or snap at me to figure it out on my own. I was incredibly frustrated that my questions about patient needs were not being addressed. I felt that the office manager wasn't taking patient care seriously. As someone who had worked in the dental field for over twenty years, I had always put the patients first. At the same time, I was having to learn a new dental software program, which added another layer of challenge to my job. The office manager offered no help or support with this transition. (*Like what did you make my password? It would be super helpful to be able to log in!*) In truth, she barely lifted a finger to assist anyone. It seemed that her only goal was keeping up appearances in front of patients and Dr. Gentle. I have worked with amazing office managers in the past, many of whom oozed warmth and compassion and worked hard to keep everyone on the same page so that we could all concentrate on patient care, but that was not this manager's style.

Thankfully, the dental assistant I worked with in the back was very knowledgeable with the computer programs and willing to help me in a pinch.

———

As the days went by, I grew more accustomed to Dr. Gentle's preferences and practices and began to feel like part of the team. I loved that we would write the tooth number and surface of the tooth we were restoring on the tray liner for each patient, or the tooth number of the permeant crown we were going to deliver, this was a way to dually confirm the proper tooth was being worked on. I was secretly flattered that Dr. Gentle would double check before removing a temporary crown, because I crafted such authentic looking temporary that she sometimes mistook them as permanent crown! Acknowledging and complimenting my hard work meant the world to me—I hadn't been treated in this way since I worked with Dr. Huntington.

As we moved through the day, I was happy to keep busy and help my coworkers as time allowed. I strongly believe that being part of a team means helping where and when you can. One such task was cleaning up the hygienist's room after patient care when she ran behind schedule. Although she had yet to acknowledge my presence, my good intentions were met with an unexpected reaction. Instead of showing any appreciation for my helpfulness, she became quite agitated and pointed out minor infractions, such as where I placed the patient bib and bib chain on her treatment tray. She ignored the fact that I had just wiped down her room and set it up for her next patient, saving her at least ten minutes and getting her back on schedule. Instead, she snorted in disapproval that no one had ever cleaned her room for her and stomped off. *Noted.* This, my friends, is why some hygienists get a "prima donna" label from me, and a reputation for being hard to work with in the dental field. I learned my lesson and didn't offer to help her again.

Doctor continued to earn my respect as I observed the way she listened to her patients, considered their concerns, and exercised a gentleness that put them at ease. She practiced dentistry with confidence and skill and took her time when treating each patient.

Within just a few weeks, the spunky and helpful co-dental assistant's enthusiasm for her work began to wane. In the beginning, I had considered her my upbeat partner in crime. She typically ran the low-production room and often, when not with a patient, could be found at the computer in the lab (where she was visible to all) just staring at the screen. Sometimes when I was knee deep in a long procedure with Dr. Gentle, I would see her at that desk, propping her chin up with her fist and napping, while seemingly deep in thought, trying to look busy. I knew that she had once been responsible for running the high-production room, getting lab cases sent out, and handling all treatment-related shipments. She may have been relieved to no longer have such a big workload, but instead of helping me clean my room, bag instruments, run the autoclave, or set up trays—which I did for her whenever I had a free minute—she now seemed content to just take it easy. It was a very one-sided arrangement.

Meanwhile, the office manager and I were still struggling to find common ground, try as I might, my attempts to engage her in conversation were rebutted with single-word or short, clipped answers. I made it my mission to get her to talk to me and frequently sought out opportunities for a chat here and there. I could see that dealing with her was an issue for most people. There had been a string of front-desk new hires that had come and gone (each quitting within a few weeks), because they couldn't take the office manager's overbearing ways. The most recent person she hired had a shabby appearance and was far from ideal in terms of being the first person patients would see when they stepped into the office. The young woman often smelled like she had skipped her morning shower and her hair was a rat's nest. The office manager made hair and makeup suggestions to try and help her align more with the office demeanor, but these fell on deaf ears.

"Can you try to look more like Joy tomorrow? Her hair and makeup are very office appropriate," she said to this gal (in front of me and the other staff) during one of our morning huddles.

By the end of my fill-in gig, the messy receptionist had been let go. As for me, it had been great while it lasted, but my temporary gig as a dental assistant had come to an end, the person I was covering for returned to work. I was once again seeking a fill-in assignment or a full-time dental job. But then Dr. Gentle called with a question: Would I consider applying for the front-office receptionist position? *Hmmmm . . .* I thought.

I told Dr. Gentle that I was excited for the opportunity to stay with the office but voiced my concerns about the friction I had felt with the office manager during my fill-in assignment. She understood, but by the end of the call I accepted the position and prepared to start immediately. The next day I was back in the office, but this time I was up front, and my every move was about to be scrutinized by the overbearing office manager. She seemed to be envious of or perhaps even threatened by the fact that I had previously worked in the back, directly with Dr. Gentle, and already had a rapport with the staff. My biggest hurdle was learning to use front desk modules in the dental software program. The way the assistants used the program in the back was entirely different from the way it was used up front, but I was determined not to let this overwhelm me. As my training began, I took notes and tried not to ask the office manager too many questions. She, in turn, made a show of telling me that ONLY she knew the entire protocol for checking in a patient. Of course it involved using the front-desk modules I was learning and included signing a HIPPA form, changing screens to sign a consent for dental work, updating their health history, and taking a quick photo. Once the lengthy process was complete, hit save and bam, the patient can have a seat.

"Well," I said, "by tomorrow I will have it down and you won't have to help me every time. And that will free you up to do other tasks."

"Doubtful," was her one-word answer.

I took my notes home and poured over them until I had the exact steps in my head and felt ready to use them the next day. When the moment finally came for me to check in a patient, I wasn't surprised to see the office manager standing right beside me, seemingly ready to swoop in and take over. To my delight and her disbelief, she watched as I gracefully executed each and every step. I was off and running, but she watched me like a hawk all day, and found plenty of reasons to nitpick and correct me:

> I mentioned to a patient on the phone that I didn't have an available appointment but would be happy to place them on the "quick call" list.
> ✓ **WRONG!** I was told to immediately place the patient on hold and then instructed to use the words "sooner if possible" instead of "quick call."

> I refilled the printer with a large stack of paper.
> ✓ **WRONG!** The printer could hold more paper than I was loading. She added *two* more sheets of paper to my stack, and then declared the paper tray "full."

> I refilled the water in the patients' single-serve coffee maker.
> ✓ **Wrong!** I didn't fill it up to the very tippy-tippy top.

> I tidied up the waiting room.
> ✓ **Wrong!** I missed a candy wrapper that was lodged in a seat cushion. (Who was eating candy at a dental office?!?)

Additionally:
She kept a space heater up front, set to "Burn in Hell," and my little personal fan aimed at only me made her cold.

This type of behavior and micromanaging went on for many weeks without so much as even one cordial conversation between us. I tried to keep my patience from wearing thin, but I reached my last straw when she made a show of chastising me in front of an elderly patient. A hygienist who was filling in had unexpectedly brought an older gentleman to the front desk for check out. I could not quickly change my computer screen at that moment, so in order to find his name, I grabbed the master schedule clipboard that was kept at the front desk. Every patient scheduled for the day was on this master list, along with notes regarding extra paperwork, co-pays, HIPPA updates, or updated photos that should be completed during their dental visit. After scanning the hygienist's column, I found the gentleman's name and properly greeted him. As I began his check-out process, I placed the clipboard in nearly its original spot. In a flash, the vigilante office manager jumped from her seat. She swept up the clipboard, clutched it tightly to her chest, and loudly declared that it was a HIPAA violation for the patient (who was standing several feet away, on the other side of the front desk) to see the names and information on the schedule. I looked at her for a moment, keeping my "receptionist" smile on my face, as I took in the scene she was causing for the whole waiting room to see. I could feel my face flush as she continued to berate me in front of the patient. Wasn't this something that could have been discussed after the patient left?!? The patient, who couldn't have seen the small print on that schedule without a telescope, watched in amazement. The office manager went on and on with her beratement of me as the patient waited to be checked out and dismissed. . Finally, I just turned away and finished up with the gentleman and sent him on his way. As soon as he left, I turned to the office manager to have a few words. My voice was firm yet respectful as I told her if she felt something needed changing or improving then she should discuss it with me in private; and after today, she would never have the opportunity to embarrass me in front of a patient again.

At the end of the day, I approached Dr. Gentle and asked for a few minutes of her time. I explained the issues I had with the office manager and how she was making it difficult for me to stay long term at the front desk. I offered to stick it out while they interviewed for a replacement, but Doctor thought it best for me to just leave. It was an incredibly difficult decision, and I was so sad that I couldn't stay with that office. I liked everything about the practice except for that one overbearing woman. It's unfortunate when one person in an office insists on making each day more difficult than it needs to be, and as someone who had been through similar situations before, I couldn't allow that kind of toxic behavior into my life again. When Dr. Huntington's hygienist was set on making me miserable I suffered mouth ulcers, hair loss, gained weight, lost sleep, and experienced anxiety over it for years. This time, I nipped it in the bud. Not today, sister!

A few months later, as I was browsing dental job sites, I came across an ad for an assistant position at Dr. Gentle's office. I knew that her happy and upbeat assistant, who was now pregnant, had decided she would move to the town where her husband had taken a job. I knew in my heart that I fit in with the office (and could tolerate the office manager and her quirks if I was working in the back). I was already familiar with Dr. Gentle's dental procedures and patient care protocols, so I thought I might just be first in line for the position. I texted Doctor and told her of my interest and that I was available to take the assisting position immediately. She texted back an elaborate and slightly formal reply, stating that she was in no rush to fill the spot and still looking at all her options. What neither of us realized, however, was that we were just days from finding out how severe the COVID-19 virus would be. It was March 2020, and the world was about to shut down.

Weeks later, my next text from Dr. Gentle stated that one of her assistants had gone out of the country on a cruise and the new COVID-19 precautions stipulated that she could not yet return to work and see patients. At that time, knowledge about COVID-19 was still limited and any potential exposure required an immediate quarantine of two weeks. Desperate for help, Dr. Gentle asked if I would be available to fill in while the assistant stayed home. (We didn't yet know if she would develop symptoms and need to quarantine longer than two weeks.) I quickly responded with a resounding "YES!" and confirmed the hours. I was excited to be back in her office, even with the onslaught of COVID-19. I truly enjoyed working with the patients and staff, even the office manager was a little more tolerable during this time. We were all adjusting to the COVID-19 safety procedures, and I made it my priority to follow the extra precautions to prevent the spread of the virus by consistently cleaning surfaces. In the dental field, for years we had been wearing masks, gloves, protective eye wear, and protective gowns over our scrubs, so the COVID-19 PPE requirements were not new to us. Really, they were just a heightened version of what my industry was already doing. I had also always been very careful not to cross-contaminate surfaces—such as not touching a cabinet door with the same gloved hand that had just been in a patient's mouth. In fact, I never really worried about catching the flu or a cold from a patient, because I had worked in full PPE since long before the pandemic. My vaccinations were up to date, and until COVID-19 the most feared virus in my industry was hepatitis.

In my first week assisting for Dr. Gentle, we still as a country knew very little about COVID-19. The general public was not yet wearing masks. Our state, however, had issued an order for no gatherings of over ten people. Despite warnings from medical experts, it took longer than expected for the public to accept and follow this advice. Into the office came a male patient who shared with me all the details of the big St. Patrick's Day party he had attended at an Irish pub the night before, along with hundreds of other people. As I masked and gloved up and grabbed the high-volume suction, I felt myself becoming more on edge. Any minute now, the Doctor would pick up the handpiece and begin treating this patient, a man who had spent hours at a crowded party despite a global pandemic, and all of those germs from every asymptomatic person he exposed himself to would become airborne all around us. Did those partygoers really think they could safely celebrate St. Patrick's Day without passing around the virus? How was I supposed to protect myself and my family? Though I was happy to be back in Dr. Grace's office, I was starting to think about how I would be spending extended amounts of time working chairside in patients' mouths. At this point, there were still no reliable testing methods or a vaccine. As these thoughts circled through my mind, an even more pressing issue weighed on me: Was I endangering my family because this guy couldn't skip one party during the start of a major, worldwide pandemic? Once the patient left, I voiced my worries to Dr. Gentle. To my surprise, she was not concerned at all! She thought we should carry on unless we started showing any symptoms. Although I followed every wipe-down and sterilization protocol, I felt a sense of looming dread every time someone coughed or sneezed in the chair. Were they just suffering from allergies, or did they carry something more serious? Despite the ever-growing count of confirmed cases, I was relieved to make it through those weeks without being exposed to the virus that had already taken such an immense worldwide toll.

Even though COVID-19 cast an overwhelming sense of fear and uncertainty over life as I knew it, I still had my eye on the assisting position. I hoped to replace the pregnant assistant who would be moving away. I thought I should be a shoe in. Why wouldn't Doctor hire the person who was right there in front of her and already familiar with the office? However, on my last day of the fill-in assignment, Dr. Gentle conducted a rather lengthy interview with another candidate. Nothing like being on a date with your boyfriend when he tries to pick up another girl. What was I, chopped liver?!? Let's just say I felt like I had gone from winning an Oscar to getting an honorary participation plaque as Doctor said goodbye to me with a promise of being in touch . . . yeah, right! My feelings were certainly hurt, here I was putting my health at risk to help at the very start of a worldwide viral outbreak, yet I was clearly being snubbed.

And then it happened. Dental offices were ordered to close, along with all other nonessential medical services, so I didn't just go home because my fill-in gig ended, I went home to a lockdown that halted my entire industry in its tracks—along with restaurants, hotels, optometrists, retail stores, schools, and more. The national order mandated that all offices and restaurants remain closed until further notice, leaving with no other choice but to stay home.

As the world changed overnight, I joined so many others in filling my next days and weeks with home projects, but I was not able to simply go without income. I couldn't work in my industry, so . . . well . . . I sort of fell off the wagon—the "no nanny gigs" wagon, that is—and I became a nanny to two newborn *twins*. Go big or go home, right?!? The mom was a healthcare professional, working in an essential role within the medical field, so she continued to go to work. Her husband worked out of the home in an industry that didn't involve interacting with people, so his job continued also.

As a nanny, I was excited to snuggle with the eight-week-old babies. What I wasn't excited about was the aggressive Doberman puppy the family adopted toward the end of Mom's pregnancy. It was clear that while caring for multiple babies would be difficult enough, the addition of a rambunctious and untrained puppy would greatly complicate matters. It was a lot to handle. I certainly couldn't care for the twins and train their dog for them. The babies were my priority, first and foremost, and I dove into juggling many tasks each day. Baths, feedings, endless diapers, so much laundry, making dinner, caring for that beast of a puppy. High five for me when I got the twins on the same sleeping and eating schedule! And feeding time was an absolute juggling act! The puppy needed a lot of attention and training, neither of which he was receiving. Whenever I had him inside, the five-foot-tall beast would jump on the counters and chew up anything he could get his paws on, including the bottle nipples. One day while I was rocking the babies, he chewed up one entire leg of the kitchen table. Even the playpen had a hole chewed through the mesh (but that did not happen on my duty)! When I put him outside in the fenced yard, the little yapper would bark his head off—spoiling any hope of a proper naptime for the babies and annoying the neighbors. Adopting a puppy, especially such a high-energy breed, with twins on the way would not have been my choice. I looked forward to going for twice daily walks with the twins tucked into their double stroller, just to get away from that oversized aggressive puppy. We would come back and do tummy time, read books, and I would dress them up in cute outfits and have mini photo sessions to text to Mom. Meanwhile, the puppy was growing fast and getting more out of control. I discussed with the parents my difficultly in keeping the puppy from chewing on everything or barking loudly and waking the twins. They both agreed with me that something should be done, but Mom felt the puppy had the right to be in his home and roam freely. So, nothing changed.

From the start, it was evident Mom was having some difficulty paying me. She would continuously promise to drop by my house with what I was owed, handing me ones and small bills days after a payment was due. Or she would write a check and ask me to not deposit it for a few days. So, isn't that like being paid, but not really?

As the months went by, I perfected a daily routine of feeding the babies, changing them, doing the laundry, cleaning the house, making dinner for Mom and Dad, and bathing the little ones before the parents arrived in the evening. We all agreed things were running well. But then there was that puppy. He was now almost as tall as me and felt free to jump up and put his paws on my shoulders, even if I used my knee to get him down. No amount of kneeing or blocking him made any difference. He was all muscle and far surpassed my strength and agility. If he jumped on me in Mom's presence, she would take him by the collar and tell him "no" very weakly, so he learned nothing. I was afraid he would jump on me while I was holding one of the twins and we could have potentially dangerous consequences. One day, I let him out the back door to the fenced-in area while I fed the babies and endured his constant barking through both bottle feedings. I knew the neighbors had been complaining about the barking (I couldn't blame them), so after their feedings I put the babies in their swings and let the dog in. As I opened the back door, that Doberman came flying into the house and ran through the kitchen like a Tasmanian devil. I turned to close the door as he zipped back into the kitchen at full speed. Before I knew what was happening, he body slammed me from behind, sending me crashing to my knees with my right arm catching my fall. The force of the impact took my breath away, leaving me temporarily stunned and struggling to get the dog off my back. When I finally got him off me, I opened the back door, and he zoomed outside barking and sprinting around the yard. I texted Mom and let her know I very easily could have had one of the babies in my arms when that four-legged beast jumped me.

When the parents came home that evening, they made it abundantly clear that they didn't want the puppy to be crated or spending so much time outdoors. Then I made it abundantly clear that it was impossible for me to take care of the twins and deal with an uncontrollable dog at the same time. After a serious discussion, the parents ultimately decided to put the babies into daycare. And that brought the curtain down on my nannying days. The dog won.

CHAPTER 30

Interviewing 101

Way back when I took drama in high school, we often began each class with an Ice Breaker card. These cards had intriguing questions that encouraged us to think deeply. I thought of those cards now as I prepared to start interviewing again. "Would you work for the best dentist for ten years if you knew that for the next ten you wouldn't work with someone half as kind, ethical, or as much of a good human? Yes, was my answer. Those were ten very good years.

Job interviews are much like dating, and it's important to know what you're looking for as you prepare for them. I go into the first meeting with certain expectations, while also keeping an eye out for any red flags. There truly is so much to consider in a short amount of time, which is why the one day working interview (PAID!) is a grand idea. You want to make sure they are personable, kindhearted, compassionate, and will treat you with mutual respect. Additionally, I like to pick up on any quirky details about the dentist, staff, or office in general. Remember you are interviewing them as much as they are interviewing you.

After the babysitting gig went sideways, I had an interview for a front desk position at an oral surgery clinic. I sat in a frigid conference room waiting to meet with two experienced specialty dentists. I had already devoted over an hour to being introduced to the staff, talking to the office manager, and being given an office tour. I generally feel confident in an interview setting because I know what I bring to the table, so I wasn't overly nervous. On this day, the two oral surgeons were finishing up a very long workday and now were required to sit and interview me before going home. The older dentist spent most of the interview scrolling through his cell phone, only glancing up occasionally to give me a *Why aren't you finished talking yet?* look. The younger, more attractive dentist who was conducting the interview, made it apparent that he had extensive specialty training and an impressive list of credentials. He flipped through my resume . . .

"I bet you really think you are something." The young Dr. said.

He looked at my extensive resume and wanted me to know how my background *paled* in comparison to his. Umm, I would hope so after he went through a crazy number of years of college for his specialty. I sat there with a smile on my face as he droned on and on about his accomplishments. I pondered why he didn't have a statue erected in his honor at the entrance to the practice.

He emphasized the importance of being friendly and courteous when interacting with patients. He explained that, as a self-pay office, the practice was able to make more money since it wasn't bound by insurance companies' fees and, therefore, the patients were treated with extra care. He also highlighted how I would be the primary point of contact for patients arriving and leaving the clinic, stressing my friendliness played a major role in making sure everyone felt comfortable and cared for. *Okay, okay . . . I get it . . . be a good human . . .*

After he pointed out for the ninety-ninth time that I must always be friendly, I threw up my hands and tongue in cheek said, "Well, I'm a mean person, so I don't know."

He quickly bucked up, taking on a suspicious tone, "Then why did you apply for this position?"

I was kidding. It's called a sense of humor and yours, Sir, is missing.

The interview continued to spiral in the wrong direction. The young dentist continued to lay out his expectations wanted me to get a few things straight. He *wanted* me to understand that this interview would be the most personal contact we would ever have, as he felt a certain this would keep the office gossip and petty arguments down. I couldn't imagine *not* having a personal relationship with someone I worked with every day.

Quirks and deal breakers had been steadily piling up, but the last straw was the pay: thirteen dollars an hour with very few benefits and extended workdays. I understand a potentially new employer doesn't know if I am a slacker or a hard-working overachiever, so the pay starts out on the low end. I would like to point out though, when employees are adequately compensated for their efforts, they tend to be more loyal and motivated.

I walked out of that office and sat in my car and cried. *Is this all that is out there for me?* I wondered. I quickly called Dr. Huntington, who was fully retired at this point, to ask his advice. As always, he was the calm voice of reason.

"That isn't the place for you," he said. "Keep on looking."

Quirk List (Interview Style)

- Impersonal bosses with zero sense of humor.
- Low pay.
- Focus is on patients' wallets, not the patients.
- The hours were not ideal.

- If he erected a statue of himself, would I have to polish it daily?

Working in dentistry can be a cutthroat world where outsiders are seen as potential threats. Staff members sometimes display unkind behaviors toward one another in what is supposed to be an environment of care and compassion. Adding insult to injury, dentists may try to pay employees low wages while working them to death. I have observed both of these scenarios and been on the receiving end of them more times than I care to remember. This is why the working interview is so important. I must be able to observe how people treat each other, see who is helpful and kind, who returns my morning greeting, and get an idea of how hard I will work for a dollar.

When I answered an ad for yet another oral surgeon, I was asked to stop by the office to have a quick chat with the specialty dentist and his lead assistant. We had already set up a day at the end of the week for a working interview, but they wanted to briefly meet me in person. I arrived fifteen minutes early and greeted the woman at the front desk who shared my name. I have not actually crossed paths with many people named Joy. What struck me about this "Joy" was that she didn't seem very happy despite her name, or joyful—there were no smiles, no warmth in her voice, not even a hint of excitement. I think that when you have a name that people associate with HAPPINESS, you have a certain responsibility to be happy or at least appear happy. In the limited contact I had with her on that day, and later in the week during my working interview, she was not a joy. She even told me that felt she was wrongly named, and sometimes thought she should go by her middle name.

I met with the dentist and the assistant, and our visit went well. The dentist was well known around town and had a good reputation. The assistant had caring eyes and a kind smile. We all agreed that I was qualified for a position in the back, so I would return at the end of the week to do a working interview. It is customary to pay a candidate to come in for a working interview. This would be only the second time in my twenty-nine years that I was not paid for such a workday. Lesson learned, always ask prior to agreeing to a working interview what the rate will be.

When the day arrived, I jumped right in, determined to be helpful and show this new office my skills. The back staff was incredibly warm and welcoming. They gave me helpful directions and told me about the job expectations. Despite feeling a little bit intimidated by being able to "see behind the curtain" at this office, I was eager to learn more about their processes and procedures. I jotted down notes in my notebook, asked questions, and tried to make sense of all the details. These women handled their jobs in such a manner that their tasks and routines had become second nature. I had so much information coming at me that it took two days for my brain catch up. The human body is amazing and the doctors that work on it and understand it always have me in awe. I helped with surgeries, sterilizations, and the dismissing of surgery patients. It was an extraordinary opportunity to see exactly how the world of oral surgery works on a daily basis.

Things were going well and by now we were a few hours into the workday, until . . . I was assisting with one of the procedures, when embarrassment washed over me. Suddenly, the oral surgeon looked up from giving an injection to numb the patient, his head light shined directly on my face, the beam centered on my forehead, as he peered over the dental loops that he wore to magnify what he sees in the patient's mouth. He stopped the procedure. I froze, like a deer caught in a headlight, but this headlight wasn't from a car, it was from the Dr.

"What am I seeing?"

With three other assistants standing around the patient, doing various jobs, everyone stopped and looked in my direction.

"There's a dark steak of something on your forehead." He directed at me.

He removed his sterile operating gloves, retrieved a handheld mirror and asked me to address the issue. I froze. *What is he looking at? What is on my forehead?!?*

One of the assistants spoke up immediately, "Oh, it's just some makeup! Let's wipe it off." As she handed me a tissue. I was mortified at the thought of this surgeon halting a procedure and causing the entire staff to stare at me, with his head light shining on my face. If they had only known what it really was! That morning I had used a brown hair spray to cover my gray roots, and when I put my protective eyewear on top of my head it must have rubbed off directly onto the frames. When I put the glasses back on my eyes, the brown residue had gotten all my forehead!

After the doctor gave me a kind thank-you for taking care of the matter, everyone in the room resumed their focus on the dental procedure. We finished up the dental surgery as if nothing out of the ordinary had happened. I was really surprised that he had taken the time to make me correct a streak of makeup on my forehead.

After an exhausting day of work, I was presented with a potential opportunity by the oral surgeon and office manager. Doctor had "big plans" for me, suggesting that I attend a class in another town an hour away to receive certification in placing IVs for patient surgeries. I would do this on my own time, and I would pay for the course myself, but would get a dollar an hour raise once

I was certified. The starting wage would be fourteen dollars per hour. He thought this was a fabulous deal and told me to think about it and have a good evening. I asked if he needed my home address or any other information for my check, for the day of work I had just completed. He shooed away the notion with a wave of his hand, saying they did not pay for working interviews. As a dental professional, I'm sure he would not work eight hours for free, unless it was at a volunteer clinic. I volunteer my own skills at free dental clinics quite often, and when I do, I know I won't get paid. A lack of pay is very different when it comes as a surprise.

I considered the immense level of responsibilities the oral surgery assistants had in this office, such as filling syringes with medications that were used to sedate patients. That got me thinking. What if I made a mistake? I know the dentist manages this closely, but what if he overlooked something and I was the one who caused a patient to have some sort of distress? He also mentioned the fact that young people are often hesitant to divulge any illegal drug use in their health histories, for fear of their parents finding out, and this puts them at risk when being sedated. My list of "what if" scenarios grew longer than my confidence in taking the job, especially where IV sedation was concerned.

I decided to pass on this opportunity, but appreciated my day of learning their world, even if it was without pay.

CHAPTER 31

Testing ... Testing

I became aware of a younger male dentist who had recently opened a practice through some creative, out-of-the-box, and humorous advertisements. These catchy billboards were posted everywhere. When I met him at a dental event, he seemed like an okay person, maybe a bit cocky for someone who just got out of dental school. He claimed that assistants and hygienists were clamoring to work in his office, and that getting hired was "a process" and he was very selective. *Hey, whatever floats your boat,* I thought.

I was on the job hunt many months later when I noticed a posting on an online employment site for an opening in his dental practice. I thought I might as well throw my hat in the ring and see what Dr. Cocky's hiring "process" was all about. I applied and a few days later received a response.

The email, which was a form letter to all prospective dental assistants, stated that I had been selected to come in for an interview and to arrive wearing professional clothing, not scrubs. The time (11:00 a.m.) and the date to report to the office were listed, as well as a notation stating that this would be a group interview. I had never taken part in a group interview. I thought of the group auditions I had participated in for community theater productions, with multiple people competing for the same role in a play. Trying out for a lead character had never bothered me, but "trying out" for a dental assistant position was quite an interesting concept.

Before going on a job interview, it is important to look and dress professionally. Sandals, flip-flops, or any other type of open-toe shoes should be avoided as they can give off an unprofessional vibe. And while we're at it, the first impression you make with your prospective boss should not include or allude to your breasts in any way. A blouse with an appropriate neckline is the most professional.

On the day of the interview, I dressed for success and drove to the dental office. As usual, I arrived fifteen minutes early, so I had time to get the lay of the land. *Wow!* I thought, as I walked into a room already brimming with nearly a dozen women of a variety of ages, all competing for this one opportunity. I guess Dr. Cocky was right, candidates *were* clamoring to work in his office. After handing off my resume to the office manager, I took a seat in the waiting room where all the chairs had been arranged in a circle formation. As we all sat and glanced at each other you could have cut the tension with a knife. Knowing that we were all equally nervous and in the dark as to what to expect, I decided we needed an activity to pass the time. I spoke up and suggested that we introduce ourselves. This gave us something to focus on as the final two applicants arrived, and we all prepared to start "the process."

At exactly 11:00 a.m. the front door was locked. No more applicants would be allowed to join our group (several knocked on the door to be let in, but no dice). The office manager stood before us and gave a little background on the office. Then, she proceeded to hand out a two-and-a-half-page test. *A TEST?!? UGH!!!*

I took my clipboard and dove into the multiple-choice questions. The test covered proper sentence structure, word definitions, converting weights and measurements . . . you know, things you hopefully remembered from your SAT back in high school! I could not believe it. We had ten minutes on the clock. My personal test-taking philosophy is to complete the answers you know first, then go back and work through what's left. Honest to goodness, there were questions like "If a train leaves such-and-such station at 10 a.m., Greenwich Mean Time, going 50 miles per hour, what time will it arrive at such-and-such station in Eastern Australian time?"

At exactly the ten-minute mark, the office manager collected our tests and introduced the dentist. He gave us a very detailed run down of his life, I mean who uses colorful adjectives when they are introducing themselves?

"I stepped on my blue boat wearing size ten flip flops and noticed the yellow sail wasn't tied properly. I made sure my eighteen-month-old dog, Jack who was wearing a red bandana was safely onboard, before my wife of six years and I set sail." He said.

Look, typically when you introduce yourself, the first thing I forget is your name. I can assure you I won't remember your dog is eighteen months old. I am always one to write things down so that I don't miss anything, plus I was going to give my intel to Dr. Huntington next time we spoke. After the dentist finished his speech and left the room, the office manager gave us each a piece of blank paper. We were asked to write down what had been said by both parties since arriving, to assess our "ability to retain crucial details surrounding patient care accurately." Attention to detail. I've spent a lot of time in the dental field and I'm very familiar with gathering patient information and relaying it back to the dentist. While some of the other candidates were intimidated by this task, it didn't faze me. I'm the go-between for the patient and dentist. I take down what the patient says, typing it into our dental program as a patient relays the information to me, then give the dentist a condensed version from my written notes. It amazes me the number of times I edit chart notes because there are many, many times when the patient's story changes.

"Do you have any teeth bothering you?"

"No."

Dentist to patient, "Do you have any teeth bothering you?"

"Yes, this lower left molar, and this one . . . and this one sometimes is cold sensitive." As they use their tongue to point to a general area. Ya'll know you might as well use your elbow instead of your tongue to pinpoint the exact tooth causing an issue, right? No offense, but we can't see where your big fat tongue is zeroing in on.

After I finished the task, I looked around to take in my surroundings. On my left sat a promising prospect; she was dressed professionally in an eye-catching blouse, black slacks, and closed-toe shoes. She spoke enough, but not too much. Sadly though, the two contenders on my right didn't quite make it onto my list: one played on her cell phone throughout most of the interview and the other wore a super short skirt and a tight low-cut shirt and never said a word.

The interview had now passed the one-hour mark. *Surely this is going to wrap up soon,* I thought.

Nope! There's more!

Next, we were told to work in groups of three. We were given riddles to solve . . . and I wasn't too optimistic on my ability to do so. Not my strong point or anything I am even remotely interested in doing, but I am a team player and didn't want us to not have an answer. I was in a group with a shy, quiet young gal, and someone whom I'd worked with fifteen years prior who was quite annoying to say the least; (and honestly that hadn't changed). But it was up to Ms. Annoying and me, as our shy partner gave no input whatsoever. The purpose of this activity wasn't about finding the right answers, but rather seeing how we interacted as a team. Ms. Annoying wanted credit for her work and took our losses to heart. She was loud and outspoken and hellbent on solving every riddle, even after the exercise was over. Kudos for your tenacity.

When all the riddles had been answered, I thought surely we would be done. We had been tested, lectured, quizzed, and put in groups. What more could we do?

Oh, goodness, there *was* more! Hang on! Drum roll please . . .

It really was like a grand finale. Each candidate, we were told, would now answer a question aloud in front of the rest. *You've got to be kidding me!* I thought. *And what will they follow this with? Swimsuit?? Evening gown?!?*

My question was: What has been the greatest accomplishment of your dental life?

My answer came to me quickly and my confidence showed as I described my greatest accomplishment to the group. I immediately thought of a patient who Dr. Extraction and Dr. Huntington treated at a surgery center with me being the lead assistant. The case was a very involved upper and lower all-on-four implant surgery and I had helped with every aspect in the operating room. Mental high five for me! Of course, I did not refer to the patient by name, but I was proud to share his story.

At last, we were freed and told we could expect calls by the following week. Barely an hour after I left the office, while I was picking up some groceries, my phone buzzed. The office manager was calling to set up a working interview, and also mentioned that the dentist was just starting out and therefore would not be able to pay staff very much and was offering no benefits. Oh, and I would be asked to work some late nights and Saturdays as needed. Yikes! On top of that, as he couldn't yet afford a dental software program, I would be tasked with helping piece together a free program to use in the meantime. *Huh?* This job that everyone was "clamoring for" turned out to be a rover assisting position, doing menial tasks and helping where needed. That meant during the day I would be pulled in all directions without an assigned room, juggling tasks all day with someone sure to become unhappy because I wasn't able to make their demand a priority. Not that the work was beneath me, but I had been under the impression this was a lead assistant position. I couldn't believe I literally wasted hours of my life enduring "the process"—taking a test and doing that song-and-dance interview for an "elite" position that so many other hopefuls were supposedly brawling over—just to have it turn out to be the lowest rung on the ladder, with the lowest compensation. My reply? Respectfully, I'll pass. Go ahead and call the next clamoring hopeful on your long, long exclusive list!

CHAPTER 32

Corporate Dental

I was back to square one! For about six months I had been using a popular online site to apply for dental assisting and receptionist jobs, while also working from home and doing fill in dental jobs. I became so familiar with the site that I could tell when a new hire hadn't made the cut at an office and the job had been reposted. I wondered—after seeing certain dental offices post the same opening over and over—if the dentists were difficult to work with, the staff had a bully running people off, or if they were just having a streak of bad luck.

One day, as I was checking the site, I found a direct message in my inbox. It read:

> *Hello.. I have a position in your area pls contact me if interested Strong relationship with M*** Advance*
> *Dental assistant dutiez.*
> *JOB DETAILS:*
> *Title: Dental Assistint*

Company: Dental
If you passionate Elderly patient care, we have the
focus
Full responsibilities of all dental assistant/good pay.

I noticed that the spelling was a bit off, and I knew this could be a red flag. You really have to watch out for scams on job posting sites. I also found it odd that it came as a direct message with no actual job posting linked to it. Another red flag, typically. But at the same time, my curiosity was piqued. *I'll bite,* I thought. *I do like the elderly, and maybe this job just isn't listed yet. Maybe I'm getting in on the ground floor . . .*

That evening, some friends and I ventured out to catch up at a local pub. While enjoying my beer and nachos my cell phone vibrated in my pocket. An unfamiliar number with the same area code as the ad I had responded to earlier in the day was flashing on the screen. Knowing that it might be important, I excused my-self from the conversation and answered the call. The caller intro-duced himself and asked if this was a convenient time to speak. I told him I was at an event and asked if he could call me back at another time. He agreed to call the following day, which was a Saturday. I remember thinking it was odd for an interviewer to pursue you on a weekend for a dental assistant position.

———————

My phone buzzed bright and early the next morning with the same unknown number. I answered the call, expecting it to last only a few minutes at the most. An hour and a half later, I had agreed to an in-person meeting with a dentist that this husband-and-wife management team had just hired for their new dental office.

---

*The red flags continued to pop up
during the call. In fact, they were all
over the barnyard. It didn't walk
like a duck, or even talk like a duck,
not even when they were explaining
their vision for the practice.*

The management couple, calling from New York City, had a unique story. They had been hired by a major insurance company to open an office that would cater specifically to elderly patients who carried the insurance company's plan. To fill the dentist vacancy, they had hired a locally established dentist who suddenly lost his office lease and needed a place to practice. He was seeing his own patients two days a week, and this company's patients two days a week. Sounded like a conflict of interest to me, right off the bat.

They were super interested in my knowledge of specialized dentistry and my many years of prosthodontics experience. The husband and wife, who were both on the phone with me, dually agreed that I would be the ideal candidate to train a second dentist they were about to hire fresh out of dental school. *Me? Train a dentist?!? Ugh . . . NO!* So . . . basically, they were looking to have me give him direction while he brought in the big bucks. At the end of the call, they casually mentioned that the office hours would include nights and Saturdays. I had been in the dentistry field for almost three decades at this point. So . . . working nights and weekends wasn't something I was looking to do anymore!

Mr. and Mrs. NYC tossed around common dental terms like confetti, but it soon became clear that they didn't have a clue about dentistry. While they attempted dental shop talk, all too familiar to my ears, something seemed off-kilter; they were mixing up terms and phrases in ways that didn't quite jive.

The following Monday I arrived at the dental office to meet the office manager. The building was old, yet the waiting room had been renovated with comfortable seating and a pleasant atmosphere. As I ventured further into the dental office, however, it became obvious that beyond the waiting room this place hadn't seen any renovations in decades—it was downright outdated and shabby. The receptionist's area was a total disaster with the largest mess of papers I'd ever seen haphazardly stacked on every surface. This office made my son's room look tidy! Large boxes were busting at the seams with contents that seemed desperate for escape. My heart dropped at the sight; disorder gives me a panic attack! I introduced myself to the office manager and stepped back out of the way of a patient waiting to check out. He seemed agitated because he didn't know the name of the dentist who performed his dental work, was confused about the dental procedure that had taken place in his mouth, and what the out-of-pocket cost would be. This is never a good sign. I watched as the office manager worked through answering his questions while the dentist himself showed up with an appointment card for him—only, it turned out that he had booked a follow-up on one of his own professional workdays instead of a day when he would be working as their corporate dentist. The office manager quickly viewed the card and pointed out to the dentist that the patient couldn't be seen on that day. This confirmed my suspicions about an underlying conflict of interest.

As I toured the office, I was immediately overwhelmed. The mountain of supply boxes and complete disorganization waiting to be tamed for the incoming hire (me?) and would be a daunting task. I knew the story all too well; a new dentist, freshly graduated and ready to start their own practice, would be hired by a corporate dental office and get a sixty (corporate)/forty (dentist) cut of whatever profits they earned. The dentist would build their patient base while gaining experience (especially dental prosthetics, if I were to share my secrets), only to leave and open an independent practice to get 100% of the pie. All my time and training would be just so they can watch this dentist walk out the door. I had seen this movie before, so I knew exactly how it would end. Then another dentist, fresh out of school would be hired and the cycle would start all over.

The office manager explained their current model was based around elderly plans which didn't provide much coverage; they were hoping to expand into HMO-based services to get more traffic through chairs each day. *Oh, Lord!* I knew what this meant: twenty or more patients a day—all day, every day—in each chair. My thirteen years working for Dr. HMO flashed before my eyes. *Been there, done that, got the T-shirt and the souvenir glass!* I thought. After thirteen years in the last HMO dental office, I still hadn't completely recovered from the mental trauma caused by that eccentric dentist. I also knew I couldn't work for an office where my knowledge and skills would be used and exploited, but never appreciated.

I drove home with a heavy heart. All the red flags had been waving at me since I first opened that typo-ridden direct message. And deep down, I think I knew all along this hadn't been a path I was meant to follow. I was so mad at myself for putting time into this "non-opportunity," but I also knew that I had just missed an asteroid hitting the spot where I stood on this earth. *Better to find out now,* I reasoned to myself.

But I still needed to find a job.

Oh well, I thought, *back to square one.* This mantra was becoming all too common. I went home and sent a professional email to the corporate agency (complete with proper spelling and punctuation), respectfully declining the position.

Quirk List (Corporate Style):
1. A big ol' Texas Hell No! to training someone fresh out of school.
2. Weekends are a no.
3. The office was next level disorganized and a mountain of a mess.
4. Dentist didn't communicate with patient on so many levels before starting treatment.
5. Shady corporate company running the business.

CHAPTER 33

My Dream Job

Before setting out on more interviews, I decided to take a step back and really consider what my dream job might look like. I have cast my wishes out into the universe and prayed for many things in my life, and ya'll hear me when I say, if there's one thing I've learned: *You must be specific.* What would my dream job look like? What would the components be? I had worked in offices that were a living nightmare and others that were ideal. I wrote out a list and kept adding to it as a new desire came to me. I wanted to construct that perfect scenario—the work environment we all dream of no matter the profession—and get my wish list down on paper. All in all, my dream job would be an opportunity to bring out the best version of myself while making a difference in others' lives. I wanted something that had most of the elements that were important to me.

Dream Job:

- ✓ Four days a week (Dental office days are long and draining), No weekends

- ✓ Small staff (less drama)
- ✓ No bosses' spouses or kids working in the office (With the exception of Dr. Huntington's wife, family in the office is just a recipe for stress)
- ✓ Adequate pay
- ✓ Friendly staff (no bullies!)
- ✓ A dentist who does quality dental work and interacts with me on a human level & doesn't make me push products
- ✓ Vacation time / paid Holidays would be a nice perk
- ✓ Challenges my mind
- ✓ Nice patients
- ✓ Not insurance driven (otherwise patients only want the "free stuff")
- ✓ Plenty of products provided to sterilize rooms, office, and to protect staff
- ✓ Short distance from home
- ✓ HAPPY VIBES

My career in dentistry was my life's passion, so I refused to accept that my dream job couldn't be found. I cherished my memories of the years I spent working for and assisting many dentists. I wanted to have that same feeling in an office again, to know I mattered and was part of a dynamic patient care team. I also wanted to work beside a dentist whose company I truly enjoyed, and who appreciated me *and* my sense of humor. I was determined to find my dream job! #GOALS!

CHAPTER 34

Still Interviewing

While I was looking for the perfect dream job, I took a data entry position working from home. The hours were good, and it left me time to help my husband with his business. We were even traveling again, as the COVID restrictions had been somewhat lifted. When we drove to his meetings in the Northeast, I would bring along a bag full of antibacterial wipes, masks, hand sanitizer, and anything else we might need to kill germs.

I spent days pouring time and energy into online dental assistant applications, complete with skill-testing exercises that were timed before you could hit send to apply. Then one day . . . Whoo-hoo, I got a bite! I received a reply with some appointment options for an in-person interview with an office near my house. I chose a time on an upcoming day that would have me arriving at the office just after they closed, around 5:30 p.m.

On the day of the interview, I went through my usual "prep-for-success" routine:

- Clean hair
- Minimal makeup
- Professional-looking outfit with closed-toe shoes
- Extra copies of my resume
- Notebook with my list of questions
- (And once I arrived) cell phone off

I walked into the office fifteen minutes early, ready for the meeting, but what I wasn't prepared for was the warmth and hospitality of the dentist himself. He welcomed me into his office, leaving the door open, and we sat and talked for almost two hours. I had already done my research on his practice, finding out all the information I could on the office hours, accepted insurances, dental programs, where he went to college, and even if he had a wife and kids. Most of this sleuthing was the result of calling several other dentists I knew to ask what they thought of him. *Note to self: Add "Dentist must be a good human." to Dream Job list.*

I thanked the dentist for taking the time to interview me and then dove into my list of questions. One by one he thoughtfully answered them. Then I explained to him that, in my view, finding a job was like dating.

"After all, when you're searching for that special someone, you're essentially 'interviewing' potential partners."

"Interesting assessment."

"When two people start dating and getting to know each other better, they often find five things about the other person that bug them as well as five things they adore—it's up to each person to decide whether or not those five annoying things are something they can live with over the long haul. They must ask themselves: Is this worth tolerating those little annoyances or do I move on?"

He sat there and stared at me.

"Everyone has five things, and no one should assume that they don't."

It was my mission to find another employer that could live up to Dr. Huntington's example as a good boss, a good dentist, and a good human.

He continued to just stare at me. Blink, blink.

"I have a few questions. How are assistant duties split up? Who presents the treatment plans? How do you deal with office drama? How do you reward your staff for a job well done?"

"I admire you for being prepared," he said. "If I'm not mistaken, you are interviewing me with all the questions you are asking, rather than me interviewing you."

"Guilty as charged," I laughed, but then I looked him steady in the eye and continued, "I have a lot of experience and I am very good at my job. So, it boils down to two things: office personalities and pay. Can you and I get along and have a good professional relationship day in and day out? And will I be treated fairly by your staff, or is there a bully? I do not want to work in an office with a bully." I was done beating around the bush during these interviews, and equally done with counterproductive, passive-aggressive coworkers who felt they were put on this earth to make me miserable. *That's right, fess up to your five things now, Doctor, so we don't waste each other's time.*

"So," he said after a few moments of silence, "as I think you would agree, like most dental offices, we have many strong personalities. We do have a person who has been here for many years, and I am aware that she speaks her mind and comes across as abrasive and rude." His brow furrowed as he looked at me intently, clearly, he was making sure that his message was sinking in before continuing.

He then suggested that if this person acted out toward me I should not let it hurt my feelings, but instead just let it roll off my back. He went on to explain that he too had been caught up in this person's crossfire often, but he had learned to not take it personally. I disagreed with him silently, how could anyone be expected to simply ignore such behavior? If someone is bullying another person or making them feel uncomfortable, then wouldn't that be an issue worth addressing? At least he was honest with me, and I could check off that box. A bully is a DEAL BREAKER!

When an interviewer wants to find out about more you without asking a question they aren't legally allowed to ask, they will often say something like, "So, tell me about yourself." This is an open-ended question that refers to nothing specific, but they are hoping you will say you are married, your kids are older, you own a home, and you attend a church regularly. This paints the picture of a nice, stable person who might stay in the job for a while. I have interviewed so much over the years that I have my entire "Tell me about yourself" monologue memorized—to the point that it bores me to recite it! But I know that each and every prospective employer needs to hear this spiel. I also see it as an opportunity to say certain things that are designed to make me stand out as a candidate.

What I say: "I'm from way West Texas, where my family still lives."
What it means: I pop this in to let them know I will take time off now and again to go and visit my family.

What I say: "I have been with the most amazing man for many years."
What it means: I am in a good, stable relationship, not out catting around.

What I say: "I have a son in college."

What it means: I am letting you know two things:

1. I won't be taking days off to stay home with a young child who was too sick to go to school.
2. I need to work because college is expensive.

What I say: "I own a home on the east side of town that I am in the process of fixing up."
What it means: I am handy, creative, and investing in my home, so I'm not likely to move away anytime soon.

During this interview, the dentist told me he was a theologian and the name of the church he attended. I made a mental note to look up the definition of *theologian* but was pretty sure it had to do with the study of the Bible and not a Greek God. He became rather excited when I mentioned to him that my son and I had attended divorce-recovery classes at his very church, which had helped me through a tough time. His enthusiasm soon turned into a question as to whether we still visited the place of worship. I had to admit that we weren't anymore because during one of the Bible-study classes I took there I was informed by the teacher that I would be going to hell for getting a divorce. I couldn't see the point of attending a church that thought divorce was an unforgivable sin. He quickly replied with "Well, there is argument for that . . ." and after all he was a theologian.

And that is a perfect example of a deal breaker—oh, we're way past a quirk with this one. A boss who thinks I'm going to hell?!? A theologian with no interest in helping me save my everlasting soul?!? A boss who will picture me as doomed every time he looks at me?!?

He was glad to hear that I was now in a stable relationship and threw in, "What church did you settle on attending?"

Despite my impending eternal damnation, the interview continued. Over the course of our conversation, I asked him if he was right or left-handed. I wanted to know because I am left-handed and assisting a left-handed dentist is a struggle for me. I have to switch and use my less dominant right hand. Turned out he was right-handed, so I mentally checked the "yes" box on that point. I was surprised, however, when he added that he felt ninety-nine percent of his assistants didn't use the high-volume suction to his standards. His comment left me nearly speechless. I mean, that is the number-one task a dental assistant performs during a dental procedure: suctioning the field to allow the doctor to see what he or she is working on in the mouth. Another share: He also thought that in the prosthodontic dental field the assistants don't have as many duties, really, because prosthodontists want to do all the work themselves. That tidbit more than puzzled me and I asked what on earth he meant? Dr. Huntington had given me quite a bit of responsibility and groomed me to be an expert assistant and perform work that represented his standard of care. I listed many of these duties to the dentist and said I was very proud of the quality of my work. He flatly replied that he already didn't think, based off his knowledge of other prosthodontic assistants, that I could possibly have a very high skill set. *??? I have no box for this one,* I thought. *Nope. Nowhere to put a checkmark. Ouch!!! An arrow through my heart maybe . . .*

My issues with this dentist had been accumulating by the minute, as he seemed to be presenting himself in a positive light, but then he would make some tactless comments that did not quite align with his Christian persona. For instance, he volunteered at a dental clinic once per month, yet was quite vocal about his dissatisfaction with the lack of organization, the poor quality of the instruments, and the mediocre dental products available there.

This even led him to stop volunteering for a while. If I were in his shoes, I might have said, "I volunteer monthly at a dental clinic, and it makes my heart happy to be able to help those in need, even if the clinic is limited in the kinds of products they can provide. We always find a way to make it work, and it's truly rewarding to give back in such an impactful way."

P.S. I volunteer at that same clinic, and it relies on donations and grants to run.

The dental assistant I would be replacing had given this dentist her two weeks' notice; she was expecting to move and take a job located an hour away. Although she wasn't totally sure she had the other job. I could see that in his mind she was already gone and so he was actively seeking to replace her. He wasn't going to wait around to see if she got the other job or not.

As we went over the hiring details, he offered me adequate pay and good hours. A working interview would be needed, of course, but he was willing to pay me for my working day. On my way out of the office, I told him I would call and set something up.

I thought over all that I had learned about the office during my interview:

1. Office bully.
2. Doctor may focus on his religion & thinks I'm going to hell.
3. Doesn't think I could have much of a skill set, even after assisting for over two decades.
4. The bully counts as three quirks.
5. Bully! Bully!! BULLY!!!

I struggled with the decision to do a working interview knowing that there was a confirmed bully among the staff. This was something I had encountered in two previous offices. I knew I wouldn't handle the stress well if the bully decided to zero in on me: weight gain, hair loss, mouth ulcers, —and I had brought that unhappiness home with me every night. I thought of the dentist and how our conversation had gone. Could I see us becoming friends and respecting each other's abilities? I thought of Dr. Albright and Dr. Huntington and how each of those men had viewed the care we provided as a team effort. I pictured them laughing at my corny jokes and maintaining a professional but light-hearted air around the office—one that left the staff feeling valued while the patients enjoyed their appointments. But, dang it, the pay was good and so were the hours.

I closed my eyes and tried to imagine a day of work with this dentist. As an interviewee, I had taken on the motto: *If it isn't a HELL, YES! Then it's a HELL, NO!*

When I called the receptionist, with whom I had crossed paths over the years, I asked her about the so-called office bully. I could immediately tell that her tone had become more strained. After some prodding, she eventually confided that there were far too many days when she left the office in tears because of the bully. *Oh, no!* I thought. *I cannot step foot into this office again, not even for a working interview.* I asked her to let the dentist know that I was respectfully declining the position.

I felt immediate relief from the moment I said it. This was not the office for me. No way.

I wonder if he has horns
holding up his halo . . .

CHAPTER 35

Interviewing 102

By the time you schedule your 32nd job interview, you will have most of the questions the interviewers may ask memorized, and the answers will come easily. Typically, the office manager will be working from a cheat sheet they found online to guide them through the process. Something like this:

**SUGGESTED INTERVIEW QUESTIONS –
DENTAL ASSISTANT**

How long have you been a dental assistant?

This is always a good ice breaker because you know they have your resume in hand and they could most likely do the math themselves, but they want to hear it from YOU. After giving my answer of "twenty-nine years," I feel the need to say I started when I was twelve years old. Then, we laugh. I was told by a friend of mine, a retired dentist, that I am aging out and my days working in the back are numbered. Dentists want peppy young girls with bright white teeth to represent the practice.

What are your weakest areas?

Be careful with this one, it's a trick question. You don't want to tell your prospective boss that you talk too much, loathe assisting with root canals, need the operatory organized "your way," and do not ever steal my pen (or at least give it back at the end of the day. Dr. Huntington, I mean you). While any of these would be my honest answer, I instead give them what you might call a "pageant answer." As a young thing I did my time on the beauty pageant stage. In the interview portion, the pageant judges are looking for you to turn any answer into a positive opportunity. I like to say that my weakest qualities are that I focus too much on the details and at times find it difficult to keep patient conversations short after getting to know them. And I would rather poke my eyes out with a fork than assist with root canals. (OK, I don't actually say *that*!) These are all true statements, just polished a little to make them shine in an interview.

What are your strengths?

I've got this one in list form in my head:

- ✓ I've been dental assisting for so many years that I have the critical thinking down. When a procedure doesn't go as planned, I am able to adapt quickly to the situation and follow the dentist's lead.
- ✓ I also have a strong work ethic and you will rarely find me sitting still.
- ✓ Being a team player is important to me, as well as being able to communicate with patients and other staff members.

Why did you leave your last job?

The short answer for me is that the dentist I was working for retired. But if you left because you just couldn't take another day with an aggressive ass hat, you can say "another opportunity arose." This way, you are turning a negative into a positive and avoiding the term "ass hat," which you should never say out loud in an interview.

Tell me something about yourself.

Beware: This is a loaded question since the person interviewing you can't ask if you are married, how many kids you have, or if you own a home (but these are the things they are hoping to learn with this question). You can always volunteer this information and put their mind at ease, or you can just give them some basic facts. Depends on my mood. I like to say I am from West Texas but have lived in my current town for a while, beautiful place to live . . . blah, blah, blah . . . and that I enjoy doing volunteer work both in dentistry and other areas. Then I end with the fact that I took four years of French in junior high and high school and retained very little of the language. Now, this isn't the information they were hoping to obtain, but I've answered the question and given them enough things to think about. What they *really* want to know is if you will be staying in the area versus moving anytime soon, hence do you own a home? And they would *love* to know how many little rug rats you have, and their ages, and does your mother live near enough to babysit in a pinch, or will you be needing the day off when your little one gets sick or has a school event? Being married is a solid bonus, because it tells them you will be marching into the office every morning after a quiet night at home with your spouse, rather than dragging yourself in following a wild night of partying.

Really, interviews are more like personality tests. Will your personality fit in with the office staff who have already been there for years? You can train a person to assist or handle the front desk, but you put two Type A personalities in a small space, such as a dental office, and you will get drama. Most dental professionals are typically strong-willed Type As, so the person doing the hiring—*hopefully*—is a good judge of personalities (and if not, my friends, *that* is what the working interview is for).

Fun Fact: The Type A personality is characterized by an aversion to wasting time, competitiveness, a tendency to be a workaholic, a high level of motivation, a strong dislike of failure, often feeling stressed out, and being very goal oriented.

My most outstanding office interview to date resulted in the amazing dental assisting job I had back in Lubbock, Texas. I went through the standard question-and-answer session with Dr. Grace and her dental partner, who co-owned the practice. Once they had decided to move forward with hiring me, a team member reached out and asked me to meet the back-office staff for breakfast at a nearby restaurant (just the assistants and hygienists—no dentists or front-office staff). This was genius! I was able to observe how my future colleagues behaved outside of work and consider how my personality would fit in with them (well, for the most part). It also allowed the staff to get the inside scoop on me to share with the dentists. I got the position, and it really was a great fit, until I eloped with a guy I barely knew and . . . well, you already know that story!

CHAPTER 36

I'd Like Sugar With That, Please

I answered the ad. You know, the one that oozes syrup because it is so sweet and asks you to be that overly accommodating person who thinks outside of the box. Now, if you spend some time getting to know me, you'll find that I'm as sweet as punch, unless I'm hangry or annoyed. When someone is super sweet to me right out of the gate, however, I usually find that they are hiding something. But I answered "that ad" for a dental office manager position, with additional front desk and assisting duties. Gulp. It was a mouthful just to say it. Why was I looking to become that last bit of jam from the bottom of the jar that you have to spread sooo thin to make it cover your piece of toast?

Thinking outside of the box in dentistry is appealing, but patients are typically looking for a certain consistency to help them feel comfortable with treatment. Going to the dentist is a necessary routine: you show up, you get your teeth cleaned, you have an exam, and you hope they won't find any cavities or tell you that you need any big treatments. It's insurance driven, meaning most patients want what their insurance will cover and nothing more. In other words, just the *free stuff*.

But let's get back to the ad. If you were to read it closely, you might have noticed a little "throw in" placed in fine print at the bottom, asking you to tell the employer your favorite ice cream flavor in the subject line of your reply email. This is a test. Those who reply without including their favorite ice cream flavor have already let on that they don't pay attention to the finer details and are weeded out as candidates. I have seen this instruction many times and know they aren't looking for my honest answer. They don't care what ice cream flavor I like best. The truth is I don't even eat ice cream. I am lactose sensitive, so ice cream and I are not friends. The years it took me to discover this left me not even wanting it, ever. And I have tried the ice cream alternatives, all of which fall short on the taste spectrum. So, my honest answer to "What is your favorite ice cream flavor?" is "None." But my pageant answer that I use on a job application is "Mint Chocolate Chip" or "My homemade Cinnamon Caramel Gelato." This shows a prospective employer that I pay attention to detail, that I am not plain vanilla (Which I am!), and that I might bring something yummy to the office one day.

Back to the ad. Shortly after responding, I received an email wanting to set up a preliminary phone interview ASAP. The phone call went well. We took turns listing our strengths, expectations, and wants. As I listened to this recent dental graduate's dream of the perfect dental office, I couldn't help thinking about the mountain he would have to climb. When you start out in dentistry, you really want to make a difference; but so often along the way, that fiery spirit you started with gets dampened: your employees have issues, your patients are demanding, giving care is wonderful but running a business is stressful, a global pandemic hits. This young guy was at the bottom of the mountain, just starting his climb.

I have met and interviewed with so many new dentists that start out proclaiming all the good they will do in the community and how they will give back. They plan to have an office that will be known for taking time with their patients. This one will donate a portion of their proceeds to local animal shelters. They will do volunteer dental work in their spare time. Their new office will take every insurance known to man. They will have TVs on the ceiling above every dental chair, in the waiting room, in the bathroom. They will give their practice a catchy name and get ready to make a difference. Through my many years in dentistry, I already know what the outcome of these "idealized" dental offices will often be. They will start out strong, but insurance wrangling and paperwork will soon cause them to drop the most difficult-to-work-with providers. They will try to carry on, but between negotiating with insurance and providing the lowest possible out-of-pocket rates, their bottom line for certain procedures will start to impact the chair time. Making less on each crown, for instance, will slowly push them to get the crown patients in and out of the chair faster. And so will begin the cycle of trying to increase the number of patients per chair, per day, in a mad dash to meet their financial goals (which include maintaining the office, equipment, staff, and all those community programs they wanted to support).

Donating to local charities is a nice idea, but when a new practice is struggling to build a patient following this may start to put a strain on the overhead. The fancy televisions, newly renovated offices, single-serve coffees, new patient welcome gifts (a mug), name brand toothbrushes/mini toothpaste/floss in a cute take-home bag, and warm blankets during treatment are all impressive, but they cost money. Those blankets will need to be washed every night and adding laundry duties to a staff member's already heavy workload is just another pound on an elephant's hind end. The new patient mugs, homecare kits, and coffee pods are all consumables and must constantly be reordered, so the costs keep adding up. And dazzling patients with these trinkets will not build your practice in the way that genuine and attentive care will. The dental homecare bag is plenty for any patient, along with sound advice for keeping their teeth in the best shape between appointments. But young dentists often think they must razzle dazzle new patients to gain a foothold. They think they must put a big ol' cherry on top of the sundae when they are just starting out, even if it means putting themselves and the practice they hope to build under financial strain from day one. Want some free advice? Keep it low and slow. Open your practice with good equipment and a caring attitude, welcome the community in and treat them right and they will come back. Pay your staff a fair wage and hold regular staff evaluations so there's hope they will get a raise. Don't overextend yourself, think long term, and treat your patients and staff with respect. That is how to build a practice. You're welcome.

But I digress. . . .

Getting back to the sticky sweet office interview I just landed, to keep their dreams alive, this practice will hire the least number of staff at minimal pay. The full workload, then, will not have enough shoulders to fall on with only two hires, one to run the front and one to assist in back.

And what exactly are those front and back-office duties, you ask? Let's take a look . . .

Dental Receptionist Duties (front office)

- Greeting and welcoming patients to the practice
- Scheduling, rescheduling, or cancelling appointments as needed
- Directing patients to complete informational forms/ gathering insurance information
- Preparing patients' charts or scanning information
- Updating patient records and documenting recent treatments and procedures
- Scheduling follow-up appointments and providing reminders
- Communicating with insurance providers to determine if patients are required to make co-payments
- Verifying methods of payment and collecting payments at time of treatment
- Performing general office duties, such as answering telephones, photocopying, filing, faxing, shredding
- Reconcile end of day and any other reports
- Make bank deposit slip for deposit
- Return phone calls in a timely manner
- Present treatment plans/ call for follow-up questions and scheduling
- Check patient quick-fill list to fill in canceled appointments
- Track lab cases and mail if needed
- Submit treatment plans for predetermination of benefits
- Prepare claim forms for patients with dental insurance/ organize supporting material for electronically submitted forms (such as radiographs or written narratives)
- Assist in resolution of problems with third-party payers
- Update patient medical history, HIPPA, patient photo
- Open and close office according to protocol
- Keep waiting room and restroom restocked and tidy. Restock coffee pods/ water

Dental Assistant Responsibilities (back office)

- Preparing patients for dental work/ discussing treatment plans
- Helping with infection control by sterilizing and disinfecting instruments, setting up instrument trays, preparing materials, and assisting with dental procedures
- Tracking lab cases & coordinating lab pick up or mailing
- Assisting dental hygienists with procedures when necessary
- Providing excellent patient care!
- Recording treatment information in patient records with follow up appointment noted & providing any needed referral information
- Exposing dental X-rays and caring for X-ray equipment
- Giving patients information on dental hygiene, oral health care, and plaque control programs
- Collecting and recording medical and dental histories and patient vital signs
- Providing postoperative instructions as directed by the dentist
- Caring for dental equipment, autoclave testing & cleaning, replace disposable suction traps, run hose cleaning solutions daily
- Doing office laundry, cleaning office (office refrigerator included)
- Taking preliminary impressions for study cast and occlusal registrations for mounting study casts for all patients
- Ordering dental supplies and maintaining dental equipment inventory
- Fabricating temporary restorations and custom trays/ surgical guides from preliminary impressions
- Pouring & trimming stone models
- Boxing impressions/ pouring up/ making record bases/ confirmation jigs
- Perform acrylic repairs/ replacing teeth in prosthesis
- Pick up housings in prosthesis/ check occlusion
- Placement of temporary soft liners and long-term liners
- Assist with implant procedures & prosthodontic procedures
- Crown and bridge procedures
- Resin and amalgam procedures (place sealants)
- Oral surgery procedures, including suture removal

My initial phone call with the dentist lasted ten minutes and ended with an agreement to meet in person a few days later.

I arrived at the interview my typical fifteen minutes early. COVID-19 was in full swing and keeping masks on our faces while in public was essential. I eagerly waited outside in the heat, with my mask on and a list of questions in my padfolio. At the appointed time, the young male dentist escorted me into the building and up the stairs to the interview area. His wife, the other half of the new practice and a recent dental graduate, was waiting with her computer churning. I could tell they were going to do a PowerPoint presentation to start things off. Yippee . . .

I am an off-the-cuff type of interviewee. I'll bring a list of questions to ask, but what I really want is to get to know your personality (and I strongly recommend that you try to get to know mine). Most interviewers I have encountered ask the stock ten questions and want to hear the stock ten answers. I've said it before and I'll say it again: In the dental field, you can teach virtually anyone how to execute the job of assistant or receptionist. What really makes a good team, is having personalities that mesh. Can we all just agree on this??? Trust me, you do *not* want to breed a culture of schoolyard infighting among your staff. Dental offices are too small, and life is just too damn short.

This interview lasted an hour with the female dentist methodically reading through her PowerPoint. I felt like I was in a workshop at a dental convention as she waded through slide after slide. She even gave me a handout so I could follow along!

When they asked if I had any questions, I pulled out my list. A look of surprise crept across both of their faces when they saw what I had prepared. It still amazes me that interviewers think the process of interviewing is one sided. OK, you've outlined your expectations, now here are mine. I know what I bring to the table.

We ran through my basic questions quickly. Office hours and days, how many staff, what insurances they were contracted with, what dental program is used, paper or paperless charts, what is the age of the typical patient. Then I threw out a few dazzlers to make them think. What makes an employee great? What makes them frustrated? How do you care for a scared patient? What is your office mission statement? How do you make staff feel appreciated?

The interview went well up to a point. I knew when I started to give honest answers, and not just the "pageant answers" they wanted to hear, that they were losing hope in me. No one wants to hear the truth. The TRUTH is that I have worked for some people who were not good people. I have worked for some life-changing and amazing people, as well. No one wants to hear about the people who were not good. If you ask me why I left a certain job and I give you my honest answer it might sound unbelievable, but that is what happened. Yet some interviewers try to insist that I am making that stuff up, because it ruins the sugary sweetness of the bubble they have created. When I stopped giving the pageant answers in this interview, I felt a shift in the room. Yes, I left an office after my boss's husband tried to choke me.

As we wrapped up, the female dentist handed me a five-page questionnaire to be filled out in my handwriting, scanned, and returned via email the next day.

How many hoops are you willing
to jump through? Are you OK with
a draining, demanding, and low
paying position in which you will
always feel like you are on stage? Okay,
then. Lights . . . camera . . . action!!

It was already late in the evening when I left the office. My family knew dinner would be a carry out meal. I went home and started on the handout to show I was the efficient type who finishes a task ahead of the deadline. With a chicken leg in one hand and a pen in the other, I filled out page after page. Checkboxes for every task under the sun. What is your physician's name? How many days were you out sick in the last two years? Education, certificate history, yada, yada, yada . . . Do we have permission to talk with your physician? *Hmmm, that one's new. Talk to my physician?!?* "We can't hire Joy because she has consistently been late in getting her annual PAP smear, this shows she cannot plan accordingly." I laughed.

Finally, I reached the section set aside for employment history, which included in capital letters: DO NOT SUBSTITUTE WITH A RESUME. Ugh. This one always annoys me because I have a nicely written resume with exactly this information. I also have twenty-nine years of employment history to cover. I regurgitated my resume into the employment history section. Next, they asked for three character references. I supplied this information. When I signed my name to authorize a background check, I thought I was done. I was just about to scan the questionnaire and it email back, when I turn the last page over and found four more questions that needed very detailed answers in paragraph form. Lord have mercy!

I'm to the point in my career where the testing portion of the interview can be a deal breaker. I excelled in my college classes and knew there would be a test at the end. That was the deal. I benefitted from the professors' knowledge and proved to them what I learned. But I just don't see a reason to be tested in writing for a position I already know will pay the minimum, while expecting me to handle a disproportionate number of duties.

I answered the last questions in detail, as required, then I scanned and emailed the pages back. I followed up the next morning with a pleasant text and hoped that I *wouldn't* get the position.

I was pulling up to my house after a short weekend getaway when I got the call. I let it go to voicemail, suspecting it was the female dentist from the "sugar sweet" dental office and that she would have something rehearsed to tell me about my application status. The voicemail was just as I expected: extremely polite, no emotion, well structured. No one speaks that way in real life. "We regret to inform you . . ." It's okay though; I'm not a scripted, fake, overly sweet person. I am someone who will genuinely talk to you from my heart, off the cuff, and with kindness. I may joke with you and pick on you for your haircut, but that's just who I am.

And that dental practice? Well, I see them post ads for assistants and receptionists every few weeks.

Quirks (Dr. & Dr. PowerPoint):
1. A long PowerPoint presentation at the interview? Umm, really . . .
2. Thinking outside of the box doesn't pull in patients, solid dentistry does.
3. The lowest pay for tap dancing all day for a startup practice. Naaaa, PASS!
4. The drive alone would take two hours of my life every day.
5. I just don't think our personalities and goals matched up.

Next Question

After months of filling in at dental offices in hopes that I would find a new dental home, I saw a job posting online for an assistant position in a periodontic specialty office and emailed them my resume. In the dental world, working for a specialist is ideal because typically the practice is not insurance driven. The patients have been referred by a general dentist because they have a need for treatment that is more advanced than the general dentist offers, and you don't have to fish for patients—they come to you.

Within minutes of emailing my resume, a call came in on my phone. It was the office manager. She had just seen my information pop into her inbox and was calling to say that the dentist would be in touch with me later that day. I was familiar with this specialty dentist and had been in contact with his office many times in the past to coordinate mutual patient care. Dr. Huntington and I had referred many patients to him. I recalled that when I first came to town, I sat next to him at a local hockey game. I am a very spirited person, and he is very docile. That evening at the hockey game, I picked on him a little bit because his socks did not match. He found no humor in my pointing this out, or that I thought it was funny. I personally wouldn't have been embarrassed if someone pointed out such a thing to me. I would have made a joke out of it, had a good laugh, and then moved on with my life. He, on the other hand, sat and stewed over my teasing for the rest of the game.

This made me a little leery about applying for the position because, as I had demonstrated at that hockey game, I am a bit much to be around at first. I was on a business trip with my husband when I received the late-night call from "Dr. DifferentSocks." We chatted for about twenty minutes. The first thing I said to him was that I knew he was a more introverted person, while I am full of energy and talk a lot. He thought that wouldn't be a bad thing and it might make his patients more comfortable since he wasn't a talker. We agreed on a day to meet face to face that would include introducing me to two other members of his staff.

Prior to the interview I looked over the office website and put together a list of questions. Many things on the site seemed odd for a dentist in his specialty area. I made a note to ask him about the wide range of procedures offered by his practice. As I've mentioned before, I have found that most prospective employers think an interview is one sided: *They* interview *you* to see if you will fit their needs. But a job is a relationship, and it's important to always go into a relationship with as much knowledge of the other person as possible. Remember, everyone has five things that annoy them in any relationship. You must find someone whose five things don't drive you crazy. A boss is no different.

The day of the interview I entered the office wearing my COVID-19 mandated mask. The receptionist welcomed me and instructed me to take a seat in the waiting room until she could spare a minute to chat. After several minutes, she came over to sit with me while an assistant breezed past to say only a quick hello, as she was managing a patient in the back. When the phone rang a few minutes later, the assistant rushed out to sit with me while the receptionist answered the phone. She started by asking me several questions at mile-a-minute speed, including how I would handle delays or interruptions caused by malfunctioning equipment—something that evidently happened often at the practice due to the dentist not wanting to invest in newer equipment. At just that moment she was called to the back to help another candidate who was doing a working interview. It appeared the X-ray machine the candidate was trying to use had just malfunctioned. The assistant's frustration was evident when she returned a few minutes later, looking like she was about to have a panic attack.

The office receptionist was super friendly; I would not hesitate to hire her if I ran an office. She answered my questions honestly, pointing out that the longest an employee had lasted in the position I was applying for was three years. I had already asked around and learned that Dr. DifferentSocks was known to be an odd, eccentric, demanding boss and a super micromanager. I quickly added up the facts in my head, removing points for old equipment, and three years was not a very long time for an employee to last in this position. Ideally, you want to hear the previous employees stayed much longer because they loved their job. I worked for Dr. Huntington for nine years and would have stayed forever had he not retired.

The workday was over, and the staff members quickly left for home. Soon after, Doctor emerged and gave me a tour of the office. I noted several things like ancient dental equipment, antique dental chairs, clutter on all the operatory counters, a blood pressure cuff laying on a counter next to a stethoscope (*yikes! I'm used to an automatic wrist blood pressure monitor*), tons of instruments strewn about in the sterilization room, and general clutter throughout the office. I must, however, give credit to the hygienist for her immaculately clean and organized room!

We returned to the waiting room, where we both sat down to chat through our N95 masks. At this point, I had been at the office for forty-five minutes. Dr. DifferentSocks had me fill out a quick questionnaire with about ten items on it, including: name, birthdate, social security number, why I would be a good fit for the office, and my all-time favorite, what is the lowest pay I would accept for the position. I wanted to tell him to add the ice cream question.

I think when a prospective employer asks the "What's the lowest I can pay you?" question—and most do ask that question—it's downright insulting. I have many talents and years of experience, so even if your practice doesn't use the full range of my skills, it shouldn't mean that I deserve a low (LOW) wage. You are hiring someone with advanced skills.

The interview went on for over two flipping hours, even though at the hour-and-a-half mark I asked, "Are there any more pressing questions? I need to be somewhere in a few minutes."

I understand that you are trying to get a handle on my thought process and get to know me, but I have given you every pageant answer in the book. There isn't anything we haven't discussed, and I always answer questions honestly and thoroughly, so . . . should we call it a night?

But the interview dragged on and I didn't have it in me to just get up and walk out. Next question please. . . . "What about this job do you think will be the most challenging?" If you are in my head the answer is, not falling asleep while you are talking. Look, my husband does this often. If I ask him for the time, he will build a watch. I JUST WANT THE SHORT ANSWER—WHAT TIME IS IT?

"Well, the most challenging thing would be the old school taking of blood pressure with the blood pressure cuff and stethoscope.

I just can't hear and see information accurately enough to take a blood pressure using those tools."

He looked at me like I just passed gas. Look buddy, the one on the wrist works just as well.

Next, he posed this question to me: "What kind of rewards do you need in a job?"

After giving it some thought, I answered. "Nothing is more rewarding than being appreciated. Some words of encouragement go a long way toward keeping me motivated, as well." To me, simply knowing that someone notices my hard work is important to me.

"So, you need to be petted all the time?"

Ummm . . . I would be an employee, Sir, not a dog.

I didn't want to be that person in the classroom who ask questions when everyone is ready to go home, but I was curious about his website. "So, I was looking at your website and the many procedures you do, which seemed extensive for someone in your specialty. *You do brain surgery?"* He laughed and said it was a generic website that he plugged information into when he opened the practice years ago, and that he had never bothered to look closely at it.

So, let me get this straight, you don't do brain surgery even though it says so on your website, and you've never bothered to remove that misleading tidbit?!?

Through the many questions he asked that evening, he felt the dental knowledge I shared was profound but pointed out that I wouldn't be using much of my skills in his practice because he basically did the same few things over and over. He didn't want to grow. This led him to express a concern about me not being challenged enough daily. I said I agreed, and added I was finding that to be a deciding factor throughout our interview.

After two full hours I slowly gathered my things and prepared to stand up and leave. I asked the final all-important question,

"How soon do you need someone and what does the position pay?" To my surprise, he blocked my attempt to get to the bottom line with, "I have two more pages of questions to get through before I'll answer that."

I'm taking deep breathes. I'm mentally in a field of flowers . . . I'm not annoyed.

You know that moment when you are out on a date and the other person does something that bumps your quirky and annoying meter up to ten things, so you mentally check out? At this point you know the relationship will be going no further . . .

In this interview, we were nearing that tipping point and Doctor's "two more pages" comment had just catapulted us way up and over the fence. I calmly closed my notebook, removed my reading glasses, and prepared to stand up and leave. He was taken aback, but flatly said that I would be expected on Thursday for a working interview, for which he would pay my lowest hourly rate.

"My schedule does not allow for me to be here this Thursday," I quickly shot back.

"Rearrange your schedule then," he snipped.

In my head I was not only thinking *no*, but a big ol' Texas, *"Hell, NO!"* With a smile under my mask and my keys in my hand I said, "I will call your receptionist first thing in the morning and let her know my schedule."

I worked for the most considerate, most polite boss for nine-plus years. I certainly was not about to lower my standards for a boss who couldn't even feign politeness in one interview. *Dear Dr. DifferentSocks, next time you might do better with, "Are you able to come in for a working interview on Thursday? No? What day might you be available?"*

I knew the position was an immediate fill and they were under the gun, but I am the captain of my ship; therefore, I am not told where I will be on a certain day. *Being treated with respect is a top priority for me in my life, dear Doctor. I'm sorry if that surprises you.*

The following morning I called just as the practice was opening. The receptionist answered with a pleasant but winded voice, I'm sure she had barely gotten in the door before my call. After introducing myself, I politely requested that she let the dentist know that, while I appreciated his time, I felt the position wouldn't be enough of a challenge for me, so I was declining the working interview. Well, at least the *receptionist* sounded disappointed by my decision! She complimented me on my skills and experience, added that she was sorry I wouldn't be joining their team, and wished me well.

My quirk-o-meter had been going off before my never-ending interview even wrapped up. My instincts were telling me to do a U-turn and head the other way. This wouldn't be the practice for me.

Quirks (Dr. DifferentSocks)

1. My accomplishments will never be noticed or acknowledged.
2. Very critical and bossy (my way or the highway).
3. Won't invest in updated office equipment (which makes everyone's job more difficult).
4. Disrespectful of my time (lives at the office and thinks I will too).
5. Inflexible and unapproachable. I'm not seeing any perks.

And the list went on from there.

CHAPTER 38

Dance, Monkey

If you think you are ready to get your foot in the door in the dental industry, be aware that there are many steps, skips, and jumps involved in landing a job. Really, it is not like interviewing in any other field. Knowing what to expect will help you to navigate the interview process, and with enough knowledge and a little luck on your side, you just might get that job . . . fingers crossed!

HOW TO FIND A JOB IN DENTISTRY (A STEP-BY-STEP GUIDE)

Part One: The Application Process

1. **Scour the internet for job postings.** I have used a few popular sites that are known to have legitimate postings for jobs. You must be careful. A fake posting will send you straight down a rabbit hole, then sell your information and you will start getting calls and texts for things you didn't know you needed: your car warranty has expired; we'll buy your house for cash; ocean

front property in Texas; Santa's elves need donations for the workshop; the IRS requests that you text back your bank information to avoid a penalty . . .

2. **After finding a posting for a dental job that might suit you, apply using your resume that shines a light on your skills and abilities.** Notice I did not say to send them your resume. Oh no, that would be too easy. Rather than sending them the resume you so painstakingly put together, you will instead type each and every word into *their* fill-in resume template and submit it through the application portal. This will take at least twenty minutes, likely more, and you will have to repeat this tedious task for each and every position you apply to. So, crack those knuckles and get ready to copy, paste, and type in all the many details of your career again and again. And again.

3. **But wait, there's more!** Did you think you were done? No, no, no . . . not even close! There very well might be a test, or TWO. The employer you are applying to may have paid extra to have an actual QUIZ pop up at this point in the game. You now have a three-minute timer ticking away as you answer multiple-choice or other types of questions on the site's testing page. *If Justin calls with a toothache, but can only make a Tuesday afternoon or Thursday morning appointment on months that have a "ber" in them, and his bus schedule says it takes thirty minutes to travel to the office, and he needs an hour appointment with thirty minutes of assistant time and thirty minutes of dentist time, but the dentist hunts in the colder months and is out on Thursdays, then where on this grid would you appoint the patient?*

4. **Whew, you scored well on the test!**

5. **Now, let's move on to the fine print that no one sees at the bottom of the application.** It will often ask you to describe "in a few sentences" why you are the best person for the job (AND request that you mention your favorite ice cream flavor) in a two-paragraph cover letter, to be sent in pdf form as an attachment to the office's email address. This one always gets me. Again, I am dairy sensitive, so I truly don't crave or eat any type of ice cream. But no one wants to hear about that. In fact, no prospective employer even cares what ice cream you prefer. This is just another little test to see if you pay attention to details and can follow simple directions. Does it make me sound fancy to say I make my own cinnamon vanilla gelato?

6. **Ready to hit SEND?** Hold on, another window just popped up with a few more questions. Really??? *List two or three dates and times when you are available for a phone interview. When can you start? How many years of dental experience do you have? Can you tie your shoes and chew bubble gum at the same time?!?*

7. **HIT SEND** (for real this time)

8. **Crickets** . . . Days, weeks, or months pass with no response to all to the amazing effort you put forth in applying for the position. You give up hope and eat a whole mini container of caramel swirl ice cream with chunks of waffle cone, then bloat up and feel miserable—remembering that, in fact, you don't even like ice cream.

It irritates me when I spend so much time answering these questions and taking these tests and the person can't even do me the courtesy of replying. A simple, "Hey bud, we received your application, but we want to pursue the most qualified *young* whippersnappers before we reach to the bottom of the barrel for someone like you who would, we hope, accept the absolute lowest pay possible," would be nice, right? And why am I at the bottom of the barrel when I have a wealth of experience? Well, you see, it goes like this . . . in the dental field I am seen as over the hill, opinionated, and difficult to train as a new hire. Maybe I'll croak in my assistant's chair or regularly miss work due to the medical issues that come along with getting older. Maybe I'll spend every day talking the dentist's ear off about my sciatica. Plus, younger folks have such picture perfect, pearly whites . . . and they will work for less money . . . and they are clay waiting to be molded . . . and they don't have ailments. So, this is why my chances are slim that any dentist will call me, unless their top picks don't pan out.

Young people take less money because typically they are fresh out of dental assisting school or high school—armed with a pocketful of dreams and desperate for work. Sure, they have white, shiny teeth because Mom and Dad paid to have "metal mouth bling" *(braces)* and dental care for their little pride and joy—and they don't have decades of coffee and wine stains built up on their choppers yet. I know that *you* as a dentist want to take credit for their dazzling smile, but the truth is, those choppers were already dazzling when you hired them. And from what I have personally observed, young people miss more workdays than I ever have in my entire career. When they are hungover, they call in with "food poisoning." (Yeah, from that liquid food they indulged in last night.) They get married. (Do you have no idea how many days off it takes to attend all those bridal showers and bachelorette parties? Not to mention the wedding and honeymoon!) And don't forget about babies. Little ones always seem to get sick at the most inconvenient times, leaving Mommy with no choice but to stay home—and then, of course, she ends up getting sick after all that exposure to germs! Me? I have missed four days in ten years. Two of them were because my brother passed away. I'm reliable; I'm responsible; I have a mean streak . . . *oh, ummm, I mean a mean work ethic;* I take my job seriously. But don't let that sway you. Don't take a chance on hard-working, little ol' me. Maybe you wouldn't know what to do with an employee who showed up on time every day like clockwork?!?

Back to the job-finding process:

Part Two: Landing a Job

1. **YOU GET THE CALL!** "We are interested in a phone interview. Let's set up a time."

2. **The phone interview.** This call will probably last between five and ten minutes. The goal is to find out the least amount of money you will accept and still work like a dog. Bing! Bing! Bing! They liked your answers. "We'd like to set up an in-person interview."

3. **The in-person interview.** You arrive at the office fifteen minutes early. If you are not early, you are late. You wear a solid color blouse with a sensible cardigan, slacks, and closed-toe shoes. Remember, no one wants to see your hairy toes, even if they are polished. And do not wear a white shirt! They will compare the white of your shirt to the white of your teeth. No one has shirt-white teeth, not even you young folks. Have a copy or two of your resume. Have your notebook with questions ready to ask. Prior to this in-person

interview, be sure to stalk the office on social media: Facebook, Instagram, or LinkedIn. (Look for social media site links on the practice's website and click on them, but also google to see what comes up, just as they will do for you—and read those google and Yelp reviews!!!)

4. **Your interviewer.** Know that the person interviewing you is likely worn out from interviewing candidate after candidate over the past many days or weeks—if not longer. The position may have had multiple turnovers recently, so the dentist and staff are most certainly just going through the motions by now, eyes glazed over in boredom—we're talking dead behind the eyes—as they rattle off questions to you and seem to only half listen to your answers. Don't take it personally. They will, however, be checking to see if you will fit in with their already established team, not be a threat or a drama queen, and pull your own weight . . . all for the least amount of money.

5. **Questions to ask.** You may interview with more than one person, and eventually with the dentist who owns the practice, but for now let's just talk about your initial interviewer. Hand them a copy of your resume and say, "I brought a copy of my resume for your reference." Ask your questions. They love questions. They want to see your energy and enthusiasm, after all you will be expected to establish a rapport with every patient who comes in. Example questions: *How many patients do you see in a typical day? What are the office hours? Are you contracted with any insurances? What are the main ones? Are you paperless? Do*

you have digital X-rays? *What dental program does your office use? Do you close for lunch? What color scrubs does the office wear?*

6. **"Tell me a little bit about yourself."** I guarantee they will ask you this question. This is a way of asking you to share information they can't legally ask for. They are hoping you will volunteer some details about your life. I like to jokingly lead with: "Well, I have five kids, a few medical issues that are still up in the air, and I'm hoping to marry my fifth baby daddy this summer, after he gets out of the clink. This fortune teller at the fair said we were meant to be together! And I love dentistry!" I like to know right off the bat if they appreciate my brand of humor or not. You may or may not want to follow in my footsteps here. It's up to you, but this is what works for me! Sometimes this serves to break the ice and we both relax a little. Other times I can see that this is not the way to go, so I act all serious. It's all about what feels right in the moment.

7. **"We'd like to set up a working interview."** Ah, the working interview. This is when you give up three to eight hours of your life to be a lab rat in an actual dental office. It's kind of like when zookeepers introduce a new animal into the habitat. They want to make sure it can coexist and play nice with all the other creatures before deciding if it's ready for the big league. They want to see if your resume lines up with the skills you claimed in your interview, and with how they run their office. I have found that some offices don't pay for this type of working "audition."

But they don't work for free, so I don't work for free. Speak up and ask what the rate of pay for the working interview will be. Have an amount in mind so you are prepared for this part of the discussion.

8. **The day of your working interview.** ARRIVE EARLY. Remember, if you are not early, you are late. Lint roll those scrubs before you leave the house. Pull your hair back and don't wear perfume. Arrive already knowing the entire inner workings of the office, right down to whether their toilet paper resides on a locked holder or not (and how to change a locked roll). You should intuitively know where the key to said locked holder is kept without having to ask. Questions can make you seem annoying. When they clap, you should **dance, monkey**! Somehow you should be able to guess their computer passwords, know how their dental program works, use the correct verbiage when answering the phones, be familiar with the dentist's preferred dental products and techniques, and appear to have worked in their office all your life. No pressure! At the end of the working interview they may say, "We will be in touch." Or maybe they will say, "Welcome to the team!" *Will you take $1.25 an hour?*

9. **"Welcome to the team!"** You did it! They offered you the job! Well, what are you going to do? Remember, this working interview was not only about the position they need to fill . . . it was also about whether or not you think the dentist has solid morals, performs skilled dentistry, respects the patients and staff, has a friendly staff, and if this is a place you can see yourself calling your "work home." If it's not a good fit for

you, and you choose to decline their offer, use the old *It's not you it's me,* adage. No need to burn bridges. "I like your office and you do amazing work, but I've decided to go in another direction."

10. **Or, if you decide to accept simply say, "When do I start???"**

You are off and running. Welcome to your new job! Just so you know, it will take a full year to learn the ropes and feel like you truly fit in. There will be days of struggle and you will find yourself reminiscing about former jobs where you felt more competent and knew all the inside jokes the staff keep telling each other. Don't worry about that. You *will* eventually settle in and become one of the team!

CHAPTER 39

─────────

Unsterile Sheryl

It was an unusually dreary and rainy spring morning as I drove to yet another working interview. Thankfully, this dental office was only ten minutes from my home. The office manager had asked for me to arrive at eight. I never know if I should be there at eight or my typical fifteen minutes early. I like to get the lay of the land and give them a chance to show me where things are, so I arrived early because that's how I roll. It was raining so hard that I couldn't make out which of the businesses, sitting all in a row in the office park, was the entrance to the practice, so I just made a beeline from my car to the general area in the front of the building. As we were still only in phase one of dental offices reopening after the COVID-19 shutdown, patients weren't yet allowed to sit in the waiting room. I tried to avoid getting drenched and wondered if the door would be unlocked as I approach it. Open! I thanked my lucky stars and rushed into the empty waiting room, anxious to escape the pelting rain before I became a soaked mess. I wandered through an open doorway that led to the back, trying to find someone and let them know I had arrived. I looked around

310

to see a few masked women darting away like little mice toward the back room, not one of them bothering to greet me or help me find the office manager. I wondered who they thought I was in my black scrubs and lab jacket with my name tag pinned to the left side. I continued through the office until I found another group of women, chatting through their masks with no apparent intention of greeting me or helping me out.

"Good morning!" I offered, "My name is Joy. I'm doing a dental assistant working interview today." I hoped that one of them would direct me to wherever the heck I was supposed to be.

"Oh, that has to be for the other side," said one of the women, her eyes fixed on mine which was helpful since I couldn't see her mouth. "Here, let me show you how to get there." She led me through the sterilization room to the other side of the dental office and indicated for me to continue down the hall. I thanked her and was on my way.

I would be "auditioning" for an assistant's position with a dentist we'll call "Dr. Aloof." I found his current assistant, Sheryl, busily setting up one of his two operatories. Sheryl was a tall, mature woman with wild, untamable curly hair. She appeared to be around my age, but looked like three miles of bad road, one might easily think she was much older. *Other assistant is my age: √Check. Maybe that means being "older" won't be a strike against me here.* She seemed a little frantic and impatient, unwilling to stop long enough to show me anything, so I just followed her around like a lost puppy, trying to ask questions.

"You know, you are the second working interview this week," she said flatly, clearly not in the mood for a repeat performance.

"You must get up really early to put on your makeup and do your hair," was another tidbit she threw at me.

I wanted to roll my eyes, but I slapped on my pageant-certified smiling eyes instead (knowing she couldn't see my actual smile under my mask) and just made the best of it. *Not my first two-step, Missy. Here comes the "why bother" talk . . . because most gal's don't take the time to get all prettied up if they are going to slap a mask on their face during work. I get it, but don't judge me because it makes me feel better to wear makeup.*

"I don't have time to get up and put on makeup or do my hair," Sheryl overshared. "I just roll out of bed. I'm not trying to impress anyone at work anyway."

I can see that, I said in my head, *but I bet you spackle it on when the weekend comes.*

In my opinion, it is important to show that you care about your appearance. This is my personal belief, and if I feel like slapping on some makeup and doing so makes me feel good, then I will continue to do so. Even in the aftermath of hurricanes that knock out my power for weeks, I still dabbed on some lipstick and pulled up my bootstraps to face the day.

The dental rooms were not organized, and the equipment appeared to have been around since the dawn of time. Despite the pandemic and subsequent regulations for medical and dental practices, none of the necessary protective barriers had been put into place. I noticed that this office was missing one of the most essential items: bottles of dental disinfectant spray. We had been ordered to spray it on all surfaces throughout the day and allow it to sit for at least three minutes before wiping the area down, to eliminate any viruses that might be lurking. This is standard protocol for dental offices, even without COVID. Dental disinfectant wipes were available, but they didn't allow for the same level of disinfection, and surely didn't help with every little surface that needed attention.

I asked about the daily office routine as I followed Sheryl from task to task. We soon discovered that we had a few things in common, including a family member of hers that lived near me. My heart skipped a beat when I realized who it was, but I kept my cool and didn't let on. It turned out that her "loved one" walked four or five dogs around my neighborhood every day, allowing them to do their business in any yard they pleased, including mine, and would only pick up the poo if she knew someone was watching. Years ago, I had approached her in the kindest way about cleaning up after her dogs, to which she replied, "It's God's fertilizer." *I bet if I put God's fertilizer on your lawn and YOU stepped in it, you wouldn't be thrilled!*

Then she proceeded to give me little "helpful tidbits" of advice for the flowers in my yard. [Insert sarcastic eye roll here.]

The office was cold enough to hang meat because Sheryl was having hot flashes. She told me all about her menopause, along with her other health issues. There were little fans blowing in both operatories. At least being fully masked, gloved up, and wearing a protective gown over my lab coat and scrubs kept me somewhat at a comfortable temperature.

Next, we explored the sterilization room, which was a disaster! If there was ever a place in need of a good scrubbing and tidying up, this was it. Sheryl showed her universal lack of precautions by not wearing any protective gear when she rummaged through instruments needing to be autoclaved. In fact, most of the day saw dear Sheryl without a mask or even a protective gown. Gloves? Nope. No gloves as she rifled through the instruments to be sterilized. Unbelievably gross! I just stood there judging her from safely behind my mask. It certainly highlighted my worries about the spread of the coronavirus and returning to work in the dental field. On top of this, those who did wear masks in this office only donned those thin surgical masks and did not change them between every patient. While this was somewhat typical prior to COVID-19, I would hope that with the onset of a worldwide pandemic the dentist would provide his staff with a new mask after every patient. Granted, the N95 masks were still difficult to come by, but to me that just meant even more effort was needed to keep the virus from spreading.

I offered my help many times as Sheryl navigated her morning and started to fall behind. Every offer was rejected, of course. As she seated a patient who needed his lower denture polished due to an acrylic lab repair that had left a sharp spot, she grabbed it from the patient using a paper towel in her gloveless hand and scurried off into the next operatory, with me trailing behind her. She then mindlessly placed the patient's denture directly on the countertop. *Fowl!* I thought. *At least place it on a paper towel.*

"He expects me to do, *everything*, and I'm so far behind! I still need to seat an emergency patient that has been waiting for a while," Sheryl huffed.

"I can polish the denture, I did work in a prosthodontist office for over nine years, and you can seat the next patient, or I can seat them. Whatever works best for you."

Not in any way implying you must work for a specialist to polish a denture, by the way. She smirked at me, handed over the denture (but not before I put on gloves) and left the room. I was using a slow-speed handpiece with a polishing stone when Dr. Aloof passed by the room. He stopped in the doorway and made a positive comment about my work, when Sheryl popped up behind him and said it was a project she had been working on that I had taken from her. *Ummm, that is not how I remember things going down, Sheryl.* Hand to God, I had asked her if polishing the denture was something I could help with, so she could seat the patient that had been waiting. But I didn't defend myself, I felt it best not to fan the fires Sheryl was lighting to cover her tracks.

On a positive note, at least the office was following the pre-screening protocol. Upon arrival at the office, a patient would call from their car and any necessary paperwork would be run out to them, when they were done filling everything out, they would call and let the front staff know and a staff member would run out and get it. A dental assistant would review the paperwork and then instruct the receptionist to call the patient and have them come in. Once inside, the patient would have their temperature taken with a no-contact digital forehead thermometer and they would answer a few screening questions. I observed Sheryl as she took a patient's temperature. She then held the temperature gun to show me that it was giving the reading in Celsius, which she converted to Fahrenheit using an app on her phone (unsterile). She admitted that she couldn't figure out how to make the digital thermometer give temperature readings in Fahrenheit. Later, I looked up how to make that switch and shared the information with her, which bought me nothing but a big old eye roll. So much for trying to help!

"Hey, I can do your patient's exam so you can go and do other things," I said in a desperate attempt to find something to do other than trailing around behind her all day.

Sheryl's response was, "Sure…whatever," and quick as a flash she pivoted and walked away from me.

Finally!

I chatted with the patient after taking their X-rays. The X-ray system was new to me, so I was truly punting. Dr. Aloof was very nice, but distant, as he corrected the X-rays that came up sideways on the monitor. I had tried to rotate them, but was afraid I might delete them, so I thought it best to just let the dentist see them as is. When in doubt, STOP.

As the morning progressed, I assisted Doctor with a few fillings. He wasn't as polite as Dr. Huntington. Instead of saying, "Suction, please," Dr. Aloof said, "PICK UP YOUR SUCTION." It's all in the delivery. Also, Dr. Aloof was the kind of dentist who didn't care if you felt a little twinge of pain when he administered your dental injection. Instead of using pre-numbing gel to help with the discomfort of the needle piercing the tissue, he took the minimalist approach and simply went to town with the injection. Double fisted at that. "Double fisted injections" mean he used both hands with his thumbs on the syringe plunger to quickly engage it down to give a fast shot. The result? Anesthetic blasts into the tissue, which can't expand fast enough, so it builds up pressure and hurts the patient. With Dr. Huntington, you literally never knew he gave you a shot until you felt an odd tingling in your jaw. He took great care to ensure that the topical anesthetic applied to the injection site had time to "soak in" and pre-numb the area before administering the shot. Dr. Aloof's fillings were done as quickly as possible and with a minimal amount of attention to detail; this stark contrast to my experience with Dr. Huntington left me feeling a bit disheartened about the standard of care I might witness going forward in my career. *If I am going to stay in dentistry,* I thought to myself, *then I am going to have to adjust my expectations. I may never work for a dentist like Dr. Huntington again.* This was a hard pill to swallow, but the reality was that once a person has seen and knows quality work, they just can't help but recognize quick, sloppy work.

The last patient I assisted with that morning had a toothache. I seated him and asked questions about his symptoms. He coughed the entire time I was questioning him and nearly hacked up a lung into a tissue. I was grateful for my mask! He then wadded up and launched that tissue through the air toward the trash can and missed. This office's open trash cans had already been worrying me, let alone having a patient toss a germ-ridden tissue through the air and miss the can (the tissue was now residing on the floor). If this virus could be transmitted so easily—as medical professionals and the CDC were describing every single day on the news—then the equation probably looked like this:

> A man coughing into the air + hacking up a lung into a tissue + propelling his germs into the air by carelessly throwing said tissue + said tissue landing on the floor where all its germs may now be picked up on our shoes and stamped all over the office and taken home with us = me feeling very concerned.

What if, behind this flimsy mask, I am already contracting this virus? What if I give it to my family? Unsterile Sheryl wasn't any help, either. She left numerous bur blocks (organizers that hold multiple in-mouth dental drilling instruments) on the counter and uncovered, rather than in sterilized autoclave packs, as is typical. She was also not wiping down dental chairs between patients, and she was neglecting a whole host of other safety precautions.

When my working interview ended, the office manager brought me to her desk to talk about the position. After a minute, Dr. Aloof walked in and nonchalantly welcomed me to the team! *Huh?!? Wait. When was I hired? Just now?* I politely declined, knowing that in my heart this wasn't the place for me. They were shocked, to say the least, but I just couldn't work in an office where the norm was to cut corners. It honestly felt good to walk away from this opportunity. I had to be true to myself. *I will find my forever office,* I thought as I walked out the door, *I just have to keep looking.*

Quirks (Dr. Aloof)

1. Bad vibes from staff from first moment in the office.
2. Doctor did not engage me in conversation, very cool and distant, which means he does not care who works for him. He's just looking for a pair of hands to pass him instruments.
3. Doctor is snappish when he needs something.
4. Sterilization! Sterilization! Sterilization! (or to be more accurate, a lack thereof)
5. Sheryl stabbed me in the back, and it wasn't even my first day yet. No thank you!

CHAPTER 40

Sweetheart

The COVID-19 lockdown slowed the dental world down for most of 2020. I did like every other person and used the extra time off to do home improvements.

As we neared the end of the stay-at-home order, I received a voice message from a dental office that I had applied to earlier in the year. This office was a little bit of a drive, but on a positive note to me, had a female dentist.

When I returned the call, I was put on hold and kept waiting as the person who answered was either busy on the other line or had more pressing work to attend to.

It's not like I had anything to do, but I was on hold for five minutes and I know this because I looked at my phone timer and decided I would hang up at the five-minute mark. I wanted to give the person who had taken my call and placed me on hold time to finish whatever else was going on without having my call blinking at her the whole time. About ten minutes later I called back, and the same person answered my call. She let me know how irritated she was that I hung up on her! She asked if we had gotten disconnected or if I had rudely hung up. I explained that I had only been trying to help. I wanted to give her time to finish whatever else was pulling her in another direction without worrying about me, so after five minutes had indeed hung up.

She quickly replied, "Oh, Sweetheart! You were not on hold for no five minutes, and I was speaking with the boss. When the boss calls, honey, you take that call and don't worry about the others."

Top Pet Peeve: Being called by a term of endearment by someone other than my beloved. I understand it's a southern thing. Stop it. It doesn't make me feel warm and fuzzy, just annoyed, Sweetie!

Out of the gate she was losing points with me and continued to do so for the next few minutes, until I thought about hanging up on her again! She had my resume in front of her and peppered me with all sorts of questions about my abilities. *Now, I'm not unfairly judging, but she had my information RIGHT IN FRONT OF HER, so why ask me questions about things that were clearly stated on my resume?*

"Can you take X-rays?"

It clearly states that I am highly proficient in digital X-rays *with a list of the associated computer programs I have used when taking said* X-rays. *So, the answer is YES!*

"Can you take alginate impressions?"

Again, it clearly states that I can do this, and on top of that I worked for a prosthodontist for over nine years. What do you think my days consisted of exactly? Sitting around playing solitaire?

She kinda floored me when she then asked if I needed to be "babysat" while working in the back. *Excuse me?!? As I stated before, I was Dr. Huntington's only assistant, and I worked a room by myself some days doing soft denture relines, recementing temporaries, and things I did not need the dentist to supervise. Plus, I am a responsible adult.*

"Why did you quit your last job with Dr. Huntington?"

He retired—as is clearly stated on my resume.

"Well," she insisted, "I googled it, and saw that he is still in practice." *Oh, yes! The internet full of only true facts.* I said, "Well, let me call him and ask if he has his license in Tennessee where he moved."

The phone interview wrapped up with her asking me the million-dollar question, "What was the least amount of money you would take for a full-time position?" That question drives me absolutely bonkers! I'm not giving you an estimate to paint your house, I'm wanting to be a valued employee.

So how did this one turn out? Well, she wanted to get as many resumes as possible and consider her options, and she might call me back, if I'm lucky.

I won't hold my breath.

CHAPTER 41

Catfished

Another day, another dental ad. I wasn't going to apply, but this dentist had never had an opening (at least not that I was aware of), since I moved to town two decades ago. Seeing her in various volunteer roles and knowing she was kind and professional, I decided to submit my application with a carefully crafted cover letter and hit send. Days passed without any word, so I assumed that I hadn't made the cut.

Then one day I was surprised to receive multiple calls from the office receptionist, inquiring about a potential interview. Before I had a chance to return her call, she left another message stating that they were anxious to schedule an in-person interview, and I should text the dentist directly to set something up. I quickly responded with several dates and times that worked for my availability, and the dentist called to confirm a date almost immediately. During our brief conversation, she mentioned that she was looking for an assistant and was thrilled that I applied for the position. I excitedly told her about our shared connections through dental events where we both volunteered, and how impressed I had always been by her enthusiasm and commitment to making a positive difference in our community. I added that I was grateful to get the chance to interview and possibly work with her.

Suddenly something felt off. There was an awkward pause on the phone and then she said,

---

Cue the creepy horror music . . .

"Oh, the position isn't to assist me. I have a new associate who is just out of the military and needs someone with experience to help him get accustomed to civilian dentistry."

You know that dream where you are trying to escape but you can't seem to get away? That's pretty much how I felt at this moment in our phone call. Like a bug frozen on the wall in the kitchen at 2:00 a.m., when the lights have just been switched on. Let me be clear: I had no idea that I was interviewing for a role that would require me to give advice to a new dentist on how to run a private dental practice, something that is often more draining than it is rewarding. It is exhausting to work with someone who doesn't understand how a private practice runs , in addition to helping them build a patient base from the ground up.

"Any chance you speak fluent Spanish?" she asked.

What?!? I don't even speak fluent English. I forget the names of things all day long and end up saying "thingy" or "doodad" or "whatchamacallit!"

In fact, I've been known to shout to my husband, "Honey, have you seen the thingy that scoops out soup with the long handle?!?"

With a sigh as he will slide open a kitchen drawer, hold up exhibit A and say, "We call this a ladle."

The meeting day arrived, and I'll be honest, I wasn't going to go. Interviews suck the life out of me. Since the beginning of the pandemic, I had spent more time at home than out in the world, and at this point going out seemed to require so much effort:

- You put on makeup and wear real, acceptable clothes.
- You sit in the middle of a room with a bright light shining on your made-up face.
- The "firing squad" starts shooting questions at you . . . "Tell me something about yourself."
"What do you like about dentistry?"
"What do you hate about dentistry?"
"What is your greatest strength/skill/superpower/ characteristic/flaw???"

So, I was going to cancel. I wasn't interested in helping a dentist build a practice from scratch. New practices take a lot of cheerful, perky, upbeat, fun people to get them off the ground. They require great thinkers but offer their staff low pay because the dentist doesn't yet have any patients. They sometimes push unnecessary treatment on patients to make a buck. This was absolutely the last type of situation I was interested in getting involved in. I went anyway.

———

Mask in hand, I walked up to the building fifteen minutes ahead of the appointed time. The all-female staff was already assembled in the waiting room and ready to chat with me. We all had our masks on, as this was now COVID Round II. I barely sat down before they hit me with their best questions, coming at me like the fire button on a video game.

"What part of dentistry do you like?" "Do you live near here?" "How long have you been an assistant?" "What procedures do you not like?" "Are you a team player?" "Do you throw rainbows and sunshine and glitter in all directions throughout the day?"

Then the staff exited and both dentists came in. First in line was the female dentist whom I admired and was disappointed not to be interviewing to work for. Trailing behind was her newly hired associate, let's call him "Dr. BoneDry." And the curtain lifted on yet another two-hour interview.

Now, I would gladly waltz in and assist a seasoned dentist with a solid reputation and a patient load that is steady and reliable. But when you work for a start-up practice you have to constantly dance like a monkey to show them you are worthy of being employed. And even when you prove yourself by doing everything that is asked of you and more, the dentist will still expect you to dance while balancing plates on your head. He is, after all, paying you to dazzle the patients so if his business isn't growing it's your fault.

Dr. BoneDry shared that he was looking for ways to grow his dental practice by gaining new patients in any and every way possible. He urged me to share my thoughts and ideas in this area. He wanted me to spill the beans, as they say, and reveal everything I had learned from all the successful practices I'd been a part of. *How did they make their money? What made them successful?* Oh, and he casually mentioned that he, and most of his patients, spoke fluent Spanish and hoped I would learn. And wanted ideas on how to use that skill to his advantage in the practice.

"Well, you speak Spanish, so I think you should advertise to the Spanish-speaking community," I offered.

I gave a short spiel with a few ideas. I already had more ideas swirling around in my mind . . . great ones . . . but I didn't want to just hand him my best suggestions for free on a silver platter.

They hired me on the spot. Or did they??? Well . . . maybe. Dr. Bonedry offered me the job, then the female dentist mumbled something to him, then they looked me over from across the room for what felt like a long while, and then we all shared a weird awkward moment. But the next thing I knew . . .

"Welcome to the team!" they exclaimed together. "When can you start?"

"Ummm, thanks," I said cautiously, "but I'd like to do a working interview first, just to make sure there aren't any skeletons in the closet."

With a perplexed look washing over his face, Dr. BoneDry blurted out, "What a great idea! I've never heard of that before!"

We discussed benefits and pay. After weighing the pros and cons of salaries and perks, I figured it was worth taking a chance and devote at least one day for their working interview. They informed me that one of them would be calling soon to set up a day for me to come in and work. *Looking forward to the test drive,* I thought to myself as I gathered my things and prepared to leave. *OK. Thanks. Bye.*

The next day I was out doing yard work when I received a call from their receptionist. My hummingbirds had returned, and my phone buzzed just as I was trying to put fresh food into their feeders, but I managed to answer the call. The gal on the other end of the line relayed that the dentists had decided to interview five other applicants and I wouldn't hear back one way or the other for another two weeks. *Have a great day. Click.*

What just happened?!?

I felt disoriented. After mentally preparing myself for this job—a position I had no intention of even considering until they offered it to me with decent pay (which had surprised me) and led to believe the job was mine to turn down—now they were backtracking on the offer?!? I was so confused. They hired me! I was the one who asked for a working interview to see how things flowed (which is always a good idea—for them and for me), and now they were *unhiring* me but keeping me on the back burner as the last resort? And to top it off, I gotta wait two weeks to find out which way the wind will blow?!?

I cried. Right then and there, with the container of humming-bird food still in my hand in the middle of my yard. I bawled like a baby. Big fat tears. I cried because I had put a lot of energy into that interview against my better judgement. I cried because I felt taken advantage of by people who couldn't make up their minds and were just stringing me along. Then I took a deep breath in, let it out, and got over it. I wiped my tears and thanked God for intervening and saving me from taking a job that I had known all along in my gut wasn't a good fit.

As my husband always says, "If it isn't a HELL, YES! Then it's a HELL, NO!"

I moved forward. Moved on. Went on about my rat killing, as they say. Enjoyed refilling my bird feeders for my precious birds. Continued to catch up on my yard work. I may or may not have created a plant jungle at my house. Yardwork is my therapy. Once, I planted every seed from every piece of fruit I ate over the course of an entire year. I have a tall avocado tree, a bunch of pineapple plants, a lemon tree, a lime tree, so many herbs, and even ginger. I compost, so a plant may grow in my garden without me planting a seed. I took a cooking class once and we used rosemary in the dish. The chef told us to take the remaining rosemary twigs home, score them (scratch the stems) and place in soil in a sunny area. I now have bushes of rosemary in many parts of my yard. Whenever I trim a bush or a plant, I literally shove the trimmings in the ground and watch them grow or offer them to my neighbors.

By this time in my job search, finding my self-worth outside of the typical dental job had become a goal of mine. I sought out new experiences and experimented with different activities to help me discover who I am beyond my career as a dental assistant or receptionist. This led me to watercolor painting, which has become a true passion of mine. Whenever I can, I make time to practice. I paint as often as possible to master the techniques. I even dream of starting my own little business selling original watercolor paintings, greeting cards, and stationery items. I wonder if it's time for a career change. But I still enjoy dentistry and continue to fill in as a dental assistant while searching for the elusive work-from-home gig, (like everyone else during COVID), but I never get a bite.

Then.....four days after the receptionist called to drop the bomb that I didn't have the job, the female dentist called me. She wanted me to do the working interview immediately and suggested the next day, "I will, of course, pay you for your working hours."

I hate being put on the spot. Remember the whole "you won't hear back from us for two weeks" nonsense?!? My life went on, I made plans. I mentally let the whole experience go. And now I was unexpectedly being asked to drop everything, to clear my entire next day, and rush over for the working interview that I thought was cancelled—and I had to make a split-second decision ON THE PHONE while she waited and listened for my reply. My heart was racing, and I couldn't even think of what my plans actually were for the next day, they would not come to mind, so I was just frozen with a blank mind, as she was waiting for my answer! Now, if I would just tell people, "Let me think about that. I'll get back to you . . ." or "No, that will not work for me . . ." then I would have the power to maneuver out of requests like this that don't follow my plans and cause me anxiety. But I haven't yet mastered the skill, so in this awkward moment, when I was being asked to immediately cancel my plans for the next day, I said yes.

"Oh good, we will look forward to seeing you bright and early!"

We hung up and I instantly felt my stress meter shoot straight up toward the sky. I'm a planner. I need time to make changes in my life.

The next day I arrive fifteen minutes early because, have you met me? *Here I am, again,* I thought. *Going through the motions of yet another working interview.* I walk in. The office is nice. The gal at the front desk pops up and shows me around (I never got past the waiting room when I came in for the interview). Everyone is very nice. Very southern nice.

Dr. BoneDry arrives and tells me that his entire patient base speaks only Spanish, and then he explains how we are going to get through the day. His very kind wife also speaks Spanish, so she will bring patients back from the waiting room and do all the conversing until Doctor enters the room. I will just silently assist when I'm needed. *Oh, really?? Just* assist. *No* talking. *Have you met me?!?*

I have no idea what is transpiring as the day goes on. I am thrown into a Spanish-speaking world, and I do not understand one word of what is being said. I am from West Texas and know some basic Spanish words related to Mexican food, along with some bad words. Now here I am with no way to communicate with any patient, which is eighty percent of why I love my job. And just to take it back to the old school days, this office still uses hard film for X-rays. Oh, yes, it is tons of fun to walk down memory lane and take an X-ray and wait ten minutes for it to develop. And it gets even better when, just as I get back with the X-ray he ordered, Doctor tells me to take an additional film of another area, which means another ten minutes. Good times. Glory days. I pre-fer the digital age. So, now we are running behind because the pa-tient was late and they had to complete seven pages of paperwork, and then the X-rays took twenty minutes. I can't understand a word of what is being said in the exam, so I just stare out the win-dow. *Why did I study French in high school?!? Spanish would have been a better option.*

When the day finally ends I am exhausted. My head is pound-ing was deciphering the hours of rapid-fire Spanish instructions from the dentist that have been flying at me all day: *Spanish, Spanish, Spanish . . . something to me in English (DO IT NOW) . . . Spanish, Spanish, Spanish . . . another directive fired at me . . . I'm dodging . . . I'm weaving . . . then I silently stare out the window as he and the patients chat in . . . Spanish, Spanish, Spanish . . . then English to me (DO IT NOW).* My back aches from standing all day in the operatory awaiting orders. And then . . . they do it again . . . they put me on the spot . . . they ask if I will come in again—TOMORROW—and somehow I hear myself saying, "Yes!"

Here's the thing. And it's a moral thing. He was a nice enough person, but he was bending the rules a tad on certain dental pro-cedures. For example, many of the patients we saw that day had not received dental care in their lifetime, leading to the presence of periodontal issues (their gums were jacked up) and an epic amount of hard calculus buildup on their teeth, way deep down under the gums. As a result, a more aggressive cleaning is necessary, one that would involve administering local anesthesia (to numb up the area) to ensure the procedure is pain free. A dental hand scaler or probably an ultrasonic scaler needs to be used subgingi-val (below the gumline) to remove deep down calculus deposits. On an X-ray these look like little stickers attached to the teeth, and you can cause further damage to both the bone and gums if the deposits are not properly removed. After he quickly scaled the surface tartar buildup he would have me rinse their mouth and then he would sit them up in the dental chair and dismiss them. I offered, as is typical with a cleaning, to use prophy paste and floss their teeth which would have polished and cleaned each tooth, but he said no. Morally, ethically, fundamentally, this was wrong on so many levels.

After a restless night of tossing and turning, I went back for my second daylong working interview, feeling slightly more prepared for the day ahead. I was still reeling from the contrast between Dr. BoneDry's passionate preaching about ethical dentistry that he stressed during the initial interview and his actual practices. When I got home the previous day, I spent some time contacting several of my dentist friends to ask them about some of the procedures I had observed and assisted with.

"*I mean it's not illegal, but ethically it's just not done,*" they all said.

My second day began much like my first: Dr. Bonedry barked orders at me "Hand me this." "Do it this way." He expected me to immediately catch on and know exactly how he wanted things done. During every procedure he raised his voice and snapped, "Dry the field . . . bone dry . . . BONE DRY . . . **BONE DRY**!!!" In my head I shouted right back: *I HEARD YOU THE FIRST TIME!! THE FIELD IS BONE DRY! It doesn't get any drier!!* To top, I'm annoying him as his long spider legs bumped into mine over and over as I tried to assist him. It's like stepping on the feet of your new dance partner.

This was in stark contrast to Dr. Huntington, who always spoke so politely and showed impeccable manners toward his patients as well as me. It felt odd to be assisting and not get so much as a "please" or "thank you." At lunch time he was friendly and seemed to think everything was just hunky-dory between us. We even shared a table in the break room. As we sat chatting, he mentioned almost apologetically that he knew he said "please" and "thank you" to me way too much, but he wanted me to know that he appreciated my help. I stared at him and wondered if maybe he had said it in Spanish? Honestly, he never said those words out loud to me even once on either day. I'm probably just being overly sensitive. Or maybe I'm hard of hearing. That must be it.

I do some lab work using the sparse dental tools and materials available to me to create a hard splint. These are appliances made to fit over your teeth to keep your from wearing away your enamel when you grind your teeth at night. Dr. BoneDry later brings me a broken model with a splint that I created, pointing out that there is room for improvement. I agree, admitting that it was due to a lack of access to a handpiece with a lab bur capable of cutting off the hard plastic from the model without breaking it. He reluctantly accepts my assessment, and we move on. This is another moral issue. He proposes doing this splint for all patients and charging a stupid, crazy fee. It's easy money. I would take a quick upper alginate impression and make the splint. I'm fine with that part, but he doesn't adjust occlusion (bite) and you can really jack someone's TMJ up. (jaw hinge that sometimes makes a cracking noise if you open to wide) And the price he wants to charge is seriously exorbitant!

After lunch we had an emergency patient, but since I don't understand Spanish, I had no idea what was going on. I looked out the window. I wanted to ask what Doctor was planning, but I had been told to be quiet (no talking) while he's with a patient. I could see by now that he was the type who believed a woman should be submissive and wait for the next command. That's a word no one would use to describe me. So, when he abruptly stopped talking in Spanish and looked at me with surprise in his eyes, I just stared at him.

"Where is the anesthetic?" he asked firmly.

"I don't have it ready. I thought this was only an exam."

"We are doing a filling, get it ready."

Had I understood the language they were speaking, I would have known that he offered to do a filling for the patient. I hate not being prepared. And now he was being short with me because I hadn't magically prepped for a procedure he only spoke about *in Spanish.*

At the end of the long day of patient care and doing many tasks around the office, Dr. BoneDry and I had a chat. He confessed that he was afraid that I was judging his fillings against Dr. Huntington. "No, no," I heard myself say, "you do good work." (I mean if we are being honest, he does nice fillings. I wouldn't deny him that.) Dr. Huntington did amazing artistic dentistry. But that's not what has me on the fence about accepting the position. It's all the little things. There was a laundry list of intolerable quirks, so that was the bottom line.

Quirks (Dr. BoneDry)

1. I don't speak Spanish and it's hard not to hear much English other than "DRY THE FIELD!"

2. Doctor's long spider legs nail me in the calves/knees when he pulls his chair up and leans in to start working on a patient.

3. Dry the field! DRY THE FIELD!! *BONE DRY!!!!*

4. I didn't want this job in the first place. I am not listening to my gut.

5. Doctor cuts corners in treatment, which is a disservice to the patients who put their trust in him and expect to receive proper, ethical dental care.

6. Wants me to be submissive and not talk in the operatory or while he is with a patient. Me . . . not talk.

7. Doctor constantly zips around and rushes during his procedures, as if he's two hours behind when he is not.
8. Treating me like I should know what he wants, as if we have worked together for years, and it's only day two.
9. Hard X-rays from the olden days.

Oh wait, I've gone past five things. Way past. And the list could be even longer. I was trying to justify the good pay and finally landing a job in a reputable office after job hunting for so long. *But the reputation belongs to the female dentist—the one who established the practice and the one I had hoped to work for when this whole fiasco started—not to this new guy. But maybe I'm being too sensitive? But the pay is good. But could I really do this job? Could I really work here day in and day out?!?*

As the female dentist prepared herself to leave for the day, she asked me how many hours I had worked over the two days. I told her I had them written down and would add them up, "Let me get the paper . . ."

She clapped back impatiently, "Better hurry if you want to get paid." in a tone I had not previously heard from her. I shrugged it off as I quickly looked over my hours. *It's the end of the day and maybe she's got plans.*

I gave her the total hours. She wrote out a check, handed it to me, and out the door she went. When I glanced at the amount a wave of disappointment hit me. It was for half of the agreed-upon amount. Half. I didn't work half as hard. I always gave it my all.

I grabbed my belongings and wished everyone a good night. Out the door I went just as the tears started streaming. *Here I go again . . . crying.*

Once I took part in a wilderness emergency training course and when it came time to role play, I was to come upon a person who lay dying in a building that was about to collapse. Despite the danger, I went in alone, which is a no-no, and sat with him as he was in character groaning and "dying." Tears began to stream down my face as I was overcome by emotion. Later when we were debriefing, the team leader said, "You know what, sometimes all you can do is sit with the person and cry."

The next day my phone rings and I was expecting to hear the generic "Sorry, we've decided to go in a different direction," but instead it's Dr. BoneDry with an offer for me to join his team. Is this now the third time? He was excited to learn all the great ideas I have for growing his practice and wanted us to have an open and honest dialogue. When people say this, they don't mean they want you to be brutally honest. They want a pageant type of honest.

So . . . drumroll . . . he has a question for me.

"What went through your mind during that filling procedure when I pointed out how to use the bendable micro brush?

"Well," I said laughing, "honestly, I thought you were being a "*princess.*"

I could hear the unmistakable sound of discomfort on the other end of the conversation. I chuckled nervously, trying to lighten the mood. He wasn't expecting that HONEST answer.

I didn't bend the end of the micro brush at two of the marks, only at one. I couldn't believe it when he stopped the filling procedure to show me how to "properly" bend a micro brush. He spoke to me slowly holding the little micro brush in front of my face, using exaggerated hand motions, to demonstrated how to bend it in two places, acting as if I were a child that didn't understand what he was saying. Was this how he was going to communicate with me? I knew that he could detect the combination of irritation and in my facial expression even though my face was largely hidden behind a mask.

If I would have said to Dr. Extraction, who has a jovial personality, that he was acting like a princess, he would have showed up to work in a princess dress over his scrubs with a jeweled tiara balance on his head. Having a scepter in one hand he would announce in a mighty voice: "If I am to be mistaken for a princess, then so be it!" as he strutted around the office, making sure everyone was aware of his newfound royalty.

For the record, I didn't agree to taking the job before we hung up.

That weekend, I was at a busy, loud restaurant when the female dentist called. Her message went to voice mail, as she very matter-of-factly explained that she and the male dentist had prayed on whether I was the right fit for the job and . . . wait for it . . . they have decided I am NOT. They retract their job offer, once again.

After a few minutes of feeling sorry for myself, I decided that it was probably best if they hadn't hired me anyway. That doesn't mean my feelings weren't hurt though. She also was aghast at her error of not paying me my full wages and reassured me that a check was in the mail. I knew that about her, she's a very highly respected dentist, I hate that I doubted her for a moment.

CHAPTER 42

Aging Out in Dentistry

As a young dental assistant just starting out in the field, I was eighteen and ready to set the world on fire. I wanted to help patients understand how to care for their teeth. "SAVE THE TEETH!" was my motto. I had a burning desire to make a difference. I discovered that I love teeth and realized they are the doorway to the health of our entire bodies. Having a healthy mouth can push you light years ahead in terms of longevity and overall well-being.

After thirty-one years of being in the dental field, as I approach the age of fifty, I still like teeth, but I don't love them anymore. It's not the teeth. It's me. I've changed. I lost that burning desire to educate everyone about dentistry when people stopped caring about what I had to say. Heck, I can't even get my adult kid to floss daily (but he does brush at least twice, I think). Dentistry has changed as dental schools have increasingly infused how to make a dollar into the curriculum (or in the dental world, thousands of dollars), side by side with the clinical training. Maximize earnings. Chair potential. The overall mindset seems to have shifted from "What's best for the patient . . ." to "What's best for the overhead . . ."

I'm facing age discrimination at my interviews. On paper, I have too much experience for the fifteen dollars per hour most dental offices want to pay. My son, without a degree, walked into a big sports and outdoors chain store, got a job, and started at fifteen dollars per hour. His first review took place three months later and included a raise.

Recently, a specialty dentist reached out to me on a social media platform. His office manager was planning to leave in a few months, and with my reputation he thought I would be perfect for the position. We arranged a phone call at a suitable time so we could discuss the details further. After only a few minutes of chatting, the dentist blatantly asked for my age.

Laughing, I said, "You can't ask that!"

"Well, I'll see it when you fill out the employee paperwork, don't you think?"

"I'm fifty," I admitted, hearing myself say "fifty" like it was a bad word.

"Oh, I had no idea you were that old. You don't look it. That's too old for this position. I don't like turnover and want someone younger," he said, and then abruptly ended our conversation.

Experiences like this have become all too familiar to me as I've shifted from being employed to job hunting in the dental field. In person, I strive to give the impression that I would make an outstanding employee. I carefully craft my words and demonstrate that my skills are relevant and well suited for the job. I know my stuff. My interviewers are generally friendly and smiling—until we get to my bottom line and discuss wages. All too often, it seems that dental practices want to offer me far less than what is deserved for my hard work and experience; it saddens me when they attempt to use me like a coupon—grilling me for my business expertise while paying me the lowest wage for dental assisting. I'm full price. No sales. No coupons.

The evolution of a dental assistant typically goes like this: If you "grow" with a practice (stay for many years, maybe your whole career), you start out in the back as a dental assistant. As you mature you are typically moved up front. It's the natural progression of a dental office. And if you step out of the stream, you lose your place. No savesies. No picking up right where you left off. The dental industry is a flowing river, ever moving and changing.

After more than a year of interviewing without finding a fitting dental office home, I see myself going back to my old tried-and-true approach while prepping for interviews: pulled-back hair, well-kept short fingernails, light makeup, never a white shirt, and we all know my rule about the shoes! Every piece of my presentation ritual is meant to send a message, and I want to leave no stone unturned.

1. Pulling my hair back is to show that I would never let my hair dangle in a patient's face.
2. Short nails convey that I know better than to jab at a patient's delicate gums with my nails while I am rooting around in their mouth.
3. Minimal makeup, so it looks like I care about my appearance to a patient who is studying my face (well, my eyes, which is all they see due to masking) just inches from theirs for hours at a time.
4. The white shirt is a faux pas to be avoided because in this day and age of obsessive teeth whitening, your interviewer will subconsciously compare your teeth with the white of your shirt. The teeth will always

lose. No one has shirt-white teeth. Oh! And ladies, if you want your teeth to appear whiter than they are, wear a red shade of lipstick. You're welcome.

I have yet another interview today. It feels like dating. Hi, my name is Joy. These are the things I can bring to this relationship. These are my deal breakers.

CHAPTER 43

Sunshine and Roses

I was definitely taken by surprise when one day I received a phone call saying I was in the running for an office manager position at a startup specialty dental office. Root canals ugh. I had applied some two months prior and had not even given two more thoughts to it. As COVID-19 was still in full bloom, my next step in the process would be a phone interview.

After speaking at length with the hiring manager and the dentist's wife, we all agreed that I would come in for a working interview. Remember how popular these are in the dental field? Even the coronavirus could not stop them.

I really don't care to work on Fridays—I mean, who does, really?—but I agreed to come in for an *unpaid "sit and chat"* interview on a Friday and stay up front with the hiring manager for a few hours to see if the stars would align between us. The office location was ideal for me, just a short drive from my house.

I put on some scrubs, pulled my hair into a ponytail, placed my name tag above my upper left pocket, and off I went. Up to this point I had declined job offers at some fourteen offices. I am just at a point in my life where I know my worth. It was beginning to feel like working interviews were my full-time job. Upon entering the office, I noticed that the walls were painted in one of my favorite colors, seafoam green. I wondered if this was a sign. The office was new, clean, and didn't yet smell like dentistry. I quickly saw the reason was because there was a scented plug placed in literally every outlet. *Nice touch*, I thought, *but I can't breathe!* (Turns out you *can* have too much of a good thing!) The hiring manager was so very, much younger than me (YIKES!!), but we hit it off immediately, talking about the neighborhood and dental topics in general. My first impression of her, however, was that she had a habit of trash talking other staff members. If there's one thing I have learned, it's that if people talk bad about others, they will talk bad about you. I made a mental note of this. The hours went by, and to my relief things went quite smoothly. Soon enough it was time to go home. Before leaving, I took a minute to pop by the endodontist office to introduce myself and tell him he had a nice practice. He looked up from his computer and said with a sarcastic tone, "So, it will do?" I froze for a second, not sure how to take his comment, but then I just smiled and said I had enjoyed my time spent there. He didn't say another thing. I left feeling a bit of uncertainty. Was that exchange with my protentional boss a sign of what was to come? I can be overly sensitive, so I wasn't sure if I should be worried about that little glimpse into my prospective boss's personality. *Naaaa....It's too early to tell, I thought.* Plus, it's not like I had the job.

The hiring manager gave me the standard, "We'll call to let you know . . ." speech, and I was out the door. I didn't necessarily have warm fuzzy feelings about the office, but I tried to keep my expectations in check.

Two days later I got the call. I was offered the job! And just like that, I stepped into the role of "office manager." I would be involved in helping them open and get word out for a referral based (meaning the referring dentist didn't want to do the root canal) endodontic practice—an extension of the two practices the dentist already owned and operated in towns nearby.

My first day on the job was like making a sentence out of a bowl of alphabet soup. With a steaming side dish of confusion. Almost immediately I dubbed my new boss "Dr. ASAP." He ran around the office constantly on the move from one task to another, he seemed to be in a hurry, like his hair was on fire and he was trying to put it out by passing through the office quickly. (And you know I can't react well to bosses on fire!) To each staff member, he would throw a list at each of us daily, as he breezed by on his way to something that was urgently calling to him

He brought in an office manager from one of his other locations to train me, Gabby. Gabby's presence was far from comforting. She seemed quite nervous, and I couldn't help but notice that she appeared visibly shaken whenever Dr. A. was near her. Gabby told me that on many occasions Dr. A. had made her cry, and the office manager at his third location would say the same. Oh, how I hate when the red flags start popping up so early on in a new job! I tried not to be overly sensitive toward her tales. Maybe she was thrown off by Doctor's gruff manner? I filed it away. It was too early to tell.

Gabby, who was in her mid-twenties, sat beside me for several days as she trained me on the software programs the office used. The programs were pretty basic, but the verbiage the practice wanted me use when entering information was a challenge: slash marks, specialized punctuation, symbols and an array of abbreviations made it a nightmare—it was all absolutely ridiculous. Gabby seemed far more concerned with her phone, scrolling through social media apps, getting lost in little dramas playing out across her screen then training me. It was little teenage-type drama after little drama. One morning she accidently "liked" a photo of an ex-boy-friend's ex-girlfriend, then she "unliked" it, then she spent hours trying to determine if anyone had seen or commented on her care-less click. Over the course of our time together she shared a *lot* of details about her life, from various online accounts and guys she had met through them, to juggling her job, training me, and par-enting responsibilities. The stories were often long-winded and intricate, but I listened patiently, while trying to get her to explain the systems and the office manager position to me— taking down notes. I knew my boss and the senior office manager were expect-ing Gabby to fully train me. In order to stay in her good graces, I shared a few personal tidbits from my own life, but I noticed that she only half listened when it was my turn to talk.

The office had already been in a "soft launch" for several months—open only for patients who could self-pay (no insurance) or pre-pay (pay up front, then the office would bill their insurance and reimburse the patient later). This was the office's way of initiating cash flow at the new location while building up the practice.

The soft launch also gave me time to experience certain aspects of the day-to-day operations. During this time, I noticed one ma-jor quirk: the senior office manager had the ability to tap into my computer from a remote location, and take control of my screen, overriding whatever I was currently seeing on my computer screen. I might be in the middle of scanning an insurance card or input-ting information for a patient, when suddenly my computer would freeze, and I would see the screen change and the cursor move to the folder or program she needed to work in. This was SUPER frustrat-ing, and in the midst of a busy day, this was very inefficient. And if that wasn't bad enough, she seemed to have taken it upon herself to "tidy up" my daily schedules by deleting notes I jotted down to remind me of important things pertaining to patient appointments. What's worse is that she would replace my words with her own cryptic acronyms and symbols; abbreviations familiar only to her.

One day I was at the office alone, catching up on work and answering phones, when I noticed five large boxes, each about the size of a coffin, stacked in the back room along with six smaller boxes. I didn't feel it was my place to nose through the many boxes and assumed it was something Dr. A. ordered and would deal with them when he was back in the office. Heck no! He got all twisted because it was "my office and my responsibility," I should have known without being told and taken "initiative" to figure out what was in the oversize boxes. Well, I didn't and here we are... Each "coffin" held four individually boxed, seafoam green coffee makers—matched to the office colors—twenty of them in all. Our office would be giving them to the general dentists in town who had referred patients to our practice over the previous three months. Doctor went on to say that I also should have known to make gift bags from the contents of the smaller boxes—coffee cups, coffee pods, etc.—to go with each coffee maker (not that any actual gift *bags* had come with the shipment). Oh, and why didn't I have a mapped-out route of the dental offices to efficiently deliver the gifts with the newly hired endodontist??! I must say I resented being reprimanded for not completing a task that had not yet been assigned to me. It felt like a mountain of work for one day but toughen up Buttercup we have work to do!

Doctor's wife dropped off gift bags and supplies and I quickly began organizing the items into the gift bags as I prepared to play Santa and deliver the coffee makers to so many general dentists in town, many of which I knew. I went through the previous quarter's schedule, placing marks by dentist's names who had referred patients to our new endodontic practice. I looked up each office's address and confirmed their office hours. I made a list of areas where the offices were located and mapped out a day and a half of deliveries to take place with the new female dentist Dr. A. had just brought on. I had only just met her briefly. She was fresh out of endodontic school and married with two little children. During our coffee-maker delivery tour I would find that she was very peppy and ambitious, and mentally dub her "Dr. Eager."

We drove around for two days, visiting seventeen different dental offices around town, delivering thank you gifts and introducing Dr. Eager. I had worked in many of the offices on a fill-in basis or had been affiliated with the dentist in some way over the years. No matter where we went I was warmly welcomed with many of the dentists and staff knowing that I had been selective about taking a forever job. My working for Dr. ASAP reflected on his practice and let these general dentists know that I stood behind his work, which I had now seen first-hand for many weeks. Even though I had not seen the level of care offered by Dr. Eager, as she was starting out, but I assured each practice that their patients would be well taken care of and promptly scheduled. This was a huge promise to make as most endodontic practices in the area were scheduling out weeks or even months in advance.

Fast forward to a week later, Dr. Eager's official first day. Chaos seemed to reign supreme. Dr. ASAP was not seeing patients that day but came in and hung around "just to smooth out any issues that might come up," which threw many monkey wrenches into the mix because of course he couldn't keep himself from pestering the staff with tasks all day long. On top of this we had an important piece of new equipment coming in. Why they chose that day for an expensive X-ray machine called a CBCT to be installed, I will never know. Technicians were coming and going, and a large area of the office was obstructed while they completed their task. A rep from the company was there to train staff on the machine, but we did not yet have a permanent staff hired at the office. The assistant in the back and Gabby were borrowed from Dr. ASAP's other locations that didn't yet have a CBCT. Therefore, I was told I would need to learn to use the machine and train all future staff. No problem, I told Dr. ASAP, as I am X-ray certified. Meanwhile the phone was ringing off the hook with word that Dr. Eager took almost every insurance—information that was premature for the general public because, unfortunately, it takes months to be credentialed by even one insurer and having to explain that to almost every caller takes time. I was trying to keep my word on prioritizing referred patients, get trained on the CBCT machine, and check patients in and out of in the office. Meanwhile, I was still being trained in my position. Gabby was no help on this day from hell. She just rolled her chair out of the way and said it was all up to me, then went back to scrolling through her social media accounts. The phones were ringing, patients were entering the office and needing paperwork, patients that had been seen were needing checked out, the X-ray installer needed a flashlight, the X-ray rep wanted to train me, and my computer was constantly being frozen by the senior office manager. UGH!!!!

Then, out of nowhere, a prospective dental assistant appeared and announced to me that she had come in for a working interview. She was young, upbeat, pretty, and petite. Out of his office popped Dr. ASAP to giggle and flirt with her! Now let me be clear, this man rarely demonstrated much of a personality, and he was certainly *never* outgoing. He hardly ever talked to me, but here he was getting giggly with this young gal.

Doctor: "Sara, do you have any pets?"

Working Interview: "I do! I have a dog!"

Doctor: "A dog! I love dogs! What breed?"

Working Interview, blinking her pretty eyes in Doctor's direction: "Oh, he's a mutt, I saved him from the pound!"

Doctor, with a flirty giggle: "You saved a dog from the pound? Who rescued who, huh?"

I was standing right next to them during this exchange and piped up with a little laugh and some old-fashioned ribbing due to Doctor's grammatical faux pas.

"Actually, that should be, 'Who rescued *whom*.'" I said cheekily, expecting them both to laugh and continue carrying on as they had been.

Crickets. Doctor's piercing eyes conveyed the message loud and clear, I had no place in the conversation.

Quirk Alert: Moody dentist. Runs hot and cold. Doesn't get my humor.

I stayed out of their way during the rest of Working Interview's short visit, which hardly involved any actual working—it was all giggles and glitter. She excitedly told me she was going to give notice at her present job and start in the back in two weeks, working head-to-head and knee-to-knee with Dr. ASAP. *Giggle...giggle.* I wondered how she got so far along in the hiring process without knowing that she would actually be working with Dr. Eager. Oh darn, all that flirting for nothing. I thought about leveling with her, but then I decided to let her be surprised.

I'll cut to the chase here: I lasted four months at this office. The giggle box never made it to work, so an older dental assistant,(nickname: "Ms. Bossy Britches"), from one of Dr. A's other offices, who was a thorn in my side, assisted. This assistant had wanted to be office manager, but was denied and unfortunately for me, I was stuck with her while we waited for a warm body to assist. Literally, no one applied.

In the weeks while we waited for a new assistant, Bossy Britches would constantly criticize and nitpick how I did things and give her input on how things should be done at the front desk. She wanted things upfront done her way and pointed out "helpful" advice every day she was there. She was quick to add the ways the office operated in a "not so legal" manner and that she had expressed this to Dr. A. and the senior office manager many times. No one seemed to notice or mind that, despite having been a dental assistant for six years, she still didn't have her certificate to take X-rays in the state of Florida (and yet she was doing so every workday). Our work relationship reached a high level of irritation, and I reached out to the senior office manager with my concerns about Bossy Britches. Instead of lending me a sympathetic ear, however, I was told not to stir up trouble. Then (in the interest of not stirring up trouble) she texted a recap of my complaints *to Bossy Britches*, on a day when she and I were alone in the office. SO...MUCH...DRAMA. Nothing I couldn't handle, but not a fun day by any means. *(Honey, I've been chased around a reception desk by someone who was trying to get his hands around my throat. You don't scare me!)*

Along came a day when we were unable to get a fill-in dental assistant or any additional help. I agreed to help Dr. Eager with her new patient evaluations in addition to my duties in the front office. Sometimes when you have experience in multiple areas of an office, you get stretched to cover more than your present job description requires. But it soon proved to be too much for me to handle; especially when the senior office manager from the town two hours away decided it would be the perfect time to arrange for an IT guy to come in and install some new computer programs.

Not the greatest day to do such a task with a full patient load and being short staffed (not to mention needing to use our computers throughout the day). The day prior, Gabby had been tasked with briefing the guy on which programs to install on which computer, as per instructions given to her by Dr. ASAP. I paid no mind as I had my own bundle of tasks to manage. While I tried juggling patients arriving and needing dismissed, taking X-rays and assisting Dr. Eager, I was told to forward the office phone to one of the other practices and they would field our calls, so I did just that. Before long, however, that office called to berate me over adding such devastating stress to their lives.

"We all are busy; you need to pull your own weight!" the office manager growled through my cell phone speaker.

So, the forwarding was canceled, and our phones started ringing again. My computer was constantly being taken over by the senior manager, leaving it frozen most of the time; so much that I felt like it was a losing battle trying to get any work done. *Why not have the IT guy fix that?!?* Patients were streaming in for their appointments while I was attempting to set up the CT machine, so it would at least look like I knew what I was doing when I brought a patient back for a head scan—while simultaneously running instruments, answering phones, and setting up rooms. Did I mention I have a tendency to take on too much? Eventually, I reached my breaking point. Here's why I lost my marbles:

I would bring a patient back, take their CT imaging (big X-ray machine sensitive to patient placement and needs correct buttons pushed), *remember how to save images so the images aren't lost*, seat them in an operatory, then take an individual PA X-ray with a single BWX (side image), then tell Doctor the patient was ready; then run back up front to see an inner office message blinking on the computer, saying I messed up on a laundry list of things the office manager discovered when she was tapped into my system. She was reviewing insurance claims (she was referring to coding done many months ago, prior to me) and wanted me to immediately give my attention to her discoveries; What's worse, the IT guy left without completing his allotted tasks. This tidbit of information was in a heated text from Dr. ASAP, which I was promptly blamed for because apparently I was supposed to babysit him and who knew, Gabby, the keeper of the IT instructions, didn't convey all the tasks to the IT guy? Next came the revelation that a patient had fully paid for treatment and her insurance had been billed, but during her dental appointment it was determined that the patient's tooth couldn't be saved, so the treatment wasn't done. From day one, I made it clear that an insurance claim could not be filed until the dentist had completed the procedure on a patient. Procedures often change in the moment, when the planned treatment takes a different turn, and you cannot know what will happen. She wanted her money back immediately and for her insurance to not be billed. But...they had me bill her insurance, so there was a fraudulent claim filed.

So, this was a perfect sh&% storm, as you can see. It was like a game of Whac-A-Mole. As soon as I fixed one problem, a lengthy inner office message would pop up ordering me to fix something else. At one point, I was attempting to graciously check in a patient, holding a pleasant conversation, while simultaneously reading a berating inner office message. I think I deserve an Oscar for my performance that day. The patients were never aware of the office stress "behind the scenes."

> From the regional office manager, in the midst of my busy day working in the front and the back: *Ok so I realize u don't want to answer and take blame and to be honest I don't blame u for*

ignoring the issue. But what I need to say is that your office is YOUR office, and you can't blame others for you falling short. The ball was dropped. U are not doing your job. I know now that I must monitor you and be more involved with even the smallest detail. Thanks for adding more work for me. By u ignoring me it only makes matters worse.

My reply: *I was not ignoring you or the issue. I have patients / phone calls and only me here. I'm being expected to assist in the back while also covering the front desk.*

As the day went on things only got worse and more and more intense. Run up front and help a patient. Run in the back because the Dr. needed help. Why aren't you answering the phone? Why wasn't I in the back assisting? How did the IT tasks not get done? When would I fix the months-old coding in the office system? Why wasn't I instantly answering every inner office mail message?

Lord, have mercy!

At the end of the day, I quietly collected all of my personal belongings and sent out a text to the dentists and the office manager:

After the events of today and yesterday, I am rethinking my decision to embark on a journey with a company that doesn't recognize the value of an employee.

At the start of my employment, it was not clearly outlined to me that every demand of a startup business would be my responsibility, as well as assisting duties and front desk duties, all by myself. Balancing patient care with so many other demands . . .

I followed by listing all the amazing things I had accomplished for the dental practice. I included a list of the general dentists I had professional relationships with prior to taking on my role with the endodontist, and that I had used my influence to help our practice gain referrals during that coffee maker gifting tour. I ended the message with:

> *I can't see myself crying daily for not meeting expectations that seem extraordinary, nor can I see myself enduring abusive inner office messages while I am trying to escort patients through their office visits. I feel like I deserve a pat on the back for learning a new CBCT machine on my own, scheduling patients for evaluations so efficiently, learning a new dental software, assisting, cleaning the office, and covering front desk duties.*
>
> *I need to discuss my employment.*

———

We agreed to a meeting that Monday morning. Well, not so much a meeting as a firing. Dr. ASAP acted like I was a teenager he was disappointed in because I couldn't live up to his expectations. Dr. Eager stood there looking at the floor, not defending me at all.

I returned my key.

And cried.

Then I drove out to Dr. Doright's home, a place where I would find the solace and understanding that I desperately needed in the wake of what had happened. We had remained friends since our years working for Dr. HMO and continued to do volunteer clinics together and support each other in our professional and personal lives. She reminded me that I was a capable, smart, hard-working individual who deserved better than what another dysfunctional dental office had offered me. We walked her neighborhood, and she listened as I let out all my hurt and frustration. I needed a friendly ear and to put some distance between myself and the circus I'd just left.

"Joy, the journey you took with Dr. Huntington was very memorable and rewarding, a once in a lifetime experience. You had such creative energy there, as well as mutual respect. You keep looking for that same magic, but I'm afraid you aren't going to find it. Maybe you are at a crossroads in your career. Maybe it's time to let your private practice career go and start paving a pathway forward with your other talents."

"I know, but dentistry is what has defined me for over thirty years," I cried.

"And you are good at it. But just start to consider other options."

---

*Life Lesson: Know when you are being
overworked and underappreciated.
When this happens, know where
the door is and let yourself out. If
the door is opened for you, walk out
knowing it wasn't the place for you.*

CHAPTER 44

Just Stand Up

In between searching for my next dental home, my favorite person (my husband) and I spent a few weeks in Maine, exploring the wilderness and staying in a little rustic cabin. The remote location had a few restaurants but usually only one or two of them was open on any given day, alternating staff between them. Hungry for pizza? This week they are closed on Tuesday and Thursday so the staff can work at the pub across the street. We would venture out of our cabin, eager to explore the area and go on hikes or long drives. We both enjoy fly fishing but were unfamiliar with the area, so we hired a guide, Lou, to show us the ins and outs of fly fishing in that region. On our first outing, I stressed to Lou that I am petrified of water. I don't even let water spray on my face in the shower. With that being said, I refuse to let the fear of water hold me back from doing adventurous things. So there we were with waders on in the middle of a raging icy cold stream, casting our lines into water that looked like coffee with creamer courtesy of the recent rainfall. At one point, I was up to my boobs in water that had a heavy undercurrent. Was I scared to death? Yes. Was I letting this fear cripple me?

Also *yes*, until I caught a big ol' freshwater salmon. Soon, we drove to another area with a large pond of murky water. I again stressed to Lou that I wouldn't be too keen on getting into deep water since the wading boots I was wearing had felt on the bottom with no grip but glided across the slimy rocks. I was so afraid I would fall and not be able to get back up and I would die right there on the spot, in the middle of Maine. Bless Lou's heart, he let me be dramatic and gently said, "I'll be here for you."

Of course, my husband also made sure I was safe and not having a panic attack induced by my fear of water. I signaled I was good and would stay in my area of the water as both men headed off in the opposite direction to fish in a deeper spot. Well, I have no patience, I want to catch all the fish (and put them back). I began to carefully maneuver in my boots around the sharp rocks coated with Shrek snot to get to a place where I could cast without tangling up my line. With both of my feet firmly planted in place, I prepared to cast. I lifted my right foot to step back but instead my other foot slid down into the dark ooky bottom of the pond.

EEEkkkkk!

Down I went in slow motion, forward into the water..... My greatest fear! My right arm with my precious fly rod submerged into the dark nothingness. Water quickly rushed up my right sleeve and into my waders. I was face down staring at the top of the coffee-colored water. *This is it!* my brain announced. *This is how you die. It's over. Cancel Christmas, Joy won't be there.* I start to cry. Because I always cry. But then, in the distance I heard . . .

"Just stand up!"
God, is that you? What?? What are you saying?!?
"JUST STAND UP!!"
No, I can't I'm drowning......

Then, I looked to my left and saw Lou taking great whole-body strides through the water with my husband right behind, trying to reach me. Again I hear.......,

"JUST ... STAND ... UP!"

"The water is only knee deep!" Lou says, as he's near me.

What? Knee deep? Relief washed over me as I used a walking stick that was tethered to my fishing gear to push myself up. *Oh! The water is only knee deep, I'm okay.*

Christmas is back on! *I just had to stand up!*

Sometimes we feel like we're drowning in the situations life throws our way. It can seem like we're sinking deeper and deeper into murky waters. But in reality, we often create this illusion in our minds. While the situation may appear like deep, dark waters, it's possible that it's actually just a small puddle. Once we recognize this, we can simply stand up and see the situation for what it really is. Don't let your mind deceive you and make a small puddle seem like an intimidating ocean.

Just stand up.

You'll be okay.

CHAPTER 45

The Gray Abyss, Part One

As I reflected on my dental career in private practice came to an end, I felt a deep sadness thinking I would never be in that world again. I sincerely missed my years with Dr. Huntington and all the amazing patients I had the pleasure to meet and help over the many years. I will even admit there were a few times when I parked in my spot at his old office and sat and stared at the building that still felt so familiar. I found myself missing the sound of laughter coming from our patients and the Dr., the sound of the dental handpiece and suction. How many times had I looked out the operatory window to see the tree across the street changing with the seasons? Sitting there in my car and reminiscing gave me a few moments of solitude and peace, followed by a deep sense of longing. I missed the routine of that time in my life.

When you try to navigate down a different professional path there's a lot of turns. I applied for so many jobs that weren't dental, but I lacked experience. *Thank you for applying, we have decided to move on with candidates more qualified.* Blah.

Back in my days with Dr. Huntington, we had occasionally done exams on visiting flight students assigned to our local Naval base. So, when I saw an ad for a government dental assisting position working with the flight students, I decided to apply. For sixteen long months, I worked towards a government dental assistant position for flight students stationed at the local Naval base. There were so very many steps, that I felt like I was walking over the Grand Canyon on a tight rope. I knew there was no chance I would get the position because if you missed one step, you fell off the rope and lost the job. To make it through the preliminary application process, I had to submit my resume, all my certifications, prove vaccinations, and put the needed information in the proper place while changing your passwords to the government specifications. Crossing T's, dotting I's. No way did I imagine I would get the proceed to the next level.

- ✓ *Drug test.*
- ✓ *Titer for Hepatitis.*
- ✓ *Flu shot.*
- ✓ *Phone interview scheduled with the heads of the abyss.*
- ✓ *Phone interview scheduled between the heads of the abyss and Dr. Huntington.*
- ✓ *Paperwork.*
- ✓ *Both phone interviews take place.*
- ✓ *Online continuing education taken on my personal time.*

I went on with my life, working from home and doing side jobs, as I continued to follow through with requests, as I moved up the hiring ladder. I trudged through the long and difficult process of applying for this government assistant role, which

I affectionately named *'the gray abyss.'* It felt like a never-ending task list; Take an online class, submit to a drug test, get titer tests for various vaccinations, get the latest flu shot, on and on. After all these hurdles were eventually cleared, it took a full year before I was eligible for an interview. But that wasn't the end of my challenge; additional paperwork had to be completed, phone interviews had to be scheduled, even Dr. Huntington got in on the action via a teleconference with a room full of official government hiring managers. And as if that weren't enough, I also had to obtain a special clearance badge, and an additional mountain of paperwork.

A long last, I was hired! Now I would enter a world unlike any I had existed in before. After being sworn in, with two other new hires ,we were each handed a stack of paperwork, and sent off to complete the onboarding process. My task was to complete the check-in process, which would involve me visiting each department in the seven-story facility and getting all my paperwork initialed, stamped and filed. This process was daunting to say the least, there were so many different departments, each with its own unique acronym that was difficult to remember.

As I approached a desk, hoping to quickly get the first check-mark on my list, they asked if I had my XYZ for ABC set up. *Huh?*

"I have no idea what that means," I confessed.

"Well, we can't create an account for you until you set up the XYZ and have an email account," the lady behind the desk flatly stated.

"Okay . . . who do I go to for that?" I asked.

"That's not my department."

Off I went, trudging through the winding hallways of the building in search of the second spot on my master list, trying to check off the needed box. Signature, signature, signature. There was a mountain of paperwork to complete, after all this would be a government position. When I was finished my navigator looked at me and said, "Congratulations, you are now a tuna." *Okay, she didn't actually say that, but that's what happened.*

"Hi, I'm Joy. I'm checking in," I said to someone behind a counter. I thought they would just need to sign and stamp my paperwork. Boy was I wrong! Not even close. There were seemingly endless procedures that had to be completed first, at various locations no less, before this department could even begin their process of verifying my documents. Holy cow!

"Ms. Joy you will need your supervisor to send in a signed DD4450 with the VGF," the accounting gal pointed out.

"Okay . . . how do I get the DD4450 and what is the VGF?" I asked.

"Your supervisor will know."

My first thought was that I was never going to finish the monster task I had been assigned. After bouncing from department to department, I accumulated more than 10,000 steps on my fitness tracker. Every desk I encountered seemed to require additional paperwork or approvals before anything could be done. The process felt like an endless cycle of waiting. It almost made the DMV look appealing!

I took my paperwork back to the HR person and told her I was unable to get more than a few departments to check me in. She laughed and said, "Joy, you can't complete this paperwork in one day. It will take you weeks, maybe even over a month!"

That would have been helpful information from the start.

CHAPTER 46

The Gray Abyss, Part Two

The oppressive, colorless atmosphere of the abyss was almost suffocating. As I navigated the confusing twists and turns of my bureaucratic journey, I felt like a rat in a maze, encountering dull-eyes figures behind every desk. I felt as though I was plunged into a world without any signs of life or joy. Everywhere I walked, all I could see were gray figures, moving through their daily routines with no pleasure or enthusiasm. I encountered no perky, peppy people.

You see, when I initially thought of venturing into the abyss, it seemed like a safe refuge for me. I would never have to worry about being judge on my age or looks; instead, we were all valued for our unique skills and abilities. The wages and tasks for each job were predetermined based on experience and qualifications, so there was no debate or haggling over salaries.

However, I soon realized that this kind of environment was cold and distant, devoid of personal connections. There was no interest in my sense of humor, my theory of "the five things", my favorite dessert recipes to share, nothing that speaks of being an individual. In my heart, the gray abyss was sort of my if-prom-night-arrives-and-neither-of-us-has-a-date-we'll-go-together "backup" plan.

In the abyss, no one will tell you or show you anything. It's not their job. You must figure things out for yourself, just as every employee has done before you. You navigate the labyrinth. You learn the codes and words. You learn the language, even if you've never spoken a word of it before in your life.

The gray abyss had its own language, and I didn't even know the basics. A Morse code of acronyms. As I've mentioned, I remember very little of the four years of French I took in high school. Why I thought it would be useful in my West Texas life I'll never know. At that time, I guess I was picturing a life of travel, visits to foreign lands, and maybe a chance to use a little of the language I learned. I have retained only the most basic words and phrases I studied and struggled to pronounce with my classmates. I can, however, ask you "Où sont les toilettes?"

Where is the toilet?

You wouldn't call it a bathroom, "la salle de bains," or you would be asking a waiter or stranger where you can bathe.

It would be a month from the date, when I first reported to that big seven-story building before I got to report to my supervisor and check into the gray abyss dental area with gray walls, gray floors, even gray carpet and meet the staff. At the sight of me the staff scattered like roaches when the garage light is turned on. I was surprised that they weren't more welcoming, since I knew the position had been open for such a long time, but to each his own. I knew to give it time. Not my first rodeo.

I seem to attract certain types of people in life, mostly old folks, children, and people considered to be 'eccentric', and this particular place was no different. It was one such person who enlightened me as to what was going on in the dental clinic. She appeared friendly enough; she spoke of her newfound faith in Jesus and dedication to twice-daily exercise routine. I peppered her with questions and was hopeful we could be friends.

My days at the gray abyss dental clinic were long and bleak, no patients or computer access for me. Instead, I was told just continue my check-in process and training as best I could. None of the other assistants would talk to me. If I had been a flower, I would have appeared withered and dead.

Because my supervisor was juggling many tasks, a twenty-two-year-old gal who worked in a lesser position crowned herself my delegator. She would be nice to me, give me helpful advice, and then turn on me. She competed for everyone's attention and needed constant approval. *OK, puppy. I got ya. Calm down. Here's another treat.* If another dentist engaged me in conversation, she would quickly interject her thoughts and ideas, steamrolling our discussion. In those weeks I stayed hidden and quiet, out of everyone's way, biding my time and looking forward to the day I could start seeing patients.

I'm not one to sit still but wanted to stay in my appointed lane. My supervisor would catch me working up front at times or organizing a supply closet and have a little chat with me.

"You aren't qualified yet to be up there."

"I'm just pulling charts and helping to refile them." I admitted.

"I can't allow that until you are qualified."

Walking into the supply closet the next day, he caught me again.

"Joy, you can't be in here, yet."

"I'm just organizing supplies."

How am I supposed to pass the hours? I thought. *Like the other assistant? The one who is on her cell phone from the minute she walks in until the minute she leaves?!?*

Finally, the day came when I was deemed worthy to perform simple tasks. I could now do exams. Let the heavens rejoice.

The computer program seemed simple enough, but without proper guidance, I was unable to input patient information correctly. Despite the lengthy periods of downtown I experienced, my request for someone to train me on the system fell on deaf ears. You would think that would be a priority, but you would be wrong. This caused a great deal of stress when the assigned dentist began his exam and got frustrated with me for not being quick enough. Seven minutes was the prescribed time to complete a dental exam, before he moved on to the next one. I explained that the dental program was new to me and to *calm down* (you know I'm kidding, but I said it in my head). A typical day had me performing a new exam every thirty minutes, not including X-rays (that was another person's responsibility). So, it was literally rinse and repeat all day long with exam after exam after exam. Jack pot, I'm living the dream! Or not.

Then it all came to a halt; like I had slammed head-on into a roadblock. After a week-long stint of being the exam queen, my supervisor received a notice stating that I needed an N95 mask fit test and simply pulled me out of rotation—I went from being active, to a state of complete and utter inactivity. When I asked what department, I needed to contact for the N95 fit test, no one seemed to oversee this test however, it was up to me to find out how to complete it. Weeks went by as I tried desperately to figure out which department I should contact and where the test would even be held. For weeks on end, I was stuck in limbo with no answers. I was getting paid to do endless training modules. Eventually I was put on some negligent list. I had not complied. I had not gotten the test. I could not be around patients. It was humorous in its absurdity.

Ugh.

And then one bright and sunny day, as if there had been no delay at all, the instructions arrived: Report for test on X day at X time in X location. At last! I arrived early, because one I always arrive early and two, I had nothing else to do. So, I sat for forty-five minutes past my appointment time waiting for (I didn't know who) to arrive. When this guy waltzed in looking for the person on the poo list, (me) he quickly told me that he had a trainee in tow, and she needed to learn how to administer the test. Fine, like I have a choice. I had no idea what this test would entail but figured I would try on N95 masks of different sizes, they would determine which had the best and safest fit, and off I would go. Negative ghost rider.

The gal training to administer the test was obviously not thrilled about having such a mundane task; she handed me an N95 mask without so much as saying a word or making eye contact and proceeded to take out something that looked like a thick yellow plastic bag. What on Earth? My stomach dropped as I realized this bag was meant to go over my head. As she placed the bag over my head, my heart started racing. It had a small transparent window so I could see through it, and a funky chemical smell. As she was preparing to pull the drawstring to tighten the bag around my neck, I lifted the front of it up and asked her if the bag was cleaned between uses, as COVID-19 was a serious virus. What if the last person to wear this bag was positive and I contracted the virus from breathing inside the same bag?

She dismissed my question with a roll of her eyes, pushed my hands down and tightened the drawstring. She then sprayed something in bag that made my eyes water. I glanced at my watch and noted the time before I looked up to find that my tester had left the room. She was gone for seven minutes. Do you remember that feeling when you were a child in the grocery store with your mom and you lost her? That panic of being abandoned. I could feel my heart racing, my breath growing shallow and uneven. Finally, after seven minutes, my tester re-entered the room with various cans containing different types of aromatic sprays. *Oh girl, you weren't ready with all the supplies and you just left me, another human being, with an oxygen-blocking plastic bag over my head plus an N95 mask over my nose and mouth—for an indefinite length of time?*

On minute eight, my mind went into an absolute frenzy and full-blown panic mode. When a panic attack hits, it comes on like a bear is chasing you and you are fighting for your life. Your heart races and your mind says that you are going to die from suffocation . . . *unless you do something*. You can't breathe. Panic sets in. I threw the bag and mask off while the fear and desperation escalated further with each passing second, as if each breath I attempted to take felt shallow and inadequate. As I gulped air that seemed like it wouldn't enter my lungs fast enough, I was crying and hyperventilating, all while the young lady stood staring at me holding those damn cans she left to get. I wasn't just ugly crying; I was snot slinging, make up running down my face, I'm going to die any minute crying.

A nurse from the nearby clinic was alerted to the situation and she quickly handed me a paper bag to breathe into. Oh, you would think that she was helpful, but as I tried to slow my breathing, she was in my face saying I needed counseling as obviously there was something wrong with me. *WHAT?!?*

When I finally regained my composure, tester chick stated that I had failed the test and would need to find another option to be compliant before I could get back into rotation in my job. I failed huh....You think?

Well, apparently, no one had ever failed the N95 mask fit test before. So, I waited for someone somewhere to devise a new plan. Finally, after a week, another option came in the form of fire. You read that right, *fire.* This experience was no better as I was placed in a room and had "fire" waved at me while wearing a N95 mask. I'm not kidding. The tester had a bundle of twigs that he lit on fire, then he waved the smoking bundle at my face. I was ordered to do jumping jacks, then to hop, and then to read a paragraph out loud standing up, and honestly Shakespeare is difficult to read without an N95; then I was told to bend over and recite another paragraph. It was all very odd, I just did what I was told. I took a deep breath and completed each task, all the while "holding my breath" in hopes of just getting passing grade! Hallelujah, I did!!

After passing the fire test, I was finally allowed to be around patients again. The twenty-two-year-old delegator was back in my life. She was like a moody teenager, one day she was totally unreasonable, the next day a crying emotional wreck, and most days an overall disaster. Every day she was an attention-seeking missile and the clinic dentist let her do as she pleased, which gave her a sense of power. My flighty new friend deemed me her confidant and shared all her thoughts and opinions on matters ranging from religion to politics. She was against the government yet worked there for years. She was an odd duck. I just smiled and listened.

When I wasn't busy doing dental exams, (where I was able to become proficient on my own using the charting program, thank you very much,) I was taking the mandated hours of training, feeling a little like I had been thrown into an emotionless void . I know I'm making this job sound like oodles of fun, but the reality is everyone walked around in a zombie-like state, just going through the motions until their hours were completed. Oh, but there's always that one person, who adds a dose of spice to your day, in my case it was Urna, the passive-aggressive dental assistant who had been granted immunity due to her seniority, tended to flex her power without any care. For example, during lunchtime, she would draw up a chair next to one of us and expect their food to be shared; or there would be consequences. It was like being sent back to elementary school where the playground bully would take whatever they wanted from you without consent.

She just assumed that part of your lunch would be gifted to her. Personally, I am not comfortable with this type of bullying. After a few experiences with Urna helping herself to my food I learned to sit far away from her during my thirty-minute break.

One day as I was restocking my dental operatory, I heard her voice in the next room. She was chatting with the other assistant, and they were talking about me! She was telling him how I claimed to have so much experience, but to her it didn't appear to be true since I wouldn't step up and take over her workload. Their conversation continued for about ten minutes, during which the other assistant threw in his two cents with his own unhelpful opinion of me.

I felt a deep -rooted hurt and anger beginning to bubble up inside of me. I knew that if I were to confront the two of them, I'd only make matters worse, so instead I took a few breaths and tried to compose myself before speaking. The truth was, my job was very limited as an assistant; my pay was far lower than what those two were making due to their additional responsibilities and duties. The truth of the matter was, she wanted to work less and saw me as her ticket to pawning off some of her duties, even though my job description didn't allow it. She had plenty of time on her hands for playing on her phone all day. In the end, I did calmly approach them and asked if there was anything they wanted to talk about openly with me. She didn't hesitate in responding and we moved forward from there. I was walking on eggshells around Urna, especially when it came time to change from street clothes to the scrubs that were supplied for us. She would be tucked away in her corner getting dressed while trying to critique other women's figures. "You really should consider losing some weight," I heard her say to one person who was a part of her inner circle. To another, she commented, "I like your tattoos, show me them up close." The atmosphere in the locker room always made me feel uneasy, as if every move I made was being monitored by Urna. It's called personal boundaries sister and I know for a fact one of those endless training modules went over that in detail.

I filled my days the best I could with tasks around the dental clinic (things I *was* authorized to do). Staying busy with front desk duties always helped to pass the time. Upfront I would pull charts and check out military personnel that were transferring to another duty station. One day I was by myself while the receptionist took a lunch break. A young man walked up to the window looking for the restroom. Pointing him to the nearest one, he then asked me if I was going to watch. *Excuse me, what?!?* Just as I was about to size him up as being some kind or pervert, he pulled out a urine collection cup. *Ohhhhh Ha! Ha!* Clearly, he needed to use a restroom on the medical side of the clinic, so I pointed him in the other direction.

Working in the Gray Abyss was indeed a lifeless, soul-sucking experience. The days were spent toiling away in a place without the warmth and light of the sun, with little appreciation or connection to staff and patients. It takes a certain kind of person to thrive in such an environment, and I am not that person. I take pleasure in cultivating and nurturing plants and flowers; caring for something so it can grow and flourish, by providing it with the right soil, water, air, and sunlight, it needs. But this job was devoid of those components; it existed within perpetual shadow where the environment was as lifeless as those around me.

I recall one day, with such intense heartbreak attached. I mean there were many such days, but this one still actually hurts my heart. The dental exams were done in about seven minutes. If the dentist was running behind, I might have a minute or two to chat with the patients who were all military personnel. It was during those few minutes that I felt closest to understanding what life in the military is really like for these brave men and women who give so much for our country. At the start every exam I would follow a prescribed check list of things to ask the patient. Any teeth bothering you? Last cleaning? Any tobacco use? (That one is a no-no. If the answer is yes, there's a help line, class, and tobacco literature that we were to offer. And it goes on your permanent record.) One young man sitting in my operatory chair, was pushing off answering the question before making eye contact and said " Yes." The hesitancy, combine with a sadness in his voice, was hard to miss.

"It's ok. Is this a recent thing you started?" I asked.

He bowed his head down and started to cry. He put his hand on his forehead trying to hide his emotions. *Oh my gosh!* I think, *I won't put it in your record, it's not that serious.*

"Ma'am, I started smoking cigarettes about a week ago because a little car ran a stop sign and I was driving a large truck that t-boned her. I killed her." Tears streamed down his face as he shared this heavy sadness with me. I stood by the dental chair crying with him, feeling the heavy load of his pain. We stayed talking for no longer than five minutes. The man looked so despondent that all I wanted to do was give him some time to process his feelings . Meanwhile, Urna stood a short distance down the hallway taking in the scene and was clearly perturbed by the sight of me listening to the young mans' heartbreaking story. She expressed her frustration to the director of the clinic , and soon after we were both called in to discuss my lack of self-discipline in allowing this young man to take up time by crying, when "there were far more important things that needed attention" in the clinic.

"And she cried. She cried like a baby, too!" Urna throws out there using her bawled up fist to wipe away fake tears.

I did. I hurt when people hurt. I hate when bad things happen that make you feel like the weight of the world is upon you. So yes, Urna I cried. It's who I am.

Was the gray abyss the place for me? No. Was I still on an endless search for another Dr. Albright, Dr. Grace, or Dr. Huntington? Yes. Isn't there a saying that goes something like, "Don't cry because it's over, smile because it happened?" Well, I did cry for a minute as I walked out the clinic door on my last day. There was not a hint of sadness.

Shortly after closing the chapter on that position, I had a short three-hour call with my friend Thunder Cloud. She and I shared stories of how we each were well known in our field for being the one person who can come in and wave a magic wand and make things all better. She was an outstanding Hospice nurse and well known in the field for being able to come in and make things better. She took great pride in helping those at the end of their lives, as it fulfilled her soul and defined who she was. But one day that door closed, despite her attempts to keep it from completely shutting. She was good at that job. No, she was damn good at that job. It defined her until the one day it didn't. Much like my situation.

"Joy, my Scottish Gran would say 'if the door don't open easily, don't push it."

"I know, I've been trying and trying to keep my foot in the door, so that it doesn't close on my dental career. I knew things, people asked me questions and trusted my advice."

"Well, Gran would say to you, 'What is for you won't go by you."

Thunder Cloud loves to share her Gran's Irish sayings and has found a new calling in life. Oh, she's still being an epic healthcare provider, but now she checks in on patients who are healthy.

CHAPTER 47

THE END

It has been four years since Dr. Huntington retired. In those four years I have searched in vain to find another office to match the level of comfort and respect that his office brought me. Between Dr. Huntington, his wife, the receptionist Doris, and myself, we shared many years full of laughter, and truly became a family as we delivered the pinnacle of patient care. The office motto—painted on the wall in the reception area—read, **"A DAY WITHOUT LAUGHTER, IS A DAY WASTED."** If you were fortunate enough to be a patient at our office, then you would remember the way Dr. Huntington's laugh would ring throughout the entire building. Or me cackling like a chicken (as my grandma would say) when telling a patient a funny story. The perks of working in that small office were many, at the top of the list is that my heart was happy.

I continue to compile my daily lists of tasks to accomplish, a habit I've developed from years in the dental field. While at home, I go from room to room as I did at the dental office, methodically checking off each task on my chore list. After so many years of being organized and efficient, it's still difficult to slow down.

Now, instead of fighting cavities or periodontal diseases, I'm tackling dust bunnies and doing laundry. Thankfully, when Dr. Huntington is in town he makes time for a long visit with my family and me. We catch up and still play "Name That Patient."

I have interviewed with many of the dentists in town and worked with some very good ones. I know in my heart, like Dr. Doright said, that none of them can recreate the magic of my time at Dr. Huntington's office. What you choose to look for you will see; and I see that no one will ever provide the level of optimum dentistry that he produced, along with a harmonious and respectful work environment. As a dental professional, I reached the summit of Mount Everest. Me, the gal from West Texas—the one who took a high school placement test and was told she would make a great plumber—was a lead prosthodontic assistant with advanced lab skills who weighed in on big, life-changing dental cases. I know big words and important people. I helped to change lives for the better. Many lives. I was part of a team whose goal it was to give people back their confidence, their self-esteem, to restore their smile and enable them to speak to loved ones, friends, neighbors, and even strangers without fear. I was part of that. Me!

After so many years in the dental world, I felt like I did when I fell in that river water in Maine. It took a long time, but you know what? I just stood up, and I'm okay. My career and its accompanying responsibilities didn't define who I am, but it filled my glass jar with things that made me happy. Being a mom to my son who is a good human, certainly fills me with happiness. I'm so very proud to see him pursue a successful medical career where I hope, one day, he will feel the same joy from helping others, that same feeling of accomplishment, that I did. This career path for him is a result of an amazing eighth-grade science teacher that fanned a flame, igniting my son's love for science. Oh, and he wanted to wear scrubs every day to work. The love of my life continues to peel my grapes and fan me with palm fronds on hot days. Well, okay, maybe he doesn't go that far, but he does bring me a glass of wine when we sit under the pergola (that he built!) in our backyard. Me? I'm enjoying a remote job where there's something incredibly liberating about having the ability to just take off on a whim, knowing that my absence barely causes a ripple in the grand scheme of things. This allows me to embrace the simple pleasures of life like spending a day outdoors gardening or at the beach. Or perhaps I can treat myself to a leisurely lunch with Dr. Doright.

*And she lived happily ever after,
with her glass jar overflowing with
sunshine and happiness!*

About the Author

 **Joy Moore**, a native West Texan, began her journey as a certified dental assistant in 1990 while residing in Washington State. In addition to her passion for dentistry, Joy has a myriad of interest that reflect her vibrant and creative spirit. Whether its watercolor painting, fishing, kayaking, sewing, reading, writing, gardening, going on adventures, or baking, Joy possesses a zest for life that is contagious and inspiring.

Equally important to her are the ties she has to her community; she is an active participant in community service, always looking for ways to give back and make a positive impact.

With over three decades of experience as a dedicated clinician, including over nine years specializing in prosthodontics care, Joy is known for her jovial personality and exceptional skills.

Her patients always feel at ease in her presence and establish a trust that lasts long after their appointments.

Now residing in Florida since 1996 with her husband, Chuck, and their son, Dallas, Joy has made the sun-kissed shores her home. She continues to explore her passions, both in her professional and personal life. And now, she embarks on a new journey: that of an author. Pouring the same care and dedication into her writing as she does into her dental career. Joy hopes to inspire, educate, and connect with readers through her memoir, just as she has done with her patients all these years.

Acknowledgements

I want to express my sincere gratitude to Chuck, you truly are an outstanding human being. Your encouragement and support have been invaluable in giving me the confidence to start this journey. You are not just the best part of my life, you are my life! Your unfaltering belief in me served as a tremendous source of motivation. Thank you for always being my loudest cheerleader and most of all for feeding my soul. PS: I'm glad you are always right! There, now there's written proof.

To Fred, who I've never once called by his first name, your patience in accommodating my quirks is greatly appreciated. Thanks for keeping the ship sailing in the right direction and being levelheaded when you caught on fire. I appreciate, more than you know, how much you respected my opinion, and I am truly grateful for your many years of guidance.

For Cecilia, who is so devoted to making sure her friendships remain strong and is always quick to lend a helping hand when needed. Thank you for your steadfast support; it truly has helped boost me up!

A thank you to Shawn my editor who was a crucial source of help throughout this process without her my werk would still be filled with typos and run-on sentences.......

9 798988 485209